Becky Wicks was born in 1979. She attended the Gleed School for Girls, (also known as 'The Virgin Megastore') in Spalding, England. She studied media production at Lincoln University and was freelance writing from the age of 14. Becky headed to New York City at 21 and worked a number of jobs including an interesting stint as a jello-shot waitress. Back in London, she wrote for mags and websites before heading to Dubai. She currently lives in Sydney.

For juicy Burqalicious extras,
visit www.beckywicks.com, find Burqalicious on
facebook or follow bex_wicks on twitter.

Burqalicious

THE DUBAI DIARIES
A true story of sun, sand, sex, and secrecy

Becky Wicks

Skyhorse Publishing

First published in Australia in 2011
by HarperCollins*Publishers* Australia Pty Limited
ABN 36 009 913 517 harpercollins.com.au

Skyhorse Publishing books may be purchased in bulk at special
discounts for sales promotion, corporate gifts, fund-raising, or edu-
cational purposes. Special editions can also be created to specifica-
tions. For details, contact the Special Sales Department, Skyhorse
Publishing, 307 West 36th Street, 11th Floor, New York, NY 10018 or
info@skyhorsepublishing.com.

www.skyhorsepublishing.com

10 9 8 7 6 5 4 3 2 1

Library of Congress Cataloging-in-Publication Data is available on file.

Printed in the United States of America

ISBN: 978-1-61608-589-6

Photographs courtesy of Rebecca Wicks

For M&M.

I'll never forget the good times.

Acknowledgements

Wow. A book. It's a book full of words I wrote, how bizarre! There are so many people to thank ... not least my lovely agent, the wonderful Margaret Gee in Sydney, Australia who called me half an hour after skim-reading my manuscript and promptly set about fighting for my words to reach the right pair of hands. And now, my story has reached American and Canadian shores thanks to the awesome team at Skyhorse Publishing, New York. I'm excited about this, not least because it means I have a valid excuse to come and shop under the guise of a business trip (ahem).

Then of course there's my incredible friends and family, who've supported my writing since I first starting penning shitty Christmas poems about angels for the local paper. In particular I should acknowledge Mum, Dad, Simon and Mrs Christine Fynn, my English teacher at the Gleed School for Girls in Spalding. She always gave me A grades and let me hide in her cupboard when my Math's teacher kicked me out for being thick.

I should extend HUGE thanks to the team at lastminute.com in London — the best job I ever had — who first got me hooked on blogging. Without your encouragement I wouldn't have had the confidence to leave my comfy life of blag and head to Dubai for an adventure. Or maybe you just wanted to get rid of me, hmmm?

I can't forget to thank Dubai of course, for all it taught me during my time there. I learned from the best about fierce ambition, chasing dreams and knowing when to fess up that sometimes, you bugger things up royally without meaning to. To the people I met there, who crop up in my story, you know who you are and I thank you. Some of you I'm still in touch with, some I'm not, but I'll always remember our time together and be grateful to have shared your company.

With that said, I hope you all like my story. I've tried to stay true to the way my memory serves me, to the way things really happened to me and to the people who surrounded me in Dubai. It's a place I still read about, still talk about and dream about, and even though I left as a slightly spoilt and slightly fed-up expat, my time there was a turning point in my life. In fact, even if I'd left this story in my memories, only for myself to play over and over and over, I'd still look back on Dubai as being one of the most influential, exciting and special cities in the world.

If you haven't been there yet, I hope my story will encourage you to visit. And if you have, I hope it had a lasting effect on you, too ... preferably for a good reason, and not because you're still there, banged up in a prison cell.

Becky x

An introduction to insanity ...

On that first fateful day, walking along the edge of a six-lane highway in 45-degree heat, sweat pouring from my ears, brow and belly button, I thought, *maybe a few months, I'll give it a few months*. As the cabs refused to stop and the humid air soaked my leggings, making me look more like a disoriented drunken teen who'd wet her pants than a hip ex-Londoner making the journey back from work on foot, I stared up at a billboard featuring an ominous sheikh atop a mammoth white horse, reigning supreme over the road. Wiping my face on my sleeve and only narrowly missing a speeding Lamborghini, I thought to myself, *just a few short months and then I'll go home. I'll shrug it all off as a mistake and beg for my old job (and dignity) back.*

Two and a half years and a good few pairs of sodden leggings later, Dubai is a part of me. I belong to Dubai, like a falcon does to an Emirati's shoulder. And not just because I took out a bank loan the size of Milton Keynes and would have been imprisoned if I'd left without letting my loaded Arab boyfriend pay it back.

There have been a lot of changes since I first arrived on those dusty shores with nothing but a suitcase and a head full of tax-free dreams. As far as Dubai's concerned, I've seen a rise and fall bigger than a boy band's pop career and a good few front men struggling to keep a hold on what they once assumed was theirs in limitless supply. I guess living in Dubai was a bit like starring in a cartoon — you know, where everything's exaggerated and the lines between fiction and reality are blurred? And as a prelude to what's ahead, I'll say in brief that I've become a different sort of character. This could be seen as a good or a bad thing, I suppose. Those who know me are still a bit baffled when I act surprised at having to clean my own bathroom, or remark that a house is not a home unless it has an outdoor swimming pool and a golden-crested marble bird perching on the ledge above the doorway. (I only said this once — don't judge me.)

It's not that I've changed that much … well, maybe I have, but the changes were so slow and unnoticeable in their unravelling that I surprise myself when I talk about how life once was, compared with how it is now — now that the bubble's burst on the economy.

The stories that follow began as a collection of more than 600 diary entries and articles, written from 2007 to 2009, initially meant only for the eyes of my friends. So inspiring was this land, so strange and new … and so incredulous was I at being thrown right into the midst of this mounting chaos that pages and pages poured out of me sitting in my luxurious apartments, huddling over my laptop by the pool, or even swivelling in my seat at work, bored with writing bullshit just to keep Dubai's PR force happy. What I really wanted to write was the truth. But possessing a bank loan the size of a small county rendered me pretty busy, and pretty much stuck in what's now, essentially I guess, a building site of unfinished business.

This has been a bit of a secret project, in spite of working in the media and itching to speak out to a wider group than my on-line circle. There's been lots of stuff in the papers. I've read it all with interest and so have you, probably. We've all read of sex-on-the-beach scandals and stories of successful, spoilt expats who've since seen their dreams and relationships fall into ruin like many of the plans for Dubai's now-flailing infrastructure. But there's a lot more to it than that. There are things I've seen and done that must be mentioned, things that could have potentially, had I spoken of them within the strict confines of the city's well-oiled PR machine, seen me stuck in a cell surrounded by criminals who'd committed other such unforgivable offences. These crimes might include falling pregnant outside marriage, drinking outside a bar instead of inside it, or accidentally bouncing a check.

An entire city has risen from the dust around me, along with a good few rungs of that hard-to-climb career ladder. I've learned to snowboard in the desert, spent New Year's Eve on the branch of a manmade palm tree and celebrated my birthdays in a five star blur of champagne luxury. I've lived on the landing of a mad Iranian inventor's villa. I've been a celebrity gossip editor in a land where sex definitely does not sell and I've been thrust into the crazy world of advertising, alongside the Lebanese mafia. I've been whisked around the world by a rich Arab man, who proclaimed that he'd fallen so deeply in love with me that his world shattered every time I left his side, and I've lost more friends to the transient lifestyle than I've had the chance to add to Facebook.

Now that I think of it, in a place that until recently (with the opening of the Metro), couldn't even run a decent public transport service, I've learned what it truly means to be indulged, spoilt and, ultimately, changed forever.

That said, let's go back to the beginning.

Picture if you will, the summer of 2007 …

Another suitcase in another hall ...

It's almost 6 am and I've been awake for hours. My mouth tastes weird thanks to a Caesar salad dinner and I think it might be a chewing gum day. There are too many things in my head right now — mostly mundane things, like making sure I have my passport and wondering whether it's safe to pack the Marmite. I've heard funny things about Dubai customs. There are so many random objects you're not allowed to take in (Robitussin, for example), and far too many rules to abide by once you actually make it through, by the sounds of it (no public displays of affection, etc). I shook all my clothes for traces of marijuana before Mum got here, of course, but I can't help but wonder if I'm a liability.

Mum and Dad have kindly brought more bags to my apartment so I can decide which one to take to Dubai. I've realized I've got way too many clothes. In spite of promising not to buy anything else since I landed the job, I bought a new dress from TopShop yesterday. But *awwww*. It's my new 'I'm off to glamorous Dubai so I really, really need a nice dress' dress. It's red.

I'm meeting Stacey at Heathrow once I'm all packed. Stacey and I have been hired by the same company to be 'deputy travel editors' at a publishing company. I met her for the first time the other day at a pub in Covent Garden, after another British employee already in Dubai, called Heidi, hooked us up on Facebook. We're very excited about our new titles in Dubai and both agree that had we decided to stay in London, neither of us would be 'deputy' anythings. Stacey's from Manchester and she's just finished university, but even though I'm a few years older and possibly, maybe, a rung or two further up the career ladder than her, she's skipped effortlessly to my level thanks to Dubai's unprecedented need for decent English writers. Either that or I'm just crap for my age, but you know what, at this point, I don't really care.

It's all happened so quickly. To think I met the head honcho of the publishing company just a month ago at the London Book Fair and now I'm sitting here surrounded by the remnants of my London life crammed into garbage bags. Stacey admitted the other day that she didn't even know the job she was applying for was based in Dubai at first. She was just so happy to have a 'deputy editor' interview that she didn't double-check the details when the call came through. She said she sat there before her potential employer, wondering why the strange blonde lady was talking so much about the Middle East!

Lucy'll wake up soon. I'll have to say goodbye to my flatmate of two years. I almost hope she doesn't wake up, you know — I think I might cry. I'm not very good with goodbyes. I do believe my lovely workmates were slightly miffed that the floodgates didn't open until my emotions had been inebriated with five shots of whisky last night. But on the whole I prefer to be happy about this decision. I like to stay strong. Because if I don't, I'll just think too much about what the hell I'm doing—moving to the Middle East.

Lucy reminded me the other day of how, about a year ago, she'd thought about applying for a job in Dubai and I'd scoffed at her;

told her she'd be known as 'Letterbox' and would have to cover herself from head to toe in black. Clearly, I was a selfish moron who didn't want her to leave me. And now I'm going instead, whether I can fit my life into all of these bags or not.

13/06

Travelling at the speed of Dubai ...

The first thing I'll say is that the Internet here is *soooooo bloody slow*! It appears to be powered by plodding camels, even in the office. Some pages won't load and some flash a giant BLOCKED message across the screen, so huge and sudden that I can practically feel an authority figure smacking me about the eyeballs in disgust. I'm not trying to look at anything naughty. I'm actually trying to log in to the blog I've been diligently keeping for two years. I don't know if it's my company or the country that's rendering this impossible, but I'll be very unimpressed if my blogging days are over just as my life gets vaguely exciting.

Other than that, my first week in Dubai is actually going relatively smoothly, bar an hour-long journey to work every day, ninety per cent of which is spent twiddling our thumbs in a cab stuck in traffic, and ten per cent of which is spent explaining to the driver where exactly it is he needs to go, even though we don't quite know ourselves.

Stacey and I have discovered that the roads in Dubai change so frequently that many drivers have no idea whatsoever if the route they took yesterday will still be in existence the next day. Every trip is an adventure. There's no GPS. Google Earth reveals from above what looks a little like a children's sandcastle after it's been battered by a loon with a pile of metal rods. From the ground it's not much different. With a population of almost 2 million people it's growing by the day.

It's hot outside, too. And by hot I mean the kind of hot you might experience if you installed your household oven in your wardrobe, turned the heat up to 300 degrees and sat with your face in the open door, wearing a balaclava while drinking soup. It's so humid that when Stacey and I step outside the office block, our glasses steam up instantly. We fumble about, praying we won't get hit by a car — and when a breeze does actually blow, it's like someone pointing a hairdryer at our faces.

We're told that this is something that'll get even worse during the summer, which is difficult to think about right now. Temperatures are set to soar into the high 40s and maybe even reach the 50s in July, August and September. I can't help but feel like a bit of a sucker, if I'm honest. Clearly, I was too busy buying hot red dresses and worrying about which yeasty extracts to pack to actually check the weather in Dubai from London, but it appears we've been shuttled in at the worst possible time. And there I was, dressing like a Londoner in my leggings and slouch boots, ready for a day at the office as the fashionable import from the East End's Mile End to the Middle East's middle of ... well, a little hamlet called Karama. I've never sweated so much in my life.

Justifiably, people here seem to be afraid of going outside. We offered to attempt to walk to work on our first morning, which judging by the map should have taken roughly twenty minutes (Karama is an older, residential part of the city), but we were met with puzzled looks and a shaking of the head so severe I thought the lady downstairs at our hotel apartment block was going to have a seizure. 'You don't walk anywhere in Dubai' was her warning. It seems she was right. Instead, you shut yourself in an air-conditioned car and sit in traffic for what feels like all eternity before literally turning the corner and getting out again. Occasionally, says Heidi, you're stared at long and hard by the person in the car next to you, causing colossal paranoia and an urge to cry, until you realize it's because you're showing your knees under the dashboard.

The apartment in the hotel is nice — Stacey and I were given one each, but seeing as mine was three times the size of the flat I've just left behind with Lucy, we moved all our stuff into one so we wouldn't get lonely. I've really never been the type to get homesick, but having one relatively close friend means everything at a time like this. Saying goodbye to Lucy was tough, as predicted. I'm not even sure when I'll see her again, and even though she's only a few hours away by time zone and we can chat in real time with the aid of modern technology (if any of it ever starts to work properly), this place couldn't be more different. It doesn't seem all that modern, either. I was expecting something rather glamorous and special. What little I'd heard about Dubai from other people before I got here was all extravagant and glitzy — man made islands and classy shopping malls — but then, we haven't been to many places yet. Perhaps Karama isn't the *real* Dubai.

Everyone's tanned here, though. Our coworker Heidi met us at the hotel on our first day, when jetlagged and bleary we stood with our bags at our feet, looking out at the cab drivers inching in and out of the lanes outside trying desperately to move through stationary traffic. In the light of day, Heidi is the kind of russet brown, just verging on orange, that manages to look healthy in spite of a little voice in your head screaming *premature ageing and wrinkles!*

It was nice to meet Heidi after writing for weeks via Facebook. She lives in a mammoth villa in Satwa, which is an older area in the city, some of which actually has pavements for pedestrians and roads with less than six lanes. When we arrived at her place, the maid was leaving. Heidi proudly exhibited her washed, ironed and hung-up clothing collection and announced she hadn't done any of the above since she moved in. Stacey's jaw dropped only marginally faster than my own. I imagined my room at the flat I shared with Lucy, the mess spilling over the laundry bin to the point where it was so much a part of the furniture I didn't even notice it till I ran out of knickers.

Stacey and I have decided to embark on the flat hunt on our own, once our company-sponsored hotel stay has expired. The price of rent here is shocking, though. Probably more than sharing in central London. We're hoping to share a room for a while if we can, which will make things cheaper.

As I'm writing, someone's just told me that I might not blog again. Ever. I'm feeling a little sick at the thought. Apparently, along with porn and dating sites, anyone with an opinion that might not be appreciated in Dubai is banned from expressing it via TypePad and other popular blog hosts. Facebook is allowed, however, so for now I must turn to writing notes on my favorite blue-and-white buddy. I can tell you now, it's going to take some getting used to, travelling at the speed of Dubai.

17/06
Wanted: One Bacardi with Mexican hat

It's becoming glaringly apparent that Stacey and I have indeed landed ourselves in Dubai's black hole — the quiet, older part of town that's still semi-stuck in the nineteenth century. The glitzy, glamorous hotels and dazzling nightlife we read about before arriving lie slightly out of reach at the end of an enormous highway. Having thrown ourselves almost immediately into a routine involving our hotel apartment, an office and a deliriously heated walk home, we haven't seen much of it yet.

Tonight, I would have killed for a nice cold beer back at the hotel, but there isn't even a bar. You can't buy alcohol in Dubai unless it's in a licensed establishment, and there aren't really any hotels anywhere nearby that we've seen. The days of skipping over to the shops for a bargain bottle of cheap merlot, or a cool, inviting can of Stella are over. Stacey and I already both admit we took them for granted.

Sitting at our computers and emailing each other all day, which has quickly become as routine as complaining about the job we moved here to do (to be honest, it's dull, monotonous and disappointingly doesn't appear to involve any proper deputy-type tasks at all), Stacey and I started dreaming of the mini Bacardi I smuggled into the country in my make-up bag. It's been sitting on one windowsill or another in its little Mexican hat since 2004, and when it came to packing, I couldn't bear to part with it.

The time had come, I thought, to tuck in. We'd mix it with some orange juice and break the fast with a nice rummy nightcap. But — and you won't believe this — on getting back to our apartment, mini Bacardi was missing. He'd gone AWOL. I saw him this morning, I swear. I'd placed him lovingly by the telly opposite the beds, next to a disgusting German aniseed concoction Lucy once brought me back from Hamburg. But when I reached for him, he'd gone.

The maid must have nicked him. It's the only explanation. She obviously left the German crap behind because she thought it was some sort of evil medicine, but my beautiful Bacardi baby … she swiped it for herself, to drink, no doubt, in a darkened doorway, or to exchange for a few thousand dirhams in a land where my blessed Mexican rum child is as precious as a newborn baby on the black market. I'm gutted!

At least he's gone to a good home, I suppose. At least he's been enjoyed and appreciated instead of glugged in a last-minute attempt at prolonging a night of inebriated joy. Stacey and I face another night sober, but I suppose I shouldn't be too annoyed, really. She could have taken my laptop.

22/06

Where everybody knows your name ...

Last night, Stacey and I cabbed it to a far more salubrious part of town, right near the Dubai Marina. It's currently a bit of a crane-filled construction site that happens to overlook a pool of water; a rich man's yacht-filled extension of the sea surrounded by apartment blocks. According to our guidebooks, behind a beachfront hotel called Le Méridien Mina Seyahi, hid a cocktail-lovers' paradise. We clambered out of the cab in awe of the glistening fairy lights and tottered down the sparkly path towards what was essentially a welcoming Garden of Eden to two Brits in dire need of some sweet intoxication.

The Barasti bar occupies the space between the hotel and the beach. It sprawls around swimming pools, palm trees, the sandy shore and a host of beds on well-tended grasslands that you're free to lounge upon at your leisure. In the cooler winter months it's heaving, apparently, although last night we couldn't even stand outside without dripping into a Dove-deodorised pool of our own bodily fluids.

En route to the loo, we kept passing two businessmen who were (quite stupidly) sitting outside at the bar, and with every little trip these guys looked wetter and wetter and wetter. By the end of the night, not only were they slumped in a drunken heap across the bar, one of them was sweating so profusely he looked as though he'd just taken a running jump into the nearby swimming pool. Like a couple of Homer's slurring friends from *The Simpsons*, they were getting more and more leery with every journey, and consequently less and less attractive, if that was even possible.

We met M&M* inside the bar. He's a great guy with a big smile. A friend of a colleague of mine in London introduced him to me. M&M in turn introduced us to his equally lovely work colleagues, buying us a couple of Coronas each in quick succession as we all chatted underneath the fans. Trying to ignore the beads of sweat sliding down my back beneath my new red TopShop dress, I did my best to focus on the novelty of being bought drinks without having to hint, or buy any first. This kind of thing never happens in London; certainly not in my social circles, at least! To get a drink from a male you barely know, he's either drunk, or it's happy hour and your nasty beer only cost him a quid.

There was no happy hour in Barasti last night. I instantly warmed to this man of apparent power and generosity; so different to me yet clearly thriving in a world I know absolutely nothing about. He chatted with ease and regaled us with tales of his working week that made us laugh out loud (he's funny too!). In turn, Stacey and I told the group about our experiences in Dubai so far. 'You haven't seen anything yet,' was the general consensus.

I must mention that last night we also had our first encounter with a bunch of Dubai dickheads — a group of male expats who

---

* *Looking back, this was my very first encounter with M&M, whom you'll definitely hear more about later. I changed his name. You'll know why soon enough (sigh).*

can't hold a conversation without interspersing it with how much money they're making. To top off their charms, they purchased two very expensive bottles of wine 'to share in their rooftop hot tub' and took great offence when Stacey and I refused to leave with them and enjoy it. In fact, the way they exited the bar can be described in no other way than in an 'angry strop'.

M&M seemed amused. I thought again what a gentleman he was as he saw us into a cab and promised we'd hang out again soon. I hope he means it. Thank Christ there are decent guys here, too. If we hadn't met M&M in Barasti, I would have been left with a totally different impression of the local talent.

As it was, it was an awesome night! And as we got our first glimpse of the mighty Burj Al Arab in its nightly display of changing colours, I suddenly felt excited to be in Dubai. It's been a long time coming but I actually do feel as though I'm going to love this place now!

27/06

Arduous treks and torture ...

Getting a cab when we exit work in the evenings is proving impossible. It gets even more difficult as each day passes, in fact. I'm told that expats are moving here in their droves now, clogging up the roads, forcing up the rents, causing whisperings of imposing taxes. I don't know who these people are, but they ought to be ashamed of themselves. It means Stacey and I can't get a cab for love nor money, not that we have much of either.

Perhaps the cab drivers know us now and take a small pleasure in watching our dripping, bedraggled bodies waving and wavering helplessly and pathetically from the side of the road at the same time every day. I should imagine we're a bit like one of these giant billboards you find every five feet in these parts, only moving.

Kids must love us, too. 'Look, Daddy, it's the funny wet girls again,' little Ahmed shrieks as his father frowns, thinking he's far too young to be announcing such things. And then he spots us himself, sighs momentarily and watches us flop in the wing mirror of his humble Porsche Carrera GT.

Perhaps as other more fortunate passengers witness us waning from their air-conditioned cabs, they turn the other way, knowing they should stop and let us hop on in, but fearing our persistent perspiration will rub off on them and ruin their perfect journey. I have to say that ever since I moved here, I've never felt entirely clean. Stacey and I have taken to stopping midway in our nightly trek in an air-conditioned discount clothing store. Sweat dripping from every pore we peruse the lines in the latest Arabic fashions — umming and aahing in admiration, and then leaving without buying anything.

I think the shop assistants are getting suspicious now. They're starting to recognise us. We're going to have to buy something soon, but that's OK. Most things are only 25 dirhams, which is about four quid. It's a fair trade for some cool refreshment, really. And if I get a pair of muslin slacks with detachable belly button ring thrown in, well … all's fine with me. We really don't have a choice anyway. By the time we reach this air-conditioned shelter, we're so hot we're about to die.

Which brings me to another point. The labourers here. The city would have us believe Dubai is being built to the skies and out to the surrounding desert sands by Sheikh Mohammed, the man whose face looms over the road on a series of giant billboards. He's everywhere, and everyone knows him.

These self-portrait-style advertisements would, in America, be the kind to shout the services of kooky psychics or lawyers with double-barrelled surnames. In Dubai, however, it's the rather catchy title of, 'His Highness, The Emir Sheikh Mohammed bin Rashid Al Maktoum; Prime Minister and Vice President of the United Arab Emirates (UAE) and Ruler of Dubai' that we're supposed to remember.

For all his glory, he's not building anything himself. Hell, no. The people who are actually building this crazy place are the ones standing by the side of the roads all day long (and not for an hour or so like Stacey and me). It breaks my heart to see them, lining up in their overalls like wilting blue oompa-loompas, waiting for their rickety buses at the end of a ridiculously long shift. They spend all day in this unforgiving heat, lifting, stretching, welding, hammering and braving heights that would make even pilots want to puke, in some cases. I'm told that some of them have to share beds on their labour camps, too, because they work in shifts and this is more economically sound for their employers.

My co-workers have told me that some get their passports taken away when they arrive. Many were conned into coming here, promised they would earn far more money than they ever dreamed possible in their home countries (mostly Bangladesh or India). When they rock up here, however, they're told that, hang on, no wait, your wages are far less than that, and you have to give your bed to someone else while you're at work, too — sorry!

They're set to work like slaves. They can't go home because many of them have sold their land and taken loans in order to pay for their own work visas, which are viewed as tickets to paradise (a bit like my plane ticket when I waved Dubai-bye to the folks at Heathrow). If they try to leave they'll be chucked into prison until they can pay off their debts, which they clearly can't do when they're earning less than they've been promised. I'm told that most of these offending companies are government-owned. If the workers were to try and speak out for themselves they'd be told to shut up, basically. There are no human rights laws because profit margins would inevitably be reduced if there were. Slavery's encouraged here, it seems, and looking at these people ... well, I know it's wrong but I'd rather not.

It must be about 38 degrees outside at 6 pm, when we set off on our nightly voyage. And it's dark. It's annoying and uncomfortable, and yet it's only a small taste of what these people are enduring in order to earn a pittance and turn this city of dreams into reality. It's awful, but I find myself looking away. If I look too long, or think too hard, I feel guilty.

Although it's a tedious trek, the second leg of our journey is always saved by a certain giant Arab, riding a horse — on a billboard, I might add, about halfway along the Um Zaab'eel Road. It's one of Sheikh Mohammed's brothers, I think. The thing is huge and takes up valuable Nike or Coca-Cola space. I've never seen anything like it. It's even lit up. It must cost a fortune to keep him there, grinning beneath his keffiyeh, legs wrapped tight around his wild stallion. Of course, I'm not saying there are any metaphors here, or hidden messages to be found in this curious roadside rider, but it certainly stops traffic. Well, foot traffic anyway.

To think ... the most interesting thing on the walk home from my last job was a homeless man wanking off on a bench outside Bethnal Green tube station.

Lunch break, in ten easy steps ...

As is probably becoming apparent, my life and weekday habits are unrecognisable, compared with what they were a few months, even weeks, ago. Lucy emailed, asking whether I'd become a 'Letterbox' yet. In truth, I had nothing to say about my clothing for once, besides the fact that I can now wear everything just once before having to wring it out. I find the topic of locating food in the middle of a working day far more interesting to report on. So, in response, I crafted a simple step-by-step guide to illustrate exactly how quickly the monotonous habits of old can change, depending on where you choose to lay your hat and call home.

Lunch hour in London

Step 1: Exit office via lift, step onto street outside.

Step 2: Break into instant goose pimples, folding arms against chest and performing high-pitched *brrrrrrrrr* noise for added acknowledgement of shitty weather.

Step 3: Walk/run round corner towards nearest shop featuring predetermined, desired edibles.

Step 4: Glare at local 'suits', all with more money than me.

Step 5: Peruse the numerous options on offer: sandwich, salad, sushi, burger, chips, quiche, Chinese, Indian, Thai, etc. Make purchase.

Step 6: Head to TopShop/Zara/Sainsburys/New Look/Accessorize, etc.

Step 7: Glare at local 'suits', all with more money than me.

Step 8: Spend unjustifiable amount on Visa card just because it's easy.

Step 9: Glare at local 'suits', all with more money than me.

Step 10: Head back to office, eat gorgeous, pre-packaged, hunger-busting lunch.

Lunch hour in Dubai

Step 1: Exit office via lift, step outside into office car park. Dodge speeding vehicle covered in sand.

Step 2: Break into instant sweat, flapping arms about to create human fan while feeling the unfortunate fabric under my arms develop sudden wet patch.

Step 3: Walk round corner towards four-lane motorway, developing instant tan.

Step 4: Glare at local Arabs, all with more money than me.

Step 5: Stand at crossing for twenty-five minutes, wondering if a food shop exists among the furniture stores in what was once a barren sprawl of sand dunes across said motorway.

Step 6: Cross motorway. Discover no shops selling food anywhere, except random, rundown Baskin Robbins and 'closed' Indian restaurant.

Step 7: Glare at local Arabs, all with more money than me.

Step 8: Spend no money on anything, thanks to having no bank account whatsoever and not really needing a deep scarlet, camel-printed chaise-longue.

Step 9: Glare at local Arabs, all with more money than me.

Step 10: Head back to office, narrowly missing desert safari 4 4 collision in car park. Eat another of yesterday's cheese slices.

I think that pretty much sums it up.

Car park wonderland ...

Having listened to our lunch-break woes on finding absolutely nothing food-worthy among the maze of motorways, furniture and carpet stores, the American who sits opposite me in the office kindly informed me that there's a place downstairs which sells the 'best samosas in the world' for one dirham a pop, which in London would be free. Almost. It's cheap, anyway.

With hope in our hearts, Stacey and I took the SLIT-ME downstairs. That's the Slowest Lift In The Middle East, for the uninformed. And it really is. It's one of those lifts that seems to stop at every floor, even when no one gets in or out, and when people do get in it's always at the last minute. Consequently the doors shut halfway and then slam back again as a little hand reaches through, frantically grabbing air as you roll your eyes, tutting. Annoying.

Anyway, we finally got downstairs and in spite of following his directions found nothing except even more furniture shops. There must be about six on the ground floor around a giant car park and they're always void of people except for a gaggle of Arabic men perched on stools in the doorways, waiting to sell you a bed the size of your grandmother's entire living room. There were no food shops that we could see. We asked one of the men, who then stood up and led us into the blistering heat of the car park, towards what turned out to be a coffee shop shrouded in green plants and flowers. How mysterious. He then disappeared, leaving us to push the door open and tentatively step inside.

The sight was breathtaking. We took what little breath we could through the cloud of shisha smoke that slammed our faces. All around us sat Arabs in traditional whites, puffing on pipes, shovelling food into their mouths from giant steaming plates, watching cricket. They ignored us, even as we stared like two white rabbits caught in the lights of a mesmerising wonderland.

Sadly, though, the only thing the people behind the 'bar' seemed to sell, besides hot rice-based dishes, was fruit juice and Red Bull. I don't think this was the samosa place.

We snuck back out into the car park, feeling a little bit like Alice must have felt after waking up from her dream. What a wonderful, magical place to have as a local eatery — even if we never dare to step inside again. It definitely isn't the lunchtime experience of old, when I'd wander out of the office door, through the next one, pick up a Ribena and a tuna sandwich and leave again — not so unimpressed as completely oblivious as to what I'd just done.

It's funny how heading out for food on your lunch break can become so routine; how the monotony of it all can eventually force entire hours out of your head as you drift somewhere else, *anywhere* else in what little spare time you have. But just as Narnia sleeps untouched by most inside that wardrobe, the shisha/cricket place that hides downstairs across the car park isn't even of this world. Not of my normal world anyway.

The American seemed disappointed we didn't find our samosas, but until I get a little more adventurous, and unless I want a giant bed or an energy drink for lunch in this part of Dubai, I'm probably better off just bringing a lunchbox.

Sheikh, rattle and roll ...

There are some parts of this city that take my breath away — a glamorous, special side that's far removed from the carpet stores and car parks of our office neighbourhood; a side that dazzles with the glitz of Vegas, the promise of Manhattan and the rough and ready charms of London. It might seem a tiny bit fake, some of it, but everywhere I've been this weekend I've been struck with an awesome sense of how much could be mine for the taking, whether or not I can afford it right now. I've landed in a place that's being built around me and for me, and anything I can add to help it grow will probably be welcomed with open arms.

To think that until the late fifties Dubai was a teeny-weeny port for pearl fishermen and smugglers! They got their water from wells and lived in houses made from palm leaves. Now, some of those same people are undoubtedly scratching their heads in bewilderment, just like Stacey and I were when we first found ourselves being ferried about in cab after cab after cab, owing to the lack of pavements. They surely must be wondering what's going on, these people. Their humble port is growing at the speed of light. Everywhere you look there are cranes, construction and boarded-up sites concealing absolute chaos. But rising like a phoenix from the flames, every few metres is a building of such majestic beauty you can barely believe you're allowed inside. There's an air of uprooted anxiety and excitement that definitely rubs off on you. Sometimes, even when I find myself gawping like a goldfish out of water, I feel a sort of twisting in my stomach at the prospect of getting a personal slice of such incredible success!

On Friday, Stacey and I met The Trader for our first Dubai brunch at Waxy O'Connor's. Inside, it was much like any other Irish pub you might encounter, only like an ugly sister overshadowed by her beautiful sibling, this dirty hole is attached to the side of a posh, five-star hotel. Waxy's is renowned for offering 'the booziest brunch in town' and may I add that it's got nothing to do with the pub of the same name in Leicester Square, in which I once had a rather unfortunate encounter with a box of magic mushrooms and a homeless woman on speed. But that's another story.

The Trader is another friend of a friend whom I've never met before. It's looking like everyone in Dubai is a friend of a friend, or just a friend you haven't met yet but soon will because the place is just so damn small. The Trader is raking it in already, and he's only been here a few weeks longer than we have. His company is putting him up in the Marina and he'll soon be buying his own place here with a view of the yachts and rising skyscrapers. He's just bought a Porsche 911 with terracotta seats. That's the colour, he tells us. They're not actually made from terracotta. (I nod — I know nothing about cars).

He's a friendly guy who has two mobile phones and a girlfriend overseas. Stacey and I reckon he's a pretty busy man but we sat there for most of the day in dank darkness, drinking, laughing and pretending we were nothing like the other expats congregating in the shadows, pretending in turn that they were nothing like us. In truth, I think we were all escaping the real world and trying our damned hardest not to experience the real, suffocating, intimidating Dubai. In Ireland, everyone feels at home (or is just drunk, perhaps).

We paid the equivalent of eight quid for an unlimited brunch including a full English breakfast and, after 1 pm, a lunch of roast beef with all the trimmings, plus five drinks of our choosing. I'm told it's not the gluttonous affair that some hotels afford, in which vast ballrooms draped in glittering fabrics and bordered by ice sculptures lure you to a hundred food stations, offering every dish you can imagine and even more that you can't. I'm going to one of those soon, but Waxy's, so I'm told, is a bit of a Dubai institution. An initiation, of sorts. You have to do it to prepare yourself for the rest.

When the air became too thick to breathe and the drunken expat engineers too much to handle, we got a cab to The Trader's place in the Marina. The view is to die for, although if I'm honest you have to look beyond a million cranes, bulldozers and dusty vacant building foundations to see the sea.

His place is a far cry from any apartment I ever saw in London. It's a two-bedroom flat on a pretty high floor and when he moved in not only had it been furnished (almost unheard of in a rental here), it had all been laid out like a showroom. The dinner table was even set as though he was expecting six guests, complete with fancy napkins and cutlery beside each mat. He hasn't changed it. It was a bit like walking into IKEA. I half expected to be handed a giant yellow basket and a brochure. Still, I'd love to live in a place like that, where you can literally watch the world grow around you. It's going to be beautiful, inspirational even … when it's finished.

What happened after that is a bit of a blur, but we cabbed it to the Hard Rock Café for some cocktails — something I would never even dream of doing anywhere else. I'm told that fifteen years ago the Hard Rock Café was the furthest point you could reach in Dubai. Cabs were reluctant to take people so far out of the city back then, and the place used to be attached to a seedy hotel, which is how it got its liquor licence. This part was shut down, and now the bar/restaurant sits in the middle of a spaghetti junction with central Dubai in one direction and Abu Dhabi in the other. It seems sort of lonely now. The giant guitars on the forecourt make it look a bit like a sad, abandoned theme park attraction.

It was at the Hard Rock Café that we managed to recruit two blokes from the navy — lovely guys who then joined us for a kara-oke venture at a place called Harry Ghatto's. This bar, with a name like my favourite dessert, is an exclusive, teeny little venue in the Emirates Towers, which starts pumping karaoke at 10 pm, along with ludicrously expensive drinks. By the end of the night I felt like I knew everyone in there — and I'd sung duets with most of them, too. A couple of Emirati men in full traditional dress were drinking pints and checking out the songbook. Who says sheikhs don't rock 'n' roll?

I also made friends with a private banker. He stole the mic from me with a cheeky grin and a nod of his sandy blonde head, be-fore breaking into a God-awful version of 'My Way'. He evidently had lots of money because he bought both Stacey and me drinks all night, even before The Trader went home. I'm kind of getting used to not having to buy drinks around here. There seems to be an abundance of very rich men around who are only too happy to take the job off my hands.

Speaking of very rich men, I met a project developer who works in Abu Dhabi, up the road, sort of. He drives the hour and a half to Dubai every weekend because it's a lot more interesting on the nightlife front, although I seem to remember him telling me a couple of stories that would suggest there's a lot happening there behind closed doors. A wealthy Arab he works for took him to Kazakhstan on business last week. During the trip he said they vis-ited a casino, in which the Arab man produced a bulging envelope full of US hundred-dollar bills and proceeded to gamble half away on various tables. Back in Abu Dhabi, the same guy took him to a party in a villa, which was full of rich locals and beautiful Russian hookers. These girls were allegedly paid for being there, and given a bonus if they screwed.

Still, in spite of what hypocritical nonsense might go on behind the scenes, I'm getting used to an absence of petty criminal activity. I had my bag on the floor by the bar all night in Harry's as I wandered around talking to people, and didn't worry about it once. In fact, if you hold your bag close like you have to do in London, you get a funny look here, as though *you're* the one who's shifty.

The phrase 'there's no crime in Dubai' is spoken with conviction. People are too scared to do anything that might land them in jail. One man even left his laptop next to us in Starbucks during the week, in the middle of a shopping mall, when he popped to the loo! I can't see it staying that way forever, and I wouldn't go out of my way to test the strength of someone's character by leaving my bulging wallet out in the middle of a table (if indeed it was ever to bulge), but it's definitely refreshing.

In other news, we finally checked out the Madinat, which is one of those buildings you just can't help but gasp at. It's a huge, palatial sort of affair that's built to look like a traditional souk or bazaar, sitting between two spectacularly glamorous hotels. It houses numerous shops, bars and restaurants inside and happens to have the most incredible view of the seven-star Burj Al Arab — a large hotel that looks a bit like a multi-coloured cockroach sitting on a perch. We ate a late lunch in a trendy bar with views of a manmade lagoon. Then we went for a glass of very expensive wine and watched the sun set over the sea from the terrace at the Bahri Bar in the *über*-posh Al Qasr hotel. It was brochure-like, with non-kissy couples cosying up as much as they dared on sofas overlooking the sea.

You know what strikes me as funny, thinking back? What might look like honeymooners to the untrained eye are just standard Dubai residents enjoying the way of life they've become accustomed to. I could become accustomed to it, too. What with all of these mini-adventures, I feel like I'm on holiday!

13/07

When good girls get wet and wild ...

'We have to go on ladies' night!' Heidi had enthused at work, and the entire office nodded in agreement. Ladies' night at a water park. Well, it just had to be done really, didn't it? If I'm quite honest, I thought Heidi, Stacey and I would be the only ones there. I mean, who wants to float around on a rubber ring without a boy to dunk and flirt with? Who wants to hover under a waterfall without a man to snog at sporadic intervals? Shall we just say ... the entire female population of Dubai?

Wild Wadi sits close to the Jumeirah Beach Hotel (the one shaped like a wave) and has got an even more incredible view of the Burj Al Arab than the Madinat. It's so close to this bug-shaped beauty that you can see the people inside.

I must admit, I couldn't see a bloody thing. I'm taking Stacey's word for it. I had to take my eyes out as it's no fun getting chlorine in your contact lenses, but I could decipher a colourful blur against a twinkling horizon, which made a pretty impressive backdrop when standing in line for the Jumeirah Sceirah (supposed to read as *scarer* but they've added a crafty twist). It's a terrifying

There's no need to diet before choosing
a swimsuit in Dubai.

openair slide, 33 metres above the ground. I can report that having now been truly *sceir*ed by it, the rumours of having to spend ten minutes afterwards rooting round your backside for your swimming costume are true. The gush of water hits you so fast at the bottom that your crotch sucks everything in like an inbuilt, new-edition Dyson.

Most impressive of all, however, were the people who flocked to this waterlogged ladies' night, and the swimwear they chose to exhibit. It was nothing short of burqalicious! You have to bear in mind here that even if the men are safely on the outside, this inner-world of liquid delight is still not safe from the eyes of the man upstairs. Women must cover themselves as much as possible. Just. In. Case.

Personally, I would have been pretty excited just to catch a glimpse of the great 'burkini'. This gorgeous garment is made from UV- and water-protected polyester. Unlike the bikini, it covers the whole body with the exception of the feet, hands and face, thus allowing Muslim women to swim in public. What we got, however, was a whole lot more. In the absence of men it seems these women go slightly crazy. To many, it didn't even appear to matter that they were in a water park — it was simply an exciting excuse to wear all the things that they would never usually get to wear.

We saw high heels. We saw gym pants. We saw ballet skirts. We even saw a lady in jeans, battling the water in the wave pool — with a toddler. Of course, we saw a lot of sari-scares, too — huge floaty numbers on the bodies of the bashful, billowing out and threatening to swallow surrounding swimmers, tangling them up in their masses like seaweed.

The sight of two girls bobbing along wearing shower caps was a special treat. Not even swim caps, mind. I actually mean *shower caps* — the flimsy plastic ones you get free in hotel bathrooms, no less. They doggy-paddled past, giggling gaily, seemingly oblivious to the fact that their hair was quite wet beneath these plastic sheaths. As I watched a woman in a red floral summer dress and black leggings have a go on the surfing simulator, I suddenly felt quite underdressed in my bikini. Had I known that the Wild Wadi Ladies' Night was a fancy dress affair, I would have made a bit more effort. I've got some great costumes. I could have blown them all away with my cowgirl outfit, or the Little Red Riding Hood gingham frock and cape from Halloweens past.

Anyway, aside from the hordes of children, and being the token Westerners in the water park, we really did have an awesome night. And how different my life has become from the rain-soaked London affair of just a few weeks ago! Here, just an hour or so after leaving work and wanting to scream as the sweat poured off my body and into my shopping bag, I was floating on a lazy river in a rubber ring, laughing as I bounced into other people and screaming like a hyperactive child. I was on holiday again, actually. There were no worries to dwell on, no work problems left in my head, no cares in the world.

On nights like this I can't help but feel as though I'll probably never live in the UK again. It makes me kind of sad, but I guess when you compare this fun-filled, sun-filled lifestyle to howling gales and constant rain, it's pretty much a given, to be honest.

I'll never go swimming in a sundress, though. That's just stupid.

15/07

The joys of being a woman ...

Experiencing the visit of my monthly friend at work, I trudged out into the kiln today, across the car park to the little shop in search of some tampons. Call me crazy, but being a little shop in an office car park, I expected them to stock at least a few feminine essentials. Despite housing a back wall crammed full of sanitary towels that had all been stashed out of sight like dirty porn magazines, there were absolutely no tampons to be seen. Anywhere.

I didn't really know what to do. Stacey didn't have any, neither did Heidi, and as a newbie in the company I couldn't very well go round asking everyone. It's just not the done thing. And I'm sure as hell not buying a massive wad of sanitary towels — they come in packs as big as nappies! Also, other people might think it's OK to wear a nappy under their skirt in 40 degrees, but I'm afraid I draw the line there.

I stood there, flummoxed. The tissue trick would have been OK had it not been hot, humid and altogether disgusting outside. What to do, what to do …

I remember my friend Sarah telling me once that she had a similar situation in Turkey and Egypt. It's to do with Muslim women appearing demure and modest, and some Arab men allegedly believing that pads better help achieve this status than tampons. You can buy Tampax and O.b. in the big supermarket chain, Carrefour, as well as other shops in Dubai, though. I've seen them. But remembering my friend's words made me wonder if this particular sweet-looking man was actually a secret tampon-basher, scribbling them off his weekly delivery list with hate in his eyes. I silently wished a period on him, so he too could experience the joys of bloodshed in a nappy in the middle of a sweltering car park.

It's a good thing they do actually sell tampons elsewhere in this city. I'll have to stock up. Imagine if I had to get Mum to ship them in every month from the UK. I've heard not to get necessities shipped over here, actually. Sometimes packages arrive missing tampons, decent bras and sexy underwear … and yes, these are necessities to some people. Women at the sorting office keep a beady eye out for such items and take them for themselves. It's the only way they can get them sometimes.

Come to think of it, there was a girl in the bar the other night who knows another girl, who knows a girl, who knows someone at work (I'm starting to think it was her) who was stopped at Dubai customs and made to remove a giant dildo from her suitcase. Apparently she was travelling alone, which I guess means she was spared the embarrassment of having someone who actually knew her discover how she gets her little — or big — pleasures. But on the other hand, she had no one there to witness the look of excitement in the official's eyes as she bagged it and stashed it out of sight.

Being a non-Muslim woman in Dubai so far isn't half bad, in the grand scheme of things. But if you're a kinky dominatrix with a suitcase full of pleasures, or prone to getting your period in an office block full of tampon-bashers, I'm guessing you're going to have a few off days.

17/07
Dodgy deals, desert drives and a Middle-Eastern marketing machine ...

Since arriving here four weeks ago, a guy at work has moved in and out of a place because of a lizard infestation in the corner of his bedroom. He ummed and aahed for a while before packing his bags. He carefully considered the mammoth balcony, the en-suite bathroom and the pair of Russian sisters living in the apartment next door, but still decided on the whole that his scaly roommates were too much to handle. Poor guy.

Most of the places to rent in Dubai sound incredible, but more often than not people want ridiculous deposits to move in. They also want six months' to a year's payment in advance. Who has that kind of money? Certainly not a twenty-seven year old who has spent the years since graduating from uni shopping, travelling the globe and struggling to make a living in London.

When I emailed HR at work about whether they had a policy of lending employees the money for things like this, in exchange for a monthly reduction in salary (I've heard some companies do this), the answer was, 'Most people take the money from their savings, or borrow it from their parents.' Hmmm.

I did some sums and even with my limited mathematical capabilities, there seems to be no way around the fact that the amount I would need to have saved in order to move into a room, at a monthly cost of the average 4,500 dirhams, is 7,400 pounds sterling. That's a lot of money. And asking my parents for a wad of cash equating to half the annual sum of their small-town English lifestyle would seem, perhaps, a little like taking the piss. After all, they gave me fifty quid to last the month when I moved out here.

I wrote back: 'OK, thanks a lot, I'll reconsider my options.'

I'm weak like that.

Rent has risen drastically in Dubai over the past few years. There never used to be a cap on how much landlords could increase it year by year, so they just got greedy, milking it for everything they could get. Of course, now it just means there's no cheap housing alternatives anywhere. It's just extortionate, expensive or 'bedspace' — which is basically a mattress on the floor of a hovel.

Now, I know I've lived in some hellholes in my time, the most noteworthy being a warehouse apartment I shared with a bipolar girl in Brooklyn, who had a penchant for naked nighttime rollerblading. But I kind of think that as an educated twenty-something who left a perfectly reasonable, two-bedroom East

London apartment just a few weeks ago, I automatically bypass the cockroach-ridden bed-sit situation.

A viewing last night, our first, was the miraculous result of a recommendation by the very nice Private Banker boy I met at Harry Ghatto's karaoke bar the other night. We've been sending the odd email back and forth since we bonded over 'Endless Love' (the Mariah Carey version) and he actually called to tell me there was a massive room to let in his colleague's shared villa.

We met this landlord at McDonald's near Al Safa — an area on the map that seems to consist of a road junction, two hypermarkets and a Boots pharmacy — and drove with him to the villa for what seemed like an eternity. Eventually we pulled up in an enormous driveway, next to an extremely well-tended garden and a glistening swimming pool. We were in the farthest region of an area called Al Barsha. The place was huge. In fact, the room Stacey and I were to share was the size of the entire flat I'd just vacated in London!

The only drawback, aside from a South African family, including young children, occupying the space downstairs, is the fact that it's so far away from anywhere we'd ever need to go. And the fact that neither of us really drives a car.

Also, it's so new that there's literally nothing else there. There are no landmarks from which cabs could identify our home — if they'd even travel out that far to collect us. There are no shops, the Metro won't be open for two years, the roads are literally dusty tracks and the only green things around are a few trees, perched on dirty mounds. They've left them there, apparently for a religious reason, standing tall above the ground like withered hands in a manmade sprawl of what's bound to be, I've no doubt, total luxury. We just arrived twenty years too early.

Dubai's online listings site, dubizzle.com, is full of rooms to rent. This said, I'm not quite sure if agreeing to take the one on the landing of a villa with an eccentric Iranian inventor living downstairs is the best decision Stacey and I have ever made. But this room is only 2,500 dirhams each a month if we share the space, which is less than I paid for my shoebox in London. It also leaves me even more of my monthly salary to spend on hanging out in karaoke bars and restaurants, trying to find a rich boyfriend.

I'll admit, sharing a room isn't ideal. It's sort of like reversing in status from independent career woman to student backpacker, even though Stacey and I get on well so far and clearly won't steal each other's baked beans. The room is big enough for the two single beds the landlord has promised to put in there, I suppose, and it comes with a telly and built-in wardrobes. We'll have to share the bathroom with the three or four other randoms about to move in and the kitchen doesn't have a cooker, and actually, the whole set up is situated on the landing right by the staircase … oh all right, it's a shit-hole. But we're seeing it as a temporary solution. Miraculously, we don't have to pay any ridiculous amounts up front for this place.

Back to the Iranian inventor. He seems to be a very sweet man. He's renting the upper level of this giant mansion (Iransion?) in case any clients want to come and stay. How thoughtful. By clients, I mean people who might be interested in funding his latest invention, which happens to be a vehicle that's powered by a horse running on a conveyor belt. No, seriously.

When we sat down in his ground-floor living room and he faced us, twiddling his thumbs and enquiring as to our heritage (very common here and not considered to exhibit possible prejudice at all), a quick glance around the room revealed a professionally produced display stand, featuring a certain 'fleet horse' machine. He also had a map on the wall outlining the world tour he's planning

The fabulous contraption from above (we were too scared to pose next to it in case he got angry). If you're interested in investing, get in touch.

to take in this contraption. 'I was going to start in UAE,' he told us, 'but now I think I start in America.'

Because they won't laugh at him there?

When we got outside, there was actually a 'fleet horse' on the driveway. Amazing. It looks a bit like a greenhouse on a tractor, with a strappy apparatus in the middle, presumably to hold the horse in place. Apparently, he's going to market the polythene surrounding as an advertising tool, the idea being that companies will pay him to display their logos and slogans on the side of this thing. I'm sure it will attract a lot of attention. I know I'd certainly stop and stare at a galloping horse doing a treadmill workout on the motorway … in a greenhouse. Even if I'd call the RSPCA afterwards.

I'm not sure he's really thought the whole thing through, you know. When I pointed at the suffocating, polythene sheath, trapping the desert heat inside and threatening to melt his entire invention all over the driveway, I asked: 'Won't the horse get a bit hot in there, seeing as it's 45 degrees outside?'

He looked at me for a second, then at the floor, as though a little dream had just been euthanised.

Shit, I have to start all over again, said his eyes. 'Er, yes ... I just, er ... put something inside ... um... some cooling,' said his mouth.

Yes, I think living with him will prove quite interesting. Maybe he'll even let me go on the road with him. Maybe I'll become the stable girl and recognise my true calling as a travelling salesman. Or maybe, when he pops his clogs through heat exhaustion, I'll just inherit his villa.

19/07

A Samsung fairytale

Once upon a time, on the taxi ride home from a pissed-up night in a karaoke bar at the top of a golden tower, a young girl called Stacey lost her phone.

If a sparkling gem like a Samsung phone went missing in the dangerous land of thieves and beggars from which young Stacey came, it would undoubtedly stay that way. Lost. Forever. Perhaps, she thought, the taxi driver might keep it for himself, or another Dubaian explorer would pounce upon this urban treasure with a magpie's glint in his eye and a heart of stone. She called her phone to no avail. It was switched off. Alas, alack, poor Stacey and her treasure had parted much too soon, no thanks to her Shiraz-fuelled shenanigans.

The faithful Stacey dialled her number throughout the day with hope in her hung-over heart. The verdict never changed. 'Perhaps the insurance will cover it,' she whispered into her monitor, as she scrolled through Vodafone's terms and conditions. But those unspoken words echoed around the office like a tragic love song: 'We all know it'll take fucking months for them to deliver out here.'

But little did Stacey know her luck was about to change. That night, as she sat in the food court of a palatial shopping mall, dejectedly shovelling plastic forks full of teppanyaki beef into her mouth from a Styrofoam plate, she gazed unseeingly at the passers-by, dreaming, no doubt, of a life free from mobile communications. Across the table, her good friend Becky — a stunning princess from foreign shores with full red lips, killer tits and reams of thick, shiny blonde hair — dialled her number once more, just for the hell of it. And someone answered.

The ladies almost spat out their food in surprise. 'Ah, I been waiting for your call,' said the voice at the other end. 'Your battery die. I put your SIM card in my phone. I bring you. Where are you please?'

At first, Stacey couldn't speak. In turn, Becky bit a chunk off her plastic fork and almost swallowed it. Could it be that an angel had landed in Dubai, with a heart of gold and a taxicab?

Two hours later, Stacey was reunited with her sparkling Samsung phone. The angel drove it right to her door and placed it into her welcoming hands. She noticed as he handed it over that his own phone had itself been created at the dawn of time. Its weathered screen was devoid of colour. It was so large it would probably break the lining of his trousers if he tried to keep it in his pocket, and who knows if it even doubled as an mp3 player with unlimited Internet access and a built-in Tomb Raider game with infrared headset attachment, like hers.

As she kissed her phone goodnight, back once more in its rightful place beside her pillow, Stacey swore she would never be mean to a taxi driver in Dubai again. And the moral of this story? Just because someone can't drive, speak English or navigate their way around a city for which they are paid to know every inch, doesn't mean they'll nick your mobile phone if you leave it in the back of their car.

22/07

Day one at the Iransion ...

Moving Day went relatively smoothly at the weekend, and our Iranian inventor greeted us merrily on the stairwell of the villa, ladder in hand as though he'd spent the morning renovating our bedroom. I harboured a glimmer of hope he might have invented something for us. Such was not the case, although he has now installed two single beds, each with a built-in headboard that doubles as a shelving unit. Very handy. I can fit at least three books in mine and when I lie down I lose half my head to the bottom shelf. With some clever imagining it's almost like being in a cave.

We do have a fabulous view of the fleet-horse contraption, though, still sitting proudly on the driveway. And also quite nice (although clearly not as cool) is that the Burj Dubai, soon to be the tallest building in the world, stands about half a mile away from the villa. Technically, I suppose, I could watch them build it from my bed, if my head wasn't wedged in the shelf.

Worthy of note in itself perhaps, are the channels we can receive on the telly. The Iranian has given us cable, but along with an Internet connection that's so slow it's most probably powered by another animal on a conveyor belt somewhere, the only channels that aren't scrambled are some French news stations and a whole load of porn. I'm not saying our Iranian inventor is subscribed to the porn-package, but when you can watch an Asian secretary being pounded on her office desk by a longhaired Lothario in an eighties patterned shirt, yet you can't watch the BBC, there's something amiss.

Oh, and in a separate note, we also discovered he's shagging the cleaner — an Asian girl young enough to be his daughter. Which is nice.

24/07

Girls just wanna have brunch ...

House hunts and fleet horses aside, I realise I haven't yet written about losing my extravagant Friday brunch virginity. This is probably because I'm still recovering. It can take a while, so I'm told. Waxy's was one thing, but as so many people kept telling me, a grotty Irish pub in Bur Dubai is a far cry from what this city is fast becoming famous for — an all-you-can-eat-and-drink extravaganza in a five-star beachside hotel, with requisite posh frock, high heels and an insatiable appetite for expensive food.

Even if I didn't feel it, I'm sure I looked the part as I tottered into the glimmering lobby, wearing my hot red TopShop dress and silver strappy shoes. I have to admit, although it's nice, it kind of feels a bit silly, dressing up for a daytime feed — like you're heading to a wedding where the only marriage about to take place is a variety of food to a ridiculous amount of booze.

The Al Qasr hotel in the Madinat offers a life-changing experience that has since left me floundering at the edge of reality. How can I go back from this? The brunch starts at noon and goes until 4 pm, costs the equivalent of roughly sixty quid, and sets a fairytale scene of exquisite dishes heaped in glistening crystal bowls, giant ice sculptures and cocktail stations at every turn. It's located across three different restaurants and the idea is to walk between them all, rather like the kids in *Charlie and the Chocolate Factory*, gaping in awe at all you see, loading your plate and then filling your face back at your table as the people all around you rejoice in a banquet like no other. Reservations are a must. To my virginal eyes, this brunch was heaven with angel hair pasta and a whole lot more.

Want seasoned, spiced squid, mussels in white wine, an entire lobster cooked just right, just for you? Roast beef with radishes, salad with salmon, Italian spaghetti, a petrified-looking piglet on a carving tray? (Oh yes, if you pay enough and hit the right places, you can have all the pork you want in Dubai.) Lashings of cheese, sesame seed bread, Cumberland sausages, beef sizzled in a wok before your eyes, smoking with Jim Beam sauce? Fresh watermelon, apples with ice-cream, marshmallow chunks for the chocolate fountain, no need to ask, don't be silly! Glasses of creamy custard and mini cakes that melt in your mouth, topped with a side of mashed potato sprinkled with jellybeans? Do what you want. You've paid for it. You work hard. You deserve it.

And that's just the food.

Endless champagne? Go right ahead! Bacardi cocktails? A mojito, red wine, white wine, vodka and cranberry? You want gin and tonic followed by whisky, topped up with cider by the drunken guy sitting opposite? Maybe a milkshake, a Baileys, a Breezer, or even just an orange juice? Sure! You can even have coffee, if you want. For four hours straight, you can enjoy a despicable act of gluttony you never thought was in your power to display, and then, when you're totally hammered and your clothes are stretching over bulges in all the wrong places, you can leave and fall asleep somewhere comfy. Or … you can get a cab with some very nice boys to a seventies disco night in a club called The Lodge and dance to Wham! until your ears bleed. Which is what I did.

Oh, yes, so I'm told, the partying never stops at 'brunch' — not when you're new in town. There are too many places to go, too many people to shower you with even more booze and too many egos to grace you with their business cards. I'm planning to spend every Friday like this, for the rest of my life.

27/07

Moving on up …

Tonight, Stacey and I met our new flatmates — two Indian brothers, one who works in finance and the other who runs an events company. The latter deals a lot with laser beams. He showed us no less than 300 photos taken at various luxury events here in Dubai, all involving laser and light displays, and then said I could work for him on a cricket event he's organising.

If I can get some companies to sponsor it, I'll get a cut. And we're talking three times my monthly salary, which is a pittance (if I haven't mentioned that already). I'm earning 10,000 dirhams a month in Dubai, which sounded like a lot before I got here, but when you consider rent is 2,500 every month when we're sharing, and could go up to 4,500 a month or more each when we're not, it's not that much at all. We were never told how expensive it is to live here before we left. I guess we could have done some research in that area, but sussing out the nicest bars and restaurants and making sure we had dresses to wear to them all seemed more important at the time.

Freelance on the sneaky side might just be my answer. There are tons of mags launching all around us. I also picked up some work for a funky dot com the other day, which deals in gift experiences and entertainment. The manager sounds like a great guy — the generous M&M put me in touch with him.

M&M (the sexy Corona-buying guy we met at Barasti on that hot and sweaty night) has been very nice lately, by the way, helping Stacey and me get settled and taking us out on the town. He's living in a big house on his own at the moment, apparently, so I think he must be glad of some new, impressionable friends to party with.

Anyway, I can now reveal I have applied for what I think could be my dream job, as the editor for the online version of the UAE's biggest selling glossy mag. I feel a bit guilty for wanting to leave the travel publishing company, but I honestly do feel like it's a bit beneath me at this point. Call me a demanding cow but working on an online trash mag, chatting about celebs all day and attending parties full of free cocktails, hot guys and goody bags seems far more up my street. Oh, the job description didn't contain any of that, obviously, but I know that's what it would be like. I've done it before. It would be even better in Dubai. Think of all the new places opening up every single day!

I told the Indian laser lover I'd think about his offer. It could be difficult meeting clients without a car, and I'd have to do it at weekends and after work, which could be tricky. It's funny how everyone talks business here, all the bloody time. I mean, here I am, sitting in the Iransion, flicking through endless porn, trying not to lose my entire body to the vortex created by my headboard, and I get offered a freelance job as soon as I head into the kitchen.

Doing it for our country ...

I've been here over a month now and I'll never get used to the fact that the doors to Dubai's seedy underworld open mostly from the innards of a shiny, clean shopping mall or a luxury hotel. Every time I walk into the glistening Emirates Towers, up the immaculate escalator, past the expensive watch shops and into Harry Ghatto's (fast becoming our favourite place in the whole wide world), I feel dirty inside. This is because I know that when it comes to me leaving again, I may well fall instead of walk down to level one, make un-amusing 'I'm a naughty burglar' motions in front of a watch shop, or puke on the sparkling doorstep of Starbucks next door.

Of course, it's not the done thing to be drunk and disorderly in public here. Well, it's not the done thing to be drunk and disorderly anywhere, really, unless you're wearing a football shirt, on holiday, in Ibiza. But whereas in other countries you can stumble out of a club and disappear into the depths of the darkened night, in Dubai you stumble out of a club into the pristine, floodlit glare of a sumptuous hotel and the disapproving stares of an entire Arab family enjoying some freshly squeezed orange juice.

Trying to act sober on such a public viewing platform is a true test of British twenty-something strength. And of course we all

It may look like a built in wardrobe, but it's my
second home, a karaoke bar in a shopping mall.
I miss it dearly.

know that when we feel pressured to be something we're clearly
not, we act even more guiltily.

For example:

Mum: Are you drunk?

Teen Daughter: Wachoo always washingmeee for? Donchoo
twust me?!? Dwhy look drunk choo? [*Falls over*]

Nobody wants a friend who's been in jail. I find that visualising
a set of handcuffs around my wrists is usually enough to make me
stand up straight, even when my post-karaoke status is teetering
into unconsciousness. And imagining a night behind bars with a
fleet of perspiring local fruit thieves is normally enough to ensure I resist the urge to jump on my male friend's back and yell:

'Carry me home like a pony, come on horsey, giddy-up giddy-up!' — as was so often the case back on Tottenham Court Road.

As you can imagine, it's not always easy. When I'd slurred good-bye to my mates at 3 am back in London, the usual chain of events was to stumble through the maze of Soho's back streets, load up on chips and curry sauce, wait for the number eight bus, head to the top deck, fall asleep with my head against the window and wake up three hours later, covered in condiments. I was anonymous. Invisible. Irrelevant.

In Dubai, however, if you do actually make it out of whichever exquisite hotel or shopping centre you're in without falling into a fountain or chipping someone's freshly frozen ice sculpture, you've still got to rely on someone else to get you home. There's no Metro as yet. No night bus to speak of.

A taxi ride home after a night out must of course be filled with singing, pop quizzes involving the non-English speaking driver in his eighteenth hour of ferrying morons around, and the repeated insistence that not all Brits are drunken idiots, corrupting the city's carefully constructed and highly respectable culture. There are so many risks involved — maintaining our habits and traditions, saluting our heritage, and trying not to forget who we really are as the world changes all around us. But it's something we must strive to continue, for the sake of our roots.

31/07

Musings on a sleepless night ...

When I'm drunk, I can sleep anywhere. I've slept in some pretty uncomfortable places in my time. On more than one occasion I have actually fallen asleep on a bar stool. And once, at a party on a boat, while dressed in a ball gown, I awoke to find myself lying horizontally under a pile of coats that definitely weren't there when I sat down. Also, in Arizona a few years back, I slept on a rock in a national park with no padding beneath me, and woke up to find animal droppings right next to my face.

In spite of all that, I have never, I repeat *never*, slept anywhere as uncomfortable or ridiculous as my bed in the Iransion. It's not even the vortex created by the shelving unit that bothers me anymore, even when I sit up and smash my skull on the mammoth *Welcome to Dubai* book (just to rub it in). It's more the concrete slab that the mattress resembles. Imagine sleeping on the floor with no padding underneath you. That's what it feels like. In fact, I could well be back in Arizona on that rock, should something care to shit near my face as well.

For the past few nights I've probably had about four hours of sleep in total. The rest of the time I've been shifting from side to side on my slab like a reject from *The Night of the Living Dead*, praying for some comfort. I came up with a half solution, which was to fold the duvet (a seventies yellow-and-brown affair that my friend Ric thinks looks like a Chocolate Viennese biscuit) in half, and lie on top of it. This offered moderate improvement, although rendered me without a duvet, so I've been 'sleeping' underneath my beach towel, which has the game Twister printed on it.

I can't imagine what my deceased relatives must think if they're looking down on me at this moment. And if it adds anything extra to the image, I've also been wearing an aeroplane eye mask, because the thin, white curtain lets the light in too early … and some earplugs too, because the air-conditioning unit in the room sounds like a tribe of dwarves with lawnmowers are trying to drive through the walls.

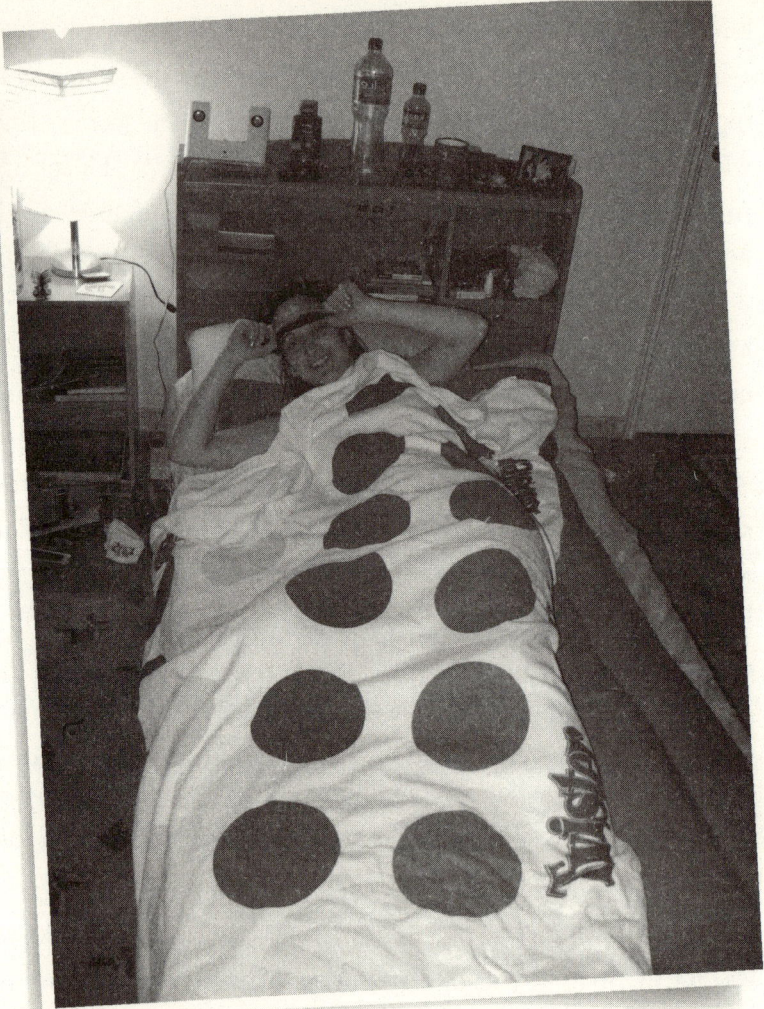

This is me trying to sleep on my concrete slab
under my Twister towel. I made Stacey take a
photo so I could look at it and feel grateful if I
was ever made to sleep in an uncomfortable place
again. Nothing has ever compared.

The cherry on top is that at 4.30 am, just when I'm finally
starting to drift off in a deformed, unborn-childlike position, the
chanting begins. It drifts over the villa-tops and through the crack

in the sliding door, bursting through my earplugs and calling the Muslims (and me) to prayer in an echoing song that quite frankly scares the living shit out of me. Parts of it would be beautiful if, as my friend The Irishman said on the phone the other day, 'I was sitting on a beach at sunrise, soaking up the soulful sounds of tradition'. I'm sure he's right. But at 4.30 am, when I'm suffering on a concrete slab, shivering under a Twister towel in an aeroplane eye mask, I can only really concentrate on the part that sounds like a moaning camel dying outside my window.

I thought about going to IKEA at the weekend and buying another mattress. It would make for an interesting expedition, trying to get it home without a car. M&M, being the generous man he is, offered to help, but like fifty per cent of men in Dubai, M&M has what I call 'a selfish car'. It's a Porsche, which only realistically has room for two and definitely wouldn't accommodate a mattress, unless it was strapped to the roof. The other fifty per cent of men in Dubai, in case you were wondering, drive cars so huge you could fit an entire bedroom suite inside, fully constructed, straight from the showroom. I don't know any of them yet though, unfortunately.

I'm going to have to lump the concrete slab for now. Having a drink before bedtime takes the edge off, at least. Hopefully I'll get used to it before I become permanently deformed.

02/08

A new-found celebrity status ...

I was in the Crowne Plaza hotel on Sheikh Zayad Road, heading to a smoky pub called The Harvester, when a man I'll call Stanley called me from the publishing company and asked me to an interview for that jazzy celebrity online editor job I applied for. I was so excited and ended up getting quite drunk with Stacey and Private Banker, who has now become a firm friend and regular singing partner in Harry Ghatto's.

I got a bit of a funny feeling from Stanley, who's the sort of man you look at and think *English ex-public schoolboy made good in a position that's probably far too superior for his skills.* I might be judging too quickly, but there are a lot of people like that in Dubai. He looked sort of nervous in the interview; his hands fumbled over little spikes in his slightly gelled hair. He also admitted he doesn't know a thing about celebrities and doesn't really care, which I did think was a rather funny thing to say when trying to big-up a brand-new position in his ever-growing department to an excited potential new employee. He brought in the editor of the magazine that I'll be responsible for putting online to talk to me about it instead.

I'll call her Hazel. She's an interesting lady, quite large, quite blunt and clearly oozing the kind of confidence that can only come from knowing absolutely everyone in Dubai's glossy mag circuit, and probably everyone in PR, too. Apparently she's been here a couple of years now, fresh from a job at a British shopping centre magazine — a powerful lady to know. She seemed to size me up before her eyes, and must have told Stanley she thought I was acceptable because he hired me the next day.

It's a salary increase of 3,000 a month, meaning I'm now on 13,000. More shopping tokens — hurrah! A whole new world awaits. It does mean I have to get to the other end of town every day, though, which is a ball-ache in traffic from the Iransion, but I'll handle it. I'm actually looking forward to getting out of carpet-and-car-park land and working in a place that has an abundance of lovely shops and eateries. Maybe someone there will even sell me tampons …

It wasn't so nice telling the boss at the travel publishers that I'd got another job already. I believe her words were, 'It doesn't show much about your character, to leave a job so quickly.' She asked outright if I was going to be working for the company I'll be working for, and when I said yes, a look of total hatred washed over her face and she told me to leave immediately, before walking off in a huff. I later learned I'm not the first person they've flown in who's stayed just a few weeks before pissing off to this certain bigger publishing company and a much better job. They clearly see the company as stealing their staff, but it's not like Stanley came swooping through my window and into my biscuit bed like a thief in the night. I applied because it sounded cool.

I do feel guilty, though. They're lovely people and it's a great company. It's just that the job's not for me. I had to pay back all the money they spent on me — the flight and the hotel stay — which basically amounted to the same as my salary. So as it happens, I've gained absolutely nothing from my time in that office and its hellish vicinity. Except, of course, a better job, a good new friend in Heidi and a couple of weeks off in the sun before starting. Yay!

06/08

Car-crash parties and the fleet-horse elite …

It had been another all-day brunch-fest and I was just thinking how good M&M was looking in his floral swim-shorts when it happened: a testament to my intoxication, perhaps. As we were splashing and laughing quite drunkenly in his pool, by the light of some intriguing neon ducks, a car literally crashed outside M&M's villa. We all ran as fast as we could to the road, where we found a sweet little lady crying and praying beside some twisted wreckage. She explained that her boss had been driving her to the airport, but hadn't made it more than a few metres — because he was absolutely shitfaced.

No one was hurt, but it was quite an event. M&M spoke to some people and acted all 'in control' as we stood dripping puddles of chlorine onto the road, and we all left the scene just as the staggering bloke was trying to explain to a security guard why he couldn't stand up straight and why his car was wrapped around a signpost, in a residential area, in a Muslim country.

That wasn't the most exciting thing to happen over the weekend, however. Hell *no*! The most exciting thing by far this weekend was being offered a partnership by the Iranian inventor.

He entered our room with a joyous spring in his step, as though the greatest idea for the greatest invention ever had just crossed his mind. His hair was kind of messy, as though he'd been staring unseeingly for many hours into the middle of a giant fan, pondering perhaps the obstacles that stood between him and the millions of things he would invent, if he only had any ideas. His T-shirt was crumpled, as though he'd been up for three days and three nights, inventing an invention to invent things (and shagging the cleaner).

He sat on the coffee table in front of us while Stacey and I perched on our concrete slabs, wondering if it was normal for a landlord to enter his tenants' bedroom on a Friday night, when they were clearly quite pissed, eye masks at the ready, getting set to embark upon another vodka-fuelled journey into unconsciousness. He rubbed his hands together and stated once more: 'I'm an inventor.'

We nodded. We had to agree. *Yes. Yes you are.*

'I come here to make money, and you come here to make money.'

We nodded. *Yes. But no. I actually came because I wanted a break from London and to see something new, and maybe to find a boyfriend, as I've been single for ages, and possibly in a few years, to maybe even buy some property …*

'Speak slower, my English is bad.'

Whatever.

'I come here to offer you opportunity. I want to take horse to America. I want you to help me take horse to America. That is the place for it. America is where I will make lots of money.'

Right.

'I am Iran. They do not like me so much in America.'

Does anyone like you here, then? Except the cleaner? You're a bit weird …

'I need you. Your personalities, your speaking. I need you two. I offer this, we help each other.'

Would you rather we just handed over our passports?

'I need you to come up with plan to take horse to America. I give you percentage. Of course, it's still my invention.'

That's OK, we're more than happy not to take ANY credit for it, but we really don't think …

'I leave you now. We talk in one week. You think of how you would take horse to America. Sorry for interrupt, I leave you now.'

And with that, off he sloped. But not before stating once again how rich he is in Iran and how he's simply here to promote 'the horse'.

Of course, Stacey and I were dumbfounded. What an opportunity, we thought. What an adventure. He even promised to sort our visas if we came up with the master plan.

I'm sure it wouldn't be that hard at all, ringing round an environmentally conscious America, plugging a sales machine involving a hot and sweaty horse on a treadmill, born from an Iranian brain. We're seriously going to put our heads together this week. I just hope we can meet his deadline. He's looking very stressed lately. So stressed is he, in fact, that upon 'fixing the Internet' for us, he swapped the fridge plug for the router, leaving our food to rot and perish overnight. Bless.

Swimming pools and breaking rules …

It would perhaps be a little too soon to say I have fallen in love. I think lust is more like it. Perhaps I've been floating on a little awe-struck cloud since I met him, but something else happened with M&M a while back that I can hardly say I was expecting. I've said nothing up until now, hoping it might go away, but it hasn't. And against my better judgment I haven't tried to stop it. Even though I should.

M&M, as I've taken to calling him, stands for Married and Muslim. And therein lies my problem.

I know I'm a terrible person, even for entertaining the notion of our drunken kiss by the pool … *his* pool, after he'd entertained us all day (again) with his barbecue skills and an unclean amount of booze. Hmmm. Well, the more I think about it, maybe I'm placing the blame on the alcohol because it stops me admitting to myself what an idiot I am.

But then, M&M is one of the nicest guys I've met in a long time. Aside from an Irishman I met briefly not so long ago, he's the first man who's actually caught my eye and stirred up any form of romantic interest. But of course you always want what you can't have, don't you? What is essentially unattainable lights a fire of intrigue inside, until you develop a mild infatuation. You start to analyse everything he says, and read between the lines of everything he types, making that man you only vaguely liked the only one you could ever imagine wanting.

M&M and I have, since we met, spent hours exchanging stupid banter on instant messenger when we're both supposed to be working. His texts crack me up. I'm not sure what it is I like the most: his easygoing nature; his brilliant smile; his kind heart and generosity; or the fact that since we've met he's shown me things I've never known before. He's so well travelled and wise, and still has time to spare for waifs and strays like Stacey and me.

He whisked me away the other night to a place called Bab Al Shams. It's the poshest resort I've seen to date and lies deep in the desert; an oasis of calm involving fountains, a planet-sized swimming pool with giant vases on ledges in the middle, and a few ludicrously expensive restaurants. It's amazing. There's even falconry, horse riding and desert camel treks, if you go in the daylight.

We only went to chat, though, not to do anything naughty. But as we sat there in the glow of a thousand candles, sharing a shisha on a terrace overlooking the pool, I realised he might be serious about carrying things on with me.

Ugh. Why does he have to be married? Why did he then, shortly after our kiss, have to pick me up in his 'selfish car', drive me away and seduce me in a hotel room about an hour's drive from Dubai, when the world wasn't looking? And why did I not think there would be consequences? Now I feel horrid and guilty, but totally unable to stop. Stacey knows because she's seen it all happen. Well, she was sleeping in a spare room when we first kissed by the pool at his house. I don't remember how it happened, really. He says I started it; I say he did. Only red wine knows the truth.

He says he hasn't been happy here for a while, in spite of being very successful, with several businesses under his belt and a good few properties that he snapped up when Dubai was less a city than a steadily growing port. Differing religious values aside, I guess it can be tough to live somewhere for so long when all your friends keep leaving. Stacey and I have experienced this already. We're always meeting people on their way out of Dubai, in spite of thousands shipping in.

I've spent the last few nights running events through my mind from under my Twister towel, on my concrete slab, waiting for sleep to arrive. My life is changing so much! I can't tell anyone else. If I don't even understand it myself, I can't expect many other people to understand it either. This isn't me, it's really not! Lucy would have killed me over this, back in London. She'd be the first to pull me up by my ear and register me on another online dating site, just to distract me, just to stop me ruining someone's life, let alone mine. We would have shared a clove cigarette, leaned over the giant open window in the living room that we used to call our balcony and chatted it all out. But the people who know me best aren't here. And what if it's the new me, doing all this stuff? And what if I'm a part of a brand-new M&M? If that's the case, well … who am I to stop him changing direction, if he wants to?

15/08

In the absence of Facebook …

My life has been thrust all too suddenly into the shadows, into a world that exists without Facebook. My new company has banned it. RIP, little blue-and-white companion. So long, buddy. Take care.

I can still access it via a clever little proxy thingy, obviously, but if I'm the only one scrolling past those happy blue banners and guffawing out loud at pictures of my pissed-up friends as everyone else punches numbers at an alarmingly sudden and increased production rate, I think Stanley would get suspicious. So I've had to wean myself off it. In my new job this week, I've had to do some (gasp) *work*.

But you know what, although my heart breaks a little more with every message that Yahoo displays, informing me of some exciting Facebook activity beyond my reach, it's actually quite remarkable how satisfied I feel in other ways, now that I'm using my time a little more constructively — albeit to write about fame-hungry, attention-seeking celebs.

I think Stanley's impressed with me so far. I'm enjoying it. Although, I have to admit I didn't expect to be based on the ground floor with all the techies. Because my job falls within the digital department, I'm actually a whole floor and set of elevators away from the glossy magazine staff. There are no celebrity posters on these walls, no crazy family photos in fuzzy frames, no laughing camaraderie or oozing goody bags on any desks. There aren't even any fake flowers in ridiculously colourful vases, or newspaper cuttings featuring colleagues' names — the kind you paste above their computer for a joke when a headline also features words like 'murdered' or 'bitten by camel'. It's nothing like the kind of stuff that was so prevalent in my glossy mag office imaginings.

Down here it's heads down, earphones on, techie-work-work, nerd alert. And flirting with M&M on instant messenger is the only decent conversation I can get.

In the absence of anything much to do besides creating a back-log of celebrity profiles and shooting my new email out to every PR company I know (which isn't many yet, as I'm expected to create all my own contacts, according to Stanley), I find myself scouring the net for more freelance opportunities and watching Facebook from the sidelines. I feel a little lost, if I'm honest. Alone. Shut out.

I guess I could always email people, but who the hell writes emails to their friends anymore? They'd all just think I was weird. I could pick up the phone for a chat, but come on, who's got time to talk to one person when they could be messaging ten at once, while attaching a photo album and a video-guided tour of their bedroom? No. I have to learn to let go, accept that things are changing. Or maybe I'll have to stay home every evening and do the night shift instead.

19/08

Confessions of a nail-biter ...

Before yesterday, I'd had one manicure in my whole life. It was a freebie, forced upon me by a PR lady who wanted a review of a brand-new London nail salon. On reflection, the guys at work were probably so disgusted at the continuous sight of my chewed cuticles and split tips bashing at the keyboard that they tricked me into it. I've just never been that bothered about them, to be honest.

Only there's something about Dubai that makes me want to look pretty. I don't know if it's M&M, or the sun and the fact that everything seems illuminated here somehow, but as I step out into a new social circle, I'm fully aware that when I'm holding that glass of champagne, engrossed in a conversation, the person I'm talking to might only be interested in the fact that half of my fingernails appear to have been eaten. Maybe I'm getting older. Maybe my priorities are changing, but it's just not very lady-like, is it?

So yesterday, after work, and after getting lost for an hour in the rabbit warren they call the Mall of the Emirates, I tentatively pushed my way through the door of a nail salon ... and discovered a whole new world.

As I was ushered into a chair by a Filipino with a stick-on smile, I stared around at the rows of polish and cleaning fluids and people stretched out on chairs being pampered from their massaged heads to their glossed-up toenails. I was afraid — and rightly so, actually. My Filipino took one look at my fingernails and practically gagged.

What the f*&k have you been doing to your hands, you disgusting, irresponsible Western ignoramus?! screamed her eyes. 'What you want done today?' said her mouth.

I scrolled through the list of options with hunched shoulders and an ignorant glaze across my face. How the hell do I know?

In the end I opted for some acrylic tips because Heidi said they were the best, but not the fill-in whitener underneath, because [*begin interesting nail fact*] the chemicals in fill-in whitener stunt your nail growth [*end interesting nail fact*]. *Will I still be able to chew?* I felt like asking, as I watched her filing my teeth's hard work away onto a bleached white towel. *Will I be able to bite my cuticles off ... you know, the bits that fray and then peel so half your finger's hanging off ... 'cause that's the best bit. Will I? WILL I?*

When she was done filing, she got the glue out. I was terrified. I watched her stick ten false nails over the top of my own carefully nibbled digits and paint over them in gold — not once, not twice, not thrice, not four times … OK, four times. Four coats. *Four.* There's more clothing on my nails than there is on my entire body right now!

She admired her handiwork with the kind of pride one assumes a mother might exhibit when looking at a precious newborn. 'Brand-new nails!' she exclaimed, beaming, and promptly stuck my hands under a drying machine for twenty very boring minutes. The good thing is, though, that at this particular place (and so I'm told now, a good few others in Dubai too) you can watch *Friends* while the entire procedure is taking place. You simply slip a comfy pair of headphones over your ears and there's Joey, Monica and Chandler having a bicker as your hands are beautified. Fabulous.

I must admit I left feeling rather exhilarated, like I'm a real woman. True, I smudged two nails when I fidgeted in my seat but it's better than the freebie session back in London, when I ruined seven before I even got to the tube.

They're not entirely practical, though. I keep hitting the wrong keys on the computer. And I feel a little dishonest, like I'm fooling the world, like I'm living a lie. I find myself wondering whether a man would be able to tell … oh, OK, one particular man if we're going to get into it. Should I scratch my nails down his back, would he recoil in disgust, sensing a fake? Would he even notice? In fact, would any man notice if a girl he saw yesterday with barely any fingernails at all suddenly rocked up with talons like a hawk?

I guess I'll quash my inner nail-biter for now, if not to impress a man but for the sake of having socially acceptable hands. Oh, and also, for all fellow bite-ees who were wondering, you can bend acrylic with your teeth if you really try. It's just not as satisfying because you can't feel it.

Money, money, money ...

Luckily, the travel publishers never got around to sponsoring me before I left to join my new employer, but now the process to grant me residency has begun through my new company. Doing this means I won't have to do a visa run to Bahrain every three months or so, which is what a lot of people seem to be doing at rather less trustworthy companies. This also means I get a proper bank account and won't have to keep cashing cheques.

I met with HSBC today in the lobby of my workplace — there's a special representative who comes and signs up every new employee. I, for one, am really very grateful for any help at all on this matter. I am absolutely rubbish with money. Anything to do with maths, numbers or finance sends me into a cold sweat. Opening a bank account in Dubai, however, was a little bit strange. No sooner had I sat down and started ticking boxes on the form, than the lovely lady started asking me how much money I wanted to borrow.

Now, can I just say that in a UK branch of HSBC, had my ears picked up this question they would have fast dismissed it as a silly fantasy, a daydream concocted by my tired brain: *They'll never let you borrow any money. You already owe about eight grand to the same bank. Don't answer her. You're clearly crazy.*

But no. It seems that HSBC Dubai has absolutely nothing to do with HSBC UK. The world's most locally recognised logo, perhaps. 'World's local bank?' Not really.

On this occasion, much like a Manchester-based KFC employee might call a man in a branch in Marrakech and find no link whatsoever in their daily duties, the UK had not been summoned to inform Dubai that while I was running amok in the sandpit, earning a tax-free salary, I was also dodging my debts. And now I was being offered more money.

This, actually, was a very good thing. And a very necessary thing for me, because in Dubai, as I've mentioned, you're not allowed to pay your rent month by month. Instead, you have to hand the whole lot over for six months or a year, in one or two cheques. And, of course, you generally need a place to live when you arrive somewhere new. And when you're the young, ambitious, self-starting type of person Dubai is trying to attract, chances are you're probably not going to have in excess of 50,000 dirhams stashed away, ready to hand over to your landlord. Luckily, I had enough saved for my stay at the Iransion, as he didn't want much in the way of a deposit. But I'm assured the next landlord will.

As it happens, I left the lovely bank lady with the promise from her that should I need a loan to pay my rent once I move out of the Iransion, all I have to do is ask. And if I need any more for a car or even a mortgage, I should please just give them a call. At the flick of a switch, they'll be only too happy to deposit however much I'd like into my account (with a ridiculously high interest rate, of course), which will enable me to pay it off every month, considering I still have a job. This will, of course, be adding to the secret debts I already find rather difficult to pay back in the UK, but really ... well, I don't really have a choice, unless I want to live on the street.

And let's face it, if I do move home, I'm sure the money I would have swiftly paid back to HSBC UK using HSBC Dubai's generous loan will make me look like an angel to my local branch. Perfect. This place is great!

Freebies make the world go round ...

The job's going relatively well, now that the site has finally launched. So well, in fact, that I'm absolutely swamped. And even if I did have access at work, I wouldn't even have time for any Facebook admin.

The thing is, what initially seemed like quite a cushy gig is actually a mammoth task, as I have no one else to help me. I kind of thought there might be someone else here by now. But nope ... I am literally writing the content for an entire website on my own. Slightly worrying. Worse still, no one upstairs on the mag has been given any incentive to help me. Hazel hasn't even spoken to me since I started. I had a great idea for a feature on the working midgets of Dubai — there's one in that club I went to after brunch that time, The Lodge, who's always getting pulled around the room on roller-skates by another man called Mr Cheese — but so alien am I in her world that she probably mistook my email for spam and deleted it.

Elsewhere in the world, you'd probably never dream of making one person responsible for an entire website, one that stretches into cyberspace in at least eight different categories. Would you? I mean, I don't know, but it feels like a huge and daunting task to me. There's also talk of me going on the radio soon, to chat about celebs and promote the website! M&M tells me it's a brilliant opportunity. I will say, he's very good at seeing the positive in every situation, and making me feel as though I can do anything I set my mind to ... even when I clearly can't.

I'm getting out and about a lot, meeting PR people and the like, who are all really excited about the site once I tell them of its existence. I have to admit, it might all be a bit bizarre, but it's better than spreadsheets and quite exciting, I suppose. Well … it would be, if anyone knew to read what I've written, or anyone in the office actually cared to talk to me, for that matter. Honestly, it's like working in a frickin' morgue with all the techie folk. No offence — I'm sure they're all ludicrously busy, punching numbers and writing code and hacking into the National Bank of Dubai — but most people prefer to break up their day with a little light banter, a giggle, or even a wheelie swivel chair race down the corridor. Not here.

I bet they're doing that upstairs. I bet there's a whole other world of glossy magazine-dom I'm just not allowed to witness in this very building. I bet they're doing all sorts of fun things up there, without me, like styling each other's hair and planning things like Mojito Mondays (virgin mojitos, of course). Could it be that there just won't ever be a job as great as the one I left behind? And even more frightening — just as my blogging days have come to an end, are my blagging days over, too?

The unseasoned blaggers among us might say I'm a spoiled brat, one who expects the world to place everything in her lap without making any effort. But anyone who works in the media will know that once you've become accustomed to such treatment, it's a painfully slow recovery process when it goes away. It hurts a little, at first. It's disgusting I know — totally spoilt-brat territory. But it's true. You know it's true. The reason we work these jobs for so little dosh is because of the perks. That's just the way it works. Take away the perks and you're just another desk-monkey, who now has to spend even more money on nice things to compensate for the misery of not having any.

I've been working in Dubai's media industry now for more than two months, and I only just got my first invite to a free piss-up this morning. I know. Shocking, isn't it? I have to admit, I felt a little flurry of joy to see a fleck of the life I once led bounce back into my inbox. But the game is played a little differently here, too. In fact … scrap that. There isn't even a game. In spite of having relatively few contacts at the moment, I still get a host of press releases every day. Most of them are in Arabic and accompanied by a badly written email, reading, 'Please publish this in your publication. Thanks a lot.'

Thanks a lot? Um … no. Hang on a cotton-picking minute, love. Where is my free holiday/dinner/CD/theatre ticket/perfume/ box of wine? You can't thank me for helping you out when I haven't actually helped you out, because you haven't helped me out first. What is it exactly that you're not getting? Did I really leave England and turn up in a place where everyone's just so nice to each other, simply because it's just such a lovely world? Because if so, I don't like it.

Regarding the site launch, M&M says this company is renowned for making a rush job of things. How infuriating!

Still, perhaps I do need to be a little more patient with things, before I wind up looking for job number three (*sigh*).

24/08

An Iranian art attack …

Wish it could be Christmas every day? Well, it jolly well can be, if you live in my villa. To be honest, I wasn't quite sure what the inventor was doing with his days, really, now that the fleet-horse is almost complete. But since last Sunday, Stacey and I have come to the sudden revelation that not only does our Iranian landlord invent mammal-powered motors, he also creates art.

I may not have discussed the serene, winged angel lady who adorns our bedroom wall. She perches on a grassy knoll between our two beds, wild fruit between her fingers, a sword in her belt and a lovely bunch of sunflowers on her lap. She also appears to have borrowed an earring from Pat Butcher in 'Eastenders' — the amber glow of which is only enhanced, I feel, by the luminous orange border on which her beauty hangs above our beds. He must have got the cardboard from the craft shop.

Behind this caring angel is a shimmering metropolis shrouded in a mysterious pink haze. I'm told it's the ancient Persepolis, just outside the Iranian city of Shiraz. M&M thinks he put it up prior to our arrival, thinking it would encourage Allah to protect us, which I think is very thoughtful (even if it gives me the creeps).

Imagine my delight when arriving home from an evening at the cinema the other night (which I paid for), I found another work of art pasted lovingly on our bedroom door. I actually had to touch it to get into the bedroom. This one features two little children — girls — who appear to have lost their way on a rather windy moor. They seem to be sisters, but gaze morosely from a loose rock, as though asking which fellow orphan took their shoes away. I'm wondering if they're supposed to represent Stacey and me, clearly at a crossroads in our lives, living on the Iranian's landing.

Both pictures have been stuck at a 'fun' angle on a cardboard background. I rather prefer the orange one to the black that surrounds the children, but as gestures from our landlord they're both very, very special. Stacey suggested that maybe they're supposed to inspire us, seeing as we haven't given him any suggestions on how to take the fleet-horse to America yet. I told her I really hoped that wasn't the point, although I fear she may well be right, because yesterday we were blessed with another two pictures!

These depict his country — the birthplace of his incredible brain. It's as if he wants to teach us, to let us know of all that could be ours, should we proceed in concocting 'The Master Plan: Bringing the Fleet-horse Home'. It's as if, through these brilliant works of art, he's shouting: 'Iran. A country of dreams! Can you hear it? I can.'

Again, like a silent soldier of the night, he mounted them as soon as we had left the building — one on the wall, just next to the bedroom door, and one on the landing, to admire as we climb the stairs. It appears as though he's experimented again with different angles because each has a slightly off-centre appeal. And he's really come into his own with the multicoloured, cloudlike backgrounds. I love how his talents are growing with every piece. It's a beautiful journey, watching him bloom.

The weird thing is, however, for the past few nights I've had really bad dreams. Last night I dreamed that Private Banker was chasing me on a boat with big claws, and an evil little doll was making my bed spin round and round — an impressive feat in light of it appearing to be made of concrete. I'm really hoping the Iranian hasn't invented a dream-altering chip, which he's using these beautiful pictures to disguise. I've looked for cameras and mind-twisting equipment … wires he might be plugging into us as we sleep … but I can't see anything out of the ordinary. Except the pictures.

If he adds any more to the gallery, I think I'm going to have to say something. I don't really think he'd be too happy if we went downstairs and pinned paintings of our own families on his walls. I don't want to offend him by taking them down; he obviously thinks he's being a kindly landlord, sharing his many talents with us. I'm actually quite enjoying these surprise new additions and await his next contribution to the art world with bated breath.

It's just that I don't want to spend the next God-knows-how-long being haunted by the people in the paintings.

I guess the nightmares mean that I'm sleeping relatively OK on the slab now, under my Twister blanket. That's one good thing at least.

Playing house ...

The Trader was kind enough to let Stacey and me stay at his luxury Marina pad last weekend. He was clearly feeling a little sorry for his tragic friends, having to sleep so uncomfortably in a house full of loons. He's off on a trip somewhere exotic to surprise his girlfriend, as she's taking a six-month tour round the world before joining him here in Dubai. When she arrives, of course, she'll get to live in his gorgeous showroom and have real dinner parties at the table that's eternally expecting guests. (It's so unfair!)

Having packed our weekend bags and waved goodbye to the circus, including the Iranian washing the fleet-horse lovingly on the driveway, and the cleaner who's now managed to shrink a large proportion of our clothes, we rocked up at the apartment and immediately opened a bottle of wine. His display-style lounge and dusty balcony with awesome view never cease to amaze me.

We played house for a while, pretending we lived there, and then M&M came to join us.

The Trader's had a good few words to say to me about M&M in the past. He doesn't really know him, but as a friend I think he's just a bit concerned about me getting hurt. Sneaking around, he says, never does anyone any good, and he's probably right. He also says we should both be careful. Getting caught in the throes of infidelity could have serious consequences for a Muslim man. But it's exciting and fun and as I may not have already mentioned, he's really quite talented in the bedroom — whichever bedroom we happen to be able to get busy in.

I know it was naughty, getting naughty in someone else's apartment, but it was also quite exciting. Our conversations lately have grown more and more intense, as have our encounters. And this time, quite stupidly, after the deed had been done and I snuggled up, I expected him to stay, which of course he quite clearly couldn't. Apologetically, M&M stood up and ventured into the bathroom as I sighed and rolled over. It was then that I heard him turn on the shower.

At midnight, on a Friday, he was taking a shower. After being with me. Ugh.

I felt disgusted. Disgusted with myself, and disgusted with him. He was washing off every trace of me and our encounter, preparing himself to sneak back to another woman's bed. And he didn't even seem to realise what a horrid thing that was to do. I felt like a cheap, seedy hooker.

I'll admit, I cried like a baby when he left. I swore to get out of this mess once and for all. The Trader was right. People are getting hurt. But strangely, as the days have passed, I've realised that this ounce of rejection, however unintentional on M&M's part, has only made me want to be with him more. I want to see him again, so he can make it up to me. Damn my new neediness. Where did that come from?

Playing house is one thing, but playing away from home … well, perhaps it's just something I'll have to get used to.

When bad beer festivals get worse ...

It was always going to be a bad idea — erecting a tent outside an Irish pub in a Muslim country and inviting a thousand expats inside to 'sample till you're ample' (interesting rhyming, by the way — ample what?). But seeing as the rest of Dubai was heading down to HopFest, I went along with Heidi and Co. to check it out.

We queued in the blistering heat for about forty-five minutes in the Irish Village, our clothes collecting an unsanitary amount of sweat in the process. I felt my hangover dripping into overdrive and found myself painfully regretting a 6 am finish the night before, after a fashion show and open bar extravaganza in the Hyatt Regency. The invites have suddenly started coming in thick and fast now, by the way, thanks to an insane amount of networking and a couple of new friends with kind hearts and heaps of contacts. It's great!

It was one of those nights that will go down in history, actually. I did a few things I probably shouldn't have done, said a few things I probably shouldn't have said, swam in a few bodies of water I probably shouldn't have gone swimming in, in my underwear ...*

Anyway, just as I was about to pass out on the pavement, we finally made it into the HopFest tent. And I wished I hadn't really bothered. Maybe I just wasn't in the mood but I was suddenly

---

* *Now that I'm out of the country, I can reveal I actually took a dip in Dubai Creek that night with my awesome and totally fun new gay friend, and then we sat in the prayer room drinking whisky. We carefully avoided the security guard's flashlight the whole time and I've still got no idea how he didn't see us splashing around the boats. I should have been deported and I'll admit, I am actually more disgusted with my behaviour now than I was with my reeking, crap-scented clothes after our swim in the sewage-ridden waterway. But nobody saw me do it. You can't prove anything.*

reminded a hundred times over why I've never been on holiday to Ibiza. Drunken men leered and sneered, jumped on tables and made those annoying 'peace out' signs above their heads in appreciation of the live band. Some were even wearing hats. I hate it when people wear hats, don't you? Well … I mean, normal hats are fine. I've got nothing against a pretty sunhat in a field of daisies, or the odd beanie on a ski slope, or even a cowboy hat, if you're straddling a camel in the desert. But when you're jumping up and down in the middle of a tent, sloshing beer over everybody, wearing a fire helmet, well, then I have a problem. Especially when you double it with that irritating 'peace out' gesture and top it all off with a squeeze of my arse. Yup … you can spot a hat-twat a mile off in the UK, and believe me, it's no different in Dubai.

[*Bit that makes me sound old*:] Some of the beers were OK, but at 30 dirhams a pop they weren't altogether worth it, in my opinion. I settled for two Leffe Blondes because Lucy and I used to drink them in the pub near our flat, and it made me miss her. Although I wouldn't have wished the experience upon her. As more and more people packed into the tent, cigarettes blazing, it was like fighting for breath at the top of an ashtray. [*End of bit that makes me sound old.*]

Needless to say, my new friend Ewan and I left after about an hour and a half, escaping to the confines of his apartment nearby to order pizza and scare ourselves, eighties-style, with a dated film about Ouija boards. Ewan is my latest confidant and I love him. He's gay and he works in the glossy magazine clan in the land upstairs — the one I'm not allowed to be a part of. He works in fashion and I emailed him from my seat in the morgue one day, hoping he'd acknowledge me because he actually used to work with Heidi a long time back. Small world.

Ewan's a true staple in the gossip mag clan and now that we're friends I feel a little less isolated, even if I'm not really allowed up to his floor. In fact, Stanley got a little annoyed when he saw Ewan and me chatting at my desk the other day. He actually commented on us being a distraction, standing there giggling in the silence. Perhaps he thought we were commenting on his latest suit jacket, another classic with sleeves so long that his fingers are covered when he stands up. It's an unfortunate item that makes him look even shorter. We were actually discussing the possibility of a trip to India together, which we've discovered is pretty cheap from Dubai.

Back to the movie. I think the mullets on the males in the lead roles were probably more frightening than any paranormal elements woven into the story, but not quite as frightening as HopFest.

Apparently, after we left there were riots. There was blood. There was a three-hour queue to get in and a whole lot of broken tables, thanks to undignified dancers, probably also wearing hats. Had this event been organised in the UK, they'd have checked bags at the entrance, offered some kind of shelter/free water affair for the people in line, and employed St John's Ambulance to stand outside, crossing their arms and waiting for the clock to strike 'shitfaced'. Only this isn't the UK.

The staff at HopFest, apparently, found it perfectly acceptable to stand on the edge of the beer-soaked battlefield, as blood spurted out from the wounded and shards of broken furniture tripped those who were actually still standing onto the sawdust-covered floor, and state that they were terribly sorry for the inconvenience, but they simply weren't expecting so many visitors.

Bless Dubai and its friendly little beer parties, coupled with an astounding faith in responsible adults exhibiting respectful behaviour. The sad truth of the matter is that had the organisers done their homework — that is, hung out in Germany in October, Clapham Common in June, and Ibiza in July — it might have been a different story.

01/09

Tube strikes in London, you say?

Surely not. That's never happened before. Reading those words from afar brings a stabbing to my heart: oh, how I miss the Big Smoke dearly. Reading anything from home when I'm sitting in the silence of the morgue has the potential to upset me greatly, especially if I'm in a bad mood. But don't think we London expats don't remember one of the main reasons for fleeing the British capital.

I may have said I've forgiven the London public transport system since moving to Dubai, but to be quite honest, that was probably in the blistering heat of the moment, when one of my friend's Porsches was being fixed, or the cab line outside the hotel was five-people-deep, or the air-conditioning wouldn't turn any higher in the limo.

With all these seemingly constant reports about strikes and various parts of various lines being extended till … well, probably till the end of time, it's enough to make anyone sizzle in the London drizzle. Everyone should come and see how we travel here. At least when we're transported around Dubai we are guaranteed:

a) a personal driver
b) air-conditioning
c) a seat
d) a seat that hasn't been pissed on.

However, I'm not so sure that's entirely consolatory when weighed against the fact that when we get into a cab, we are more often than not faced with the following:

a) a driver who doesn't speak English
b) a driver who doesn't speak at all
c) a driver who can't drive
d) a driver who's falling asleep at the wheel after an eighteen-hour shift
e) an overwhelming stench of body odour that can't be eliminated with a swift opening of the window, owing to said air-conditioning struggling to beat 100 per cent humidity.

Seriously though, I was just saying to Heidi over email that although we moan about these things, and local taxi drivers not knowing where anything is, and having to walk underneath a six-lane motorway to get to the bar, and racking up more than our travel cards ever cost us in so-called cheap cab fares … although we moan about all these things, at least we know these cab drivers will never go on strike. And even if they did, well, we'd just hire a personal driver.

I know a guy who pays a little man to take him to work every morning and pick him up every evening for a very reasonable price. He even calls him up at 3 am when he's shitfaced and gets him to collect him via KFC. Sometimes he shares his KFC. Sometimes, he says, he doesn't.

It might well seem like snobbery to you, but I think you have to be honest with yourself — if you could get the same service in London, or anywhere for that matter, you would, wouldn't you? The same way you'd pay a little lady to live in your cupboard and wash all your clothes (Heidi's actually lives in her garage). The same way you'd shun all public transport altogether in favour of a car you could run for a fiver per tank. Carbon footprints? What are those? They don't exist in Dubai.

Apparently, 'the only things that are certain in life are death and taxes'. You might not pay any taxes here, sure, but your chances of getting squished in a fifty-car pile-up are higher here than any-where else on the planet. It's a toss-up, deciding what's best. But thinking about it, I still say be grateful for the tube.

02/09

The Rage ...

It hit me this morning. Well, actually, I could feel it creeping up on me yesterday, but I managed to stifle it with a couple of Coronas and a quiet mime-along to a Filipino lounge singer in a darkened corner of the Mall of the Emirates. Today, however, I can't ignore it. I felt it as soon as I opened my eyes. Stacey didn't seem to mind as I swore like the Exorcist at my alarm clock and banged my fists on the bed. She felt it too.

They say that when women live together, they experience their Rage days at the same time. I have to say, it's true. Yesterday, The Trader and Private Banker informed us that they didn't need to know of such things, to which Stacey quite rightly pointed out that they did. If a male is to befriend cohabiting females during Rage season, he should be well informed of the dangers.

It was even stronger when I got to work this morning. Not only have HSBC screwed up my salary transfer, thus rendering me at the mercy of my friends and their much-appreciated loans, the little cleaner tried it on again.

Have I mentioned the unisex toilet at my new place of employment? It's kind of weird at the best of times, especially when I have a heated debate with Stanley about 'impending business structures and plans for future development', only to bump into him ten minutes later in the bog as I'm buffing up my hair in the mirror and he's just made all sorts of noises in cubicle number two. Most unsettling.

Anyway, it's a strange pattern but for the past few weeks, every time I venture to the bathroom, the little cleaning man is in there, scrubbing, wiping, mopping, sprinkling pointless little blue stones into the corners as a visual pleasantry — doing whatever it is that people other than pop stars and supermodels do to pass time in the company of chemicals.

Today, he asked me if I was musical. Not a good move. Any other day, this question wouldn't have phased me, but today … oooooooh, it made me angry … *really* angry. The screaming started in my brain: *WHAT DO YOU MEAN? WHY ARE YOU BOTHERING ME? WHAT DO YOU CARE? WHY DO YOU NEED TO KNOW. WHY, GOD, WHY?!*

He then informed me that he'd heard me singing at my desk, which is probably true. I've been known to hum along when listening to my iPod. But the Rage chose that moment to remind me of the fact that he's taken to cleaning the space around me in the office quite often — perhaps a little *too* often. I mean, I'm not so much of a filth-wizard that the floor behind me needs scrubbing on the hour, every hour, am I?

From his words I could only manage to decipher his ill and evil intentions. The Rage informed me that under the guise of cleaning he is actually sweeping the stray hairs that fall from my head and moulding them into a voodoo doll. *GET AWAY FROM ME, YOU FREAKISH MAN. YOU'RE WEIRD, WEIRD, WEEEEEEEIRD!*

As the internal screaming continued, he exclaimed that he wanted to sing to me. Any other day I would have just smiled politely, humoured him momentarily and walked away. Today, however, with the Rage still running through my veins, I could have lobbed him about the head with the soap dispenser. As I shut the door in his face he was still singing, 'You are soooooo beautiful, to meeeeeeee'. Quite loudly.

Why? Why must he do this? Why must he sing in the toilet, to me, today? Why must he sing at all? *Why?*

The Rage simmered as I made a little laughing noise, determined not to hurt his feelings, knowing it was me, and not him, accepting that the forces of evil were at work within me. *Fight it, fight it, fight it* said the voice in my head, as I struggled to keep my foot from kicking the door.

I'm not sure Dubai is the greatest environment for calming the Rage, sometimes. You may have a vague idea when it's going to strike, but there's no way of knowing how long it might last. *Fight it, fight it, fight it …*

04/09

The road to immediate doom …

I almost died again today. Seriously. I'm getting sick of it now. Every morning I hail a cab to work and sit there with my bag clutched against my chest, and my phone clenched in my fingers, in case I have to dial 999. The other morning, after I dropped Stacey off outside her building, we carried on towards my own office and out of nowhere came a mammoth Land Rover, speeding alongside us in the middle of two lanes. It was almost scraping the side of my cab as it swerved about, apparently not even noticing we were there. I shrieked in alarm. I think the F-word was emitted. I clutched the inside of the door and fought back tears, praying I would get to work alive.

This morning, same problem. This time it was a bus, and it almost forced us off the road and over the side of a bridge. I actually screamed today, causing much alarm among two of my colleagues in the back seat who were still drunk from last night's shenanigans and barely noticed. I literally screamed: '*NO, JESUS, NOOOOOO!!!*' And the driver just smiled as if I was a major cause of amusement in the moment preceding our imminent doom.

He even continued resting his head on his hand against the door in a sleepy, bemused fashion. And then he chuckled. Yes. Chuckled! He sees it all the time. To him, dangerous driving is a daily encounter. Near-death experiences are the norm. It's not worth batting an eyelid unless his car is literally spinning off the motorway and bouncing 50 feet across six lanes into a set of scaffolding, eliminating an entire team of construction workers like a swipe from a giant Transformer, and landing face down in a sand dune.

It's getting increasingly worse on the roads here, now that most of Dubai seems to be back from a summer away. The schools are back in action, the heat is dying down and the city has a different vibe to the sleepy place we arrived in two months ago. I'm not sure I like it as much, sometimes. However, it's bound to be a hundred times more homely once we move out of the Iransion at the end of the month (more about that later). And when the temperature really cools and the bars all open with outdoor seating, we'll be able to sit and watch day turn into night without the risk of our blood boiling and losing half of our body weight in sweat.

But it's the traffic on the roads that terrifies me. I'm a nervous passenger as it is. My friends at home will vouch for the fact that I'm a door-clutcher, even nipping round the corner for a pint of milk. I know it's because of an accident I had with an ex-boyfriend when I was eighteen, and maybe a little bit because … well, I've been known to be a bit of a control freak … but if I'm squeez-ing my eyes shut and reciting the Lord's Prayer in a spacious Volkswagen, with fifty airbags and a parachute system, imagine having me squished in the back of your Porsche.

The thing is, though, as I'm sure I've reiterated many times, you need cars to get around here. Everywhere. Take the other night, for example, when Stacey and I decided to pop out for some sushi. Oh, sweet Lord, I'm feeling the Rage just remembering.

Suffice to say, there was no 'popping out' involved in what became a two-and-a-half-hour expedition halfway down Sheikh Zayad Road, after realising the local sushi joint is closed on Sundays. We made it about a mile down the road on foot, dripping with sweat, our hungry dinner companion, The Trader, driving round numerous one-way systems to try and reach us, only to dis-cover we were blocked at all angles by a mammoth roundabout, a crumbling apartment building, a vast stretch of desert and a wail-ing mosque.

Eventually The Trader found us, sitting in a heap at the road-side, covered in dust like the victims of a volcano tragedy. It's prob-ably not even worth mentioning that by the time we'd climbed into his terracotta seats and reached another sushi restaurant, it was acoustically polluted with the sounds of a baby screaming and otherwise had only marginally more atmosphere than the moon.

Thoroughly pissed off, we made our excuses, squished back in the Porsche (not ideal for me) and sped off to the nearest five-star hotel — the Dusit — where we calmed our Rage with the sweet sounds of some live jazz, a glass of wine and a lobster pizza in a lovely restaurant called Pax.

But that's not the point. The point is that by the time that gourmet pizza blessed my mouth, almost three hours had passed. That's not popping out for dinner. That's a food-focused expedition through torture, pain and hunger, rivalled only by the ancient tribal warriors of Eastern Tibet. In rainy season.

I don't want to get a car here, even though taxis are annoying. I don't even want to be on the roads at all. But until Dubai recognises that it houses people who walk, as well as gas-guzzling, death-defying motorists, I can only keep grabbing car doors from the insides (and maybe invest in a crash helmet).

07/09

Who lives in a house like this?

One-eighth the size of the Iransion, yet still an impressive erection, a tiny house made of muddy-brown-coloured fabric has appeared quite suddenly, next door to the Iransion. I don't know where it came from. One minute, the space was a vacant, dusty patch of sand and the next, a Bedouin tent of surprise. It even has a doorstep made of stacked pink bricks, and what looks like double-glazing in a square, sliding window. There's a curtain and drape over the door, a sloping roof in case of a miraculous downpour, and a funky blue stripe spanning the width of the entire thing. I like it a lot.

I thought for a moment that the Iranian's neighbours must be a little jealous of the fleet-horse. Its astounding greatness still

The guerrilla Ramadan tent that popped up next door.
I still think it's the best house I've ever seen.

lingers on the driveway, commanding attention and diverting eyes from all the other villas on our street. I thought maybe someone's fighting back. Guerrilla-fabric housing could even be the next big thing in Dubai, until they finish all the buildings.

But M&M was quick to inform me that actually this little house of mystery is a Ramadan tent, soon to be used for prayers and evening entertainment. Apparently, very soon, this little cotton house will be filled with the sweet scent of apple shisha and if Stacey and I are very lucky, we might even be welcomed inside by the neighbours for some mint tea, for Ramadan is also a time for sharing.

I'm dying for a visit. I'm tempted to even ask if I can stay there, look after it during the day and keep the cats out. It looks far more cosy and comfy than my room, with its concrete slab, and we're used to not having a working kitchen anyway.

I'm half-considering knocking on the door or pulling back the curtain to see about rental costs. The air-conditioning system might not be sufficient, and true … we wouldn't have the Iranian's artistic creations watching over us as we slept but, in one fell swoop, Stacey and I would have graduated from sharing a shabby room to sharing a house with soft, billowing cotton walls and a welcoming patchwork doorway. I can't imagine anything better!

08/09
First comes brunch, then comes Iftar …

Those who push the lettuce leaves around their plates while breathing in until their ribs interlock with their spinal cords would be shunned, ignored and ridiculed in these parts. Thin might be 'in' elsewhere, but as you can probably tell, it doesn't take long to adopt the attitude that eating is far from cheating in Dubai. For most people, me included now, it's a lifestyle. The stick-thin lollipop heads of Hollywood could learn a thing or two from a few weeks over here.

Everyone knows about the Dubai Stone. That's how much weight the average expat gains within roughly a month of being here. But when it's far too hot to enjoy the beach, or anything outdoors for that matter, you've really only got the malls or the vast expanse of restaurants offering brunches to keep you entertained. Or the gym, but that's for losers. And I am, by now, definitely a gainer. I embrace my extra pounds. I never had this much fun with food at home.

That said, as much as I'm enjoying it, Ramadan's due to arrive just in time; some time this week, apparently. For those who aren't aware, this is a month of fasting, based on the lunar calendar.

It's against the local law to eat or drink in public between sunrise and sunset during this time. Alcohol is banned (obviously). If you so much as crack open a bottle of water on the street you could be fined or maybe even imprisoned, and as for tucking into a homemade sandwich as you browse the Internet on your lunch break … well, just who do you think you are?

At night, however, there's Iftar — the breaking of the fast. There are buffets and shisha tents all over the place now, much like the one outside the Iransion, and large marquees on the grounds of most hotels. In some places, you can sit on the sand and drink tea and eat all kinds of awesome food during parties that go on all night. It's a time when people forget about their daily concerns and sacrifice the things they love in order to spend even more time praying. It's also a time for deep thinking, appreciating all you have and giving a lot to charity. It sounds like it'll be an interesting experience, and Stacey and I are determined to stick to the daytime fasting, as the weekend feasting has most definitely taken its toll.

I don't think I've ever eaten as much in one day as I did last Friday. It was positively disgraceful. I've thought the same after every brunch I've been to, if I'm honest. And I've always felt guilty. If I were to call my mother and inform her that I was ploughing through a plate of fresh seafood, having just consumed sushi with mashed potato and a chocolate waffle, she'd be on the first plane over with the indigestion capsules and a care parcel.

But there are no rules at the impressive JW Marriott twelve-hour brunch. Yes. It lasts an entire twelve hours. I've always been excited by the all-you-can-consume concept. Four hours at Al Qasr was exhilarating, but the thought of an entire twelve hours' worth of gluttony in a five-star hotel was enthralling enough to make me lose sleep over it the night before. Eventually, the buffet tables danced through my dreams, like that scene in *Beauty and the Beast*. Be our guest, the cutlery cried, as I scooped entire wheels of cheese onto my plate, with half a Peking duck and some cola bottle sweets. OK, I will. Thanks!

In reality, we actually did sit at the same table for twelve whole hours. There were more than fifteen people there whom Stacey and I have met along the way: Private Banker, The Trader and Heidi included. We ate, we drank, we ate some more. We followed fresh oysters with strawberry cheesecake. We preceded a prawn stir-fry with a chocolate marshmallow kebab. We drizzled hoi sin sauce over octopus salads and topped our steaks with Stilton. Personally, I even marinated gummy bears in vodka for later consumption and stuffed my handbag with sweets. Next time I'm taking some Tupperware.

They actually stopped serving alcohol between the hours of 4 to 6 pm, before the second shift commenced. But the staff had no complaints when we stocked up with two hours' worth of cocktails and covered the food-splattered tables with glasses containing every spirit under the sun. And if they'd complained, we would have snuck out to the toilets in shifts and swigged from the open wine bottles they'd put on our tables earlier, which we'd then promptly hidden in our bags, complete with the caps screwed back on.

The hilarity ensued all day, from midday till midnight, with a restaurant full of what were once normal, respectful, hungry humans looking more and more like a zoo full of savage, intoxicated animals by the hour. There was cheering, there was singing, there was dancing. There were games involving dares, involving shots, involving arguments. There were girls shoving cake in guys' faces.

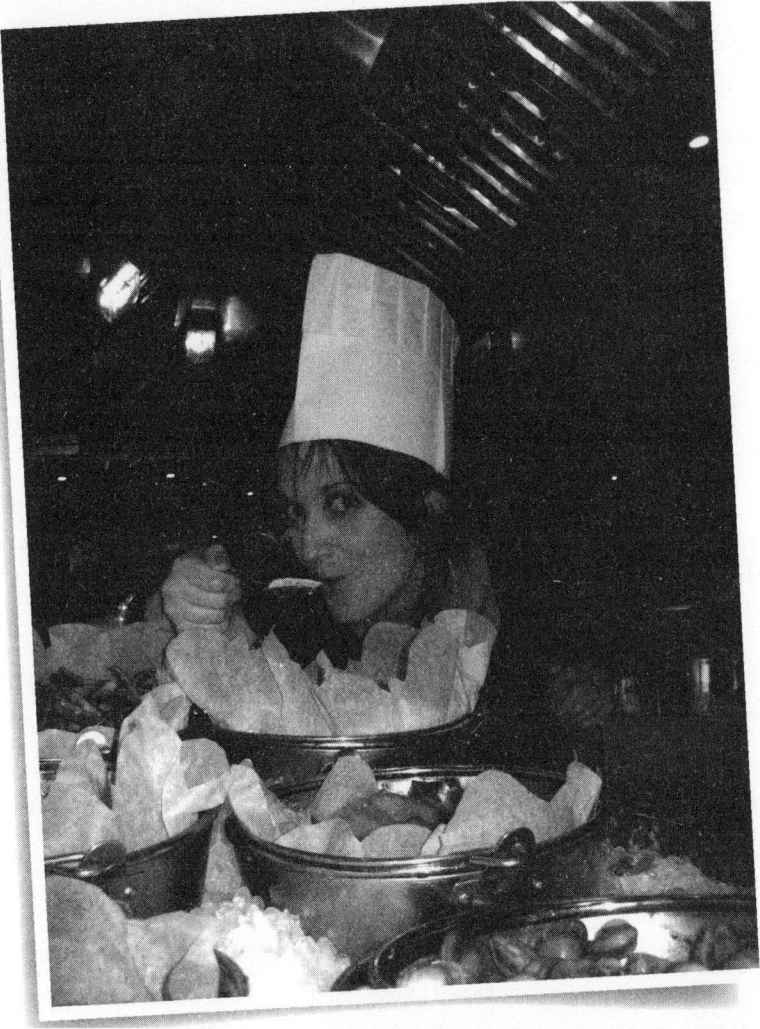

Brunch shenanigans. I have a zillion
pics like this. I needed them to remind
me what I always forgot.

But the highlight of the day came at roughly 11.30 pm, when a
bloke celebrating his birthday at a nearby table was force-fed
what's known as a Bullfrog — a lethal concoction of spirits that
left him slumped in his seat with his shirt round his head, uncon-
scious and drooling into a napkin.

Oh, grow up, that's not funny, you might think … Well, it wasn't, really … until the manager appeared with a fold-out wheel-chair and evicted him via the back exit like a Big Brother reject, as his friends cheered and sang 'Happy Birthday'. (I hear he's still alive.)

Thank goodness for a brunch-free month. An Iftar feast every night after work won't affect us as much as an all-day blowout once a week, will it? Actually, don't answer that.

12/09

Romance and the Ritz …

M&M whisked me away last night. Or rather, I whisked him away. Thanks to my new and increasingly blag-tastic job, I received an invite to review the swankiest hotel I've been to yet — the Sharq Village and Spa in Doha, Qatar. The Ritz Group run the hotel, although I think the idea was to go for a little more than tea.

Qatar is just a forty-minute flight from Dubai, so we made the trip after work and were deep in the confines of luxury by 9 pm. And I mean luxury. Not only was the bath water deliciously warm and loaded with frothy bubbles when we arrived at our room, but a heart-shaped cluster of rose petals had been lovingly sprinkled on top, which of course meant we had to get straight into it … so to speak.

It might seem a little extravagant to fly somewhere for a night's hotel review. It's definitely something I wouldn't have expected to be doing a few months ago. But then, I never thought I'd be anywhere like this with someone like M&M, who offered to pay for our flights so we could get away. Of course, I still feel guilty whenever he whisks me anywhere, as I'm sure he does. It's something we don't talk about, which gets to us in private. I sometimes wonder who the other woman is, and why he's not happy, and how he got into this situation, and whether he'll suddenly pull out of it. Or whether I'll have to, eventually.

I never, ever thought I'd be a mistress. I've barely had more than three relationships in my entire life, so trust me — the pickiest person alive — to pick this. I always pictured a mistress to be someone dark and shady with billowing breasts; the kind of woman who, whatever the weather, can always be found oozing out of a scarlet corset and perching confidently on 6-inch heels as she waits for her lover in a stationery cupboard, or an empty car park, with a whip. I might be mixing mistress with dominatrix here, but I guess they can be sort of the same ...

Not that it justifies my actions, but I'm pretty sure there are thousands of affairs happening all over Dubai, and with only a small minority of them featuring corsets or stationery cupboards. There's certainly the money to fund them all in secret, and you often see what look like totally mismatched couples dining in darkened corners of swanky restaurants, probably thinking no one they know will ever see them. I wonder if anyone's ever seen me with M&M and just not mentioned it.

If I'm honest, I think about these things all the time. I wonder when it would be sensible to stop, and I constantly ask myself why I haven't already. The fact that I think about it doesn't make it right, of course. I carry on letting him fall for me, and I really do think I'm falling for him too, unless it's just this swanky spell he's cast over my life since he walked into that bar and bought me not one but two Coronas. Something keeps reeling me in.

It's fun, doing stuff like this. Really fun. I've never been the object of anyone's desire before. Not to this extent. He buys me presents all the time. He even sends bunches of flowers to my desk, so Stanley has to stand there awkwardly, looking over the top of a huge lily when he wants to reprimand me for something. It's an amazing ego boost, if nothing else, to know that me, a normal girl from a humble hamlet in Lincolnshire, appears quite unwittingly to be rocking an Arab's world.

But then … I really don't want anyone to get hurt. Does that sound pathetic? I'm worried I'm just weak.

He's told me quite a few times now that he loves me. I really do think he means it. I'm still not sure if I love him back, though. It's kind of scary, hearing it. He makes me want to say it in return, but I know I shouldn't. The only person I can really talk to about it all is Stacey, because to the rest of the world M&M and I are separate entities, with nothing whatsoever but a few pissed-up nights on the town to link us together. And this very fact gets to me more than I care to admit.

I'm not very good at keeping secrets. I like to share my life … as you can probably tell. But I can't leave him cutesy notes on his Facebook wall. I can't call him late at night for a chat, or invite him out for dinner whenever I feel like it. I can't expect him to be there if something breaks in my bedroom, or God forbid I should wind up in hospital in the middle of the twilight hour. I can't have him bail me out if I accidentally kill a camel. I can't go home and meet his mum — and I definitely can't go to his house now that his wife's home.

But he can still do whatever he likes, of course. He can go where he pleases. He can promise me the world and then go back to her bed. And he can also, as displayed during 'that' night at The Trader's place, up and leave me feeling completely repulsive.

At the moment, you know, although I'm strangely in awe of M&M, I'm not sure how much I can handle the wall that sits between us. We're from totally different worlds, M&M and I. And if I'm truly honest, aside from a shared appreciation of the finer things in life, we don't really have a lot in common. He's very wise and knowledgeable and I'm … not. He speaks to me like a grown-up about politics and business and money, but sometimes, because none of those things excite me, I feel like a stupid child.

There were more rose petals scattered on the snowy white sheets of our enormous bed when we moved there, after dinner. I never thought I'd see a bed decorated like that until my honeymoon. And I'm not sure it isn't slightly greedy to expect it for a second time, if that day ever comes.

It's quite annoying actually, how it suddenly strikes me on the most romantic of occasions, when most girls should be planning forever with someone so incredibly wonderful and fun, that M&M, although clearly in transition, isn't really mine to speculate about at all.

13/09

Ramadan Kareem …

Everyone's been saying *Ramadan Kareem* to me all day. It's the first day of the holy month, according to the moon. *Ramadan Kareem* is a bit like saying 'Happy Christmas' really, only you can't spend five hours cooking a turkey and getting pissed on whisky. Food and drink are illegal, banned, wrong, insulting and offensive for the next four weeks, as is smoking and having sex during daylight hours (sigh — I'll really miss that).

After work we can go to Iftar, which as I've mentioned is when we break the fast by stuffing our faces, but there's to be no music at all, so Harry Ghatto's is closed all month. I know. It's a tough one to deal with, believe me, but as Heidi quite rightly pointed out to me today, 'music leads to dancing, and dancing leads to sex,' so it's for the good of all mankind that it bolts its fine self up for a while.

At work, we're not allowed to eat or drink *al desko* (the act of dining at your desk — very common in these parts). Thanks to Heidi for that one. Consequently, the morgue is even quieter than usual today. I think the hunger is setting in. People haven't eaten all day, me included. I've decided to join in the fasting in an attempt to better understand the culture I'm now absorbing on a day-to-day basis. Maybe if I can feel a little of what these people are feeling, I might become a nicer person. And at the end of it, we can sacrifice a lamb together.

This is the part that intrigues me. M&M tells me that at the end of the holy month, most Muslims drive to the sheep sale somewhere in the desert, queue about four hours for the finest they can afford, then bung the bleating beauty in the back of their car. Later, they drive to the abattoir and queue for another few hours to have it slaughtered. The head goes to the lucky man who's just lobbed it off; the rest they take home to cook or donate to poor people.

Of course, some modern families now get the butcher to do all this for them, as it's far less hassle. But I prefer the romance in making a special desert voyage. It's nice that such traditions are upheld … and I'm sure that this sacrifice is appreciated. I know that if I had to drive round in a Porsche that stank of sheep shit I'd certainly expect some element of thanks.

Today I arrived at work and discovered an apple I took from the Ritz was still on my desk. Because it stood as a fruit of M&M's affections and a symbol of our dalliance in Doha, I refrained from eating it. Now, of course, it's a political testimony of my morals.

Now I don't know if the apple that should have been consumed already is offending anybody. I sent the fruit-giver an email, for I was confused.

> By having it sitting here — shiny, new and incredibly, temptingly edible — it might be changing the course of somebody's spiritual destiny. But if I move it, surely everyone will know I've been thinking too much about it, and they'll wonder where it's gone and whether I've eaten it, which might also cause offence. If I remove it from sight and put it in my drawer, I might forget about it, and then the rotting stench will most definitely offend somebody. It's a lose–lose situation. I should have just eaten it yesterday. I just didn't think it through.

The wise M&M replied that I could solve the situation by putting it into my bag and giving it to a poor person/construction worker on the way home. By doing this I would have remedied the issue of having it sitting here looking juicy all day, plus I would have helped the needy. And this would score some major points with the man upstairs.

Either that, he said, or I could stand up in the office, shout: 'IT'S ONLY AN APPLE — I CAN'T TAKE THIS ANYMORE!' and fling it across the room.

14/09

Back to life, back to reality ...

This weekend, Stacey and I are moving from the Iranian's landing and out into the real world. We've found a gorgeous two-bedroom apartment in Garhoud, near the Irish Village of HopFest fame. And better still, it's also just a hop, skip and a jump to my workplace — yay! Another friend of the Private Banker hooked us up with it, and the landlord is a smiley, round-faced Canadian who most definitely is not an inventor. Plus, the rent is semi decent at 4,000 dirhams each for six months and, unlike many places we've seen, it's furnished.

I've decided to pay a little more than Stacey to compensate for her having to take cabs to work, and plus my room has the en suite. It also boasts the biggest, most comfortable-looking king-sized bed I've ever seen — one that most definitely is not made of concrete. I am buying a duvet as soon as we move in, and throwing the Twister towel in the dumpster. I no longer view it as a towel. It's changed.

I feel we deserve this glorious destiny. Our new abode proffers no eerie paintings of twins on windy moors, no weary horses on conveyor belts, or even strange, tent-like houses billowing like flags on the land next door. By contrast, it whispers sweet nothings of evenings spent drinking red wine on the balcony, overlooking the drunks outside the Irish Village. It sings of sipping champagne in a rooftop Jacuzzi, and hums a happy harmony of built-in wardrobes, our own cleaner who won't shag anyone in the laundry room and a flat-screen TV with more to offer than subscription porn. It's going to be blissful.

The rooftop is amazing, too. Stacey reckons it looks like a hotel deck. The sun lounges are padded and plentiful. There are even tables with umbrellas around what I'm sure is an Olympic-sized pool. I'm already planning the party to end all parties up there — imagine sipping bubbles in the Jacuzzi as the DJ spins a happy, happy summer song and everyone admires my new champagne flutes from IKEA. Luxury or what?

The Iranian was understandably sad that we felt the need to move out. Thankfully he hasn't tried to give us any pictures as parting gifts, but he did say we'd be sorry one day to have missed out on the chance to take the fleet-horse to America.

I think we'll live with it.

17/09

Sin for your supper ...

I'm trying really hard this Ramadan. I did sin on Friday, unfortunately, because I thought about sex three times and I ate a salmon sandwich. But I didn't really enjoy it because Stacey was being holy. She sat opposite, watching me, not a morsel entering her mouth. That night I had about four Coronas at Barasti Bar, but redeemed myself by thinking about how poor people couldn't drink them. And I made up for it all by not eating at all on Saturday and buying some really pretty new shoes instead. However, I did get stuck in a revolving door. I also fell down the steps in the cinema. Being hungry makes you clumsy.

I'm fully aware I should embrace every inch of this cultural learning curve and bask in a month without sin, without greed, without stress and strife, and I *can* do it, you know. I've failed so far ... but I can change, I can. There are so many good things in this world, so many fabulous feelings to cling to, really. I'm floating. I'm riding on a cloud, singing songs about silver linings, dancing with Care Bears and sliding down rainbows. Look at me, I'm feeling it, I'm winning!

But then ... HSBC come along; a bank staffed purely by genteel, semi-English speaking Arab ladies:

Me: 'So your bank has screwed up my cheque book request. Apparently I need to make another one in person because they can't seem to do it on the phone.'

Bank lady: 'You can do it on the phone.'

Me: 'I already did it on the phone. They messed it up. They told me to come in here and order another one in person, so I can sign a form.'

Bank lady: 'You can do it on the phone.'

Me: 'No I can't … they told me to come in here and order one in person, so I can sign a form.'

Bank lady: 'No problem, you can order one in person if you fill out this form.'

Me: 'OK, I still need my cash to give my new landlord. He's waiting for it. Can I withdraw it now?'

Bank lady: 'No, we are not teller. You can go to other branch and take it out.'

Me: 'Where's that?'

Bank lady: 'Bur Dubai, about twenty minutes in taxi.'

Me: 'Right. When do they shut?'

Bank lady: 'In ten minutes.'

Me: 'Right. So I can't get my cash, even though it's there in my account. I'm right here in the bank, you messed up my cheque book request and I can't travel at the speed of light?'

Bank lady: 'No.'

Me: 'Right.'

Bank lady: 'Can you get friend to lend you some money?'

Me: 'I have the money, it's there in my account. I'm right here in the bank. You messed up my cheque book request.'

Bank lady: 'Sorry about that.'

Me: 'And you want my friend to lend me some money?'

Bank lady: 'That would be only viable option right now, yes. You will have your cheque book in four to five working days.'

Me: 'You're my bank!'

Bank lady: 'You will have your cheque book in four to five working days.'

Me: 'I have no money!'

Bank lady: 'You will have your cheque book in four to five working days.'

Me: 'Can you not make an exception, make a few calls?'

Bank lady: 'You will have your cheque book in four to five working days.'

Keeping calm in Dubai on an empty stomach is not a skill that's proving easy to learn. Seriously. It's enough to drive anyone to the nearest drive-thru.

03/10

The word on the street is CENSORED ...

For the past few weeks, that word has been my life. Aside from my newfound friendship with Ewan, who luckily also lives in our new building just a skip away from work, my job is becoming increasingly difficult. Not only am I still stuck in the morgue with my friends unable to visit me, but Stanley doesn't seem to understand that in order to run a celebrity and lifestyle site, one must actually have a lifestyle.

The other day, he sauntered over in another ill-fitting suit, with sleeves far too long for his short arms, and tried to tell me I shouldn't be going out to meet people. I informed him of his previous words, which were: 'Go out there and meet as many people as possible!'

He has since changed his mind, however, and says I must be desk-bound, and if I want to engage the nation with new and exciting things happening in Dubai I must wait for press releases and rewrite them. I think he's jealous I got an invite to the Ritz and he didn't, quite frankly.

Anyway, these press releases are, of course, the same badly written press releases doing the rounds and giving every single publication here exactly the same news. Hardly the makings of a new, hit, ahead-of-the-game website. And of course, this now means I'm just going to have to call in sick whenever I want to do something, which is annoying.

Another issue that's starting to bug me is that I can't help thinking this would all be slightly more fun if I didn't have to censor myself. There are things I can't say here; things I would be fired for, deported over, even. And while I understand and respect the reasons, all these rules would be far easier to abide by if I'd been hired to work on, say, *Gardening Weekly*. Well, imagine writing about the whores of Hollywood all day when you can't mention the following:

Whores
Sex
Drugs — no names allowed, i.e. cocaine/weed/dope/blow etc.
Nudity
Sex
Booze
Swear words
Adultery
Sex before marriage, or any sex for that matter

Religion

Sex

Basically, anything that makes writing about celebrities vaguely interesting is a big, fat no-no. I have to just ignore all the vicious slander, the seeping poison going round my brain, rolling off my tongue and through my fingers ... and press delete.

Let's take a timeless Britney saga as an example of such restraint.

UK version:

Tears for Spears ...

Has-been Britney's spent the morning bawling after thicker-than-shit cling-on Fed-Ex gained custody of her kids — a 'win' he is probably going to regret once he realizes it'll only put him back in the public eye long enough to start the sentence: 'My next album is going to be released ...' before little Sean Preston shoots a water pistol in his face and demands he gets taken to Disney World. What a cock—and so perfectly matched to a cock-up like Spears. Their separation is the saddest thing since the Vick-Stick stuck by Beckham after he shot his balls elsewhere. Some people will do anything to stay famous.

UAE version:

Tears for Spears ...

Poor popstrel Britney spent the morning sobbing after losing her kids to Kevin Federline in a custody battle that shocked the nation. Dubai sends you hugs, Britney, and thanks for all your albums. We hope you bring your tour over here when the biggest arena in the world opens (sponsored by Sheikh Iowneverything).

Still, I guess it's all a nice distraction from the bombs/disease/ RAGE/anger/fury/hatred/religious dispute/suffering of the real world. It's still mindless fluff, and it's still entertaining.

However, perhaps I have sold my soul, slightly. Perhaps I should be writing about the bombs/disease/RAGE/anger/fury/ hatred/religious dispute/suffering of the real world, knowing that my carefully crafted words of wisdom, shot straight to the heart of the public, just might change something bigger for the better.

But if I did that I wouldn't get any free spa treatments. And that would be shit.

17/10

Parent planning ...

The parental units came to visit me last week. I was really looking forward to it, not least because Dubai likes families. Dubai doesn't like single people much and we're not really allowed to have boyfriends how we're supposed to become a family in the first place is quite puzzling. Perhaps you're meant to find a husband, have a family, and then move here ...

I digress. Dubai is very good for family-type things — so say all the billboards. Granted, half of the things haven't been built yet, but my mum still seemed pretty excited when I told her that should she have chosen to visit me in seven years, we could have all gone to Jurassic Park.

The things that lie in wait for us are indeed astounding. They're even building a twisty residential building with different levels, each of which will permanently rotate towards the sunlight. When it's completed in 2030-something it will be an incredible tourist attraction, which will undoubtedly see awestruck visitors like my mum sitting opposite it for hours, with a packed lunch and a pair of binoculars, watching it turn.

Dubailand is sounding pretty awesome, too. This is set to be a gigantic theme park, twice the size of Florida's Disney World! And they're building a Great Dubai Wheel, one of the biggest in the world apparently — even bigger than the London Eye. From the top we'll be able to view distances of up to 50 kilometres, so everyone will get a glimpse of … well, more sand dunes, probably. The air-conditioned beach is what really intrigues me, though. Imagine that! As yet unbuilt, it promises cooling pipes underneath the sand that will keep our tootsies nice and cool, in spite of the sizzling sun.

Mum said she wouldn't have wanted to visit this, even if it had been finished. She said it would have been a little weird, as the whole point of a beach, surely, is to experience heat as Mother Nature intended, appreciated and offset by a cool ocean breeze. I think she's just too British for her own good.

Prior to Mum and Dad's arrival, I put together an interesting 'adult' agenda for their well-deserved holiday. Of course, they stayed with me in my lovely en suite bedroom and, of course, I took the sofa, having grown accustomed to uncomfortable sleeping quarters anyway. But I wanted to ensure that as well as having a lovely time, they also got to experience the real Dubai. Here's what I presented them with via email:

Thursday night:

Straight off the plane and back to my flat, where we'll head upstairs to the sauna. You shall endure this for twenty minutes, without taking off your clothes, showering or putting your hand luggage down. This will ensure you fully understand the temperatures your lovely daughter had to endure upon her arrival in June. Cultural experiences are vital when exploring foreign shores.

Friday morning:

Up at the crack of noon and on to the poshest hotel for a twelve-hour all-inclusive brunch with *all* my friends. Prior to this there will be no breakfast, as it's vital to start drinking on a totally empty stomach. This ensures maximum drunkenness and the appreciation of everyone around the table. Each must concoct your own despicable mix of every food available, although it will be hard to beat your lovely daughter's winning combo of a marshmallow kebab, covered in soy and jellybeans with a side order of mashed potato. Mum will re-create baby photos as I fall off my chair, burp and puke a little on her holiday frock.

Friday night:

Off to Barasti for a live DJ and lots and lots of boozed-up Brits spouting things about rugby.

Saturday morning:

Recovery on the beach.

Saturday night:

Repeat Friday.

I was, of course, making a joke to shock them, but as I was constructing this joke I was marginally concerned that on this particular visit, seeing the real Dubai might have meant the couple who spawned me would see my true colors. And they might not have liked them.

When I lived in New York a few years ago and they came to visit, it was fairly easy to convince them that my lifestyle consisted of theatrical outings on Broadway and the odd meal in a lovely checked-tablecloth restaurant in the East Village. They needn't have had an inkling as to the debauchery that really commenced after dark. In fact, prior to reading this, they probably never had a clue about the pot-cookie bus incident, or the fire engine photo shoot, or the time I stayed out the entire night in a bar in Alphabet City, and walked straight to work again the next morning, reeking of cheap gin.

Here, however, after careful pondering of Dubai's infamous family-friendly concept, short of dropping them in a mall or depositing them outside the museum or souks — which are lovely but generally take about three hours to check off the list — I discovered that there's really not that much to do … yet. We lounge, drink, get fat, shop, eat some more and then start all over again. I can't hide it. That's just the way it is.

I think I pulled it off quite well in the end. Dad did comment that he rather liked Dubai, and that it was a little bit like Disney World without all the fat Americans. He also commented that he really liked my friends, but then he wasn't actually taken to a twelve-hour brunch and made to witness them in action round a buffet spread. He met a few of them in sober mode in an outdoor lounge called iKandy, sitting round a swimming pool in a glorious pink-lit shisha haze at the Shangri-la hotel. This was where they both had their first apple-flavoured puff, and Mum got a little giddy.

Mum liked my rooftop pool, the sunshine and the food, and bought a nice pashmina in the souk. But she didn't really like the fact that it took so long to get a cab anywhere, or that most drivers seemed to smell of B.O.

I think they got a pretty good idea of the place.

29/10

The difficult detox ...

In spite of outside influences, such as beers, brunches, late-night pies from the local 24/7 shop and inevitable mockery by those less understanding, this past week I have been determined to treat my body like a temple for once instead of a garbage disposal unit. Having spent far too many months boozing and eating badly I've long felt parts of me wobble that certainly never wobbled before. At first I thought it was the dreaded Dubai Stone that Stacey still spends evenings in the gym trying desperately to fight, but when I weighed myself it was only a few extra pounds. A few extra pounds around my thighs, I might add, which is never good. Sitting in the office I'm increasingly aware that my ass spills slightly further over the sides of my swivel seat than it used to, and I'll be damned if it's going to get any bigger.

M&M was madly opposed to my detox plan at first. He proclaims to like me just the way I am, although I choose to believe he heard this very line in *Bridget Jones's Diary* and assumed it would work on all of us. Personally, I thought it was the perfect time to take up the offer of reviewing a made-to-measure detox program for the website. All I needed to do, according to one glossy-haired voice of wisdom who concocted the program from her villa somewhere in Al Barsha, was devote seven days to ditching alcohol, caffeine, bread, meat, chocolate biscuits, Lebanese cheese manakich, chicken udon … OK, everything, absolutely everything that tastes nice, and swap it for fruit, veg, water and herbal teas.

Armed with a list of 'power foods', I hit Carrefour with a vengeance. Ewan told me which blueberries to buy. He's very good with his fruits, and is always snacking on dried apricots and weird stuff like that when he dares to pass by my desk. He even brings tofu to work sometimes, mixed with lentils and the like, which I never understand as he's a meat-eater, but apparently it has even more protein in it and less fat. He's very lean and healthy so it must be doing some good. It's just a shame it tastes like mouldy wet wallpaper.

Carrefour is the biggest supermarket in Dubai, just so you know. I tend to shop in the one in the Mall of the Emirates, although there are several dotted about the city. They're all the same. They always smell of cat food, no matter what time of day or night you go, and they're always full of Indian men, holding hands, eyeing-up the ladies. There are several other supermarket chains in Dubai. Spinneys is another. This one's slightly nicer, but far more expensive because they tend to import absolutely everything, mainly from Waitrose back home. You can walk in and pick up some Waitrose own-brand cornflakes, for example, or coffee, and Spinneys always smells of fresh bread, in order to attract wholesome expat families.

Spinneys have a pork section, too, which usually stocks own-brand bacon, ham and pineapple pizzas and a variety of other products you never even knew had any pork in them — like prawn cocktail crisps. (Shocking! I never would have thought, would you?) These items sometimes have stickers on them that Brits might recognise from home. I see bacon boasting the super-cheap price of 99p, quite often. Only in Dubai, it's marked up by about 60 per cent. You can pay the same price for a proper beefsteak as you can for the worst cut of bacon here. I refuse to buy bacon out of principle. I figure I had my lifetime's worth of it at uni, anyway. It's all I ever ate. I almost craved it. Maybe my body knew that some day I'd have to go without.

Anyway, even with my beautiful, silky-smooth friends from the cheese triangle family calling my name, I blocked my ears to all naughtiness and made a beeline for the fresh produce aisle. Shut it, cheese, I told them, broccoli's my buddy now, blueberries are my babies (it's very hard to lie to your friends, but I blocked their cries and ignored their sneers; told them I'd miss them and I'd be back soon). I did get some funny looks when I loaded it all onto the conveyor belt with a blender, but maybe that's because I also seized the opportunity to buy the new hot-pink wheelie case I've needed for ages. I zipped up my nutritious wares and wheeled off with it into the crowds. Well, you've got to improvise when you don't have a car and your day includes heavy veggie transportation.

As I passed the food court I realized that it's only when you can't have a Whopper with the works that you really want one. I was ravenous, having only eaten an apple since 9 am. Once home and away from temptation, I tucked into a lunch of melon, peppers and celery sticks, and a blueberry and banana smoothie. I ate a few pumpkin seeds, thinking they were really very chewy and bad for my teeth, before Ewan called to see how I was doing and informed me that I was supposed to take them out of their shells first.

At dinnertime I experimented with my homemade steamer — basically a saucepan with boiling water inside, covered with some tinfoil, pierced with a fork. I resisted the urge to cover my broccoli, red cabbage and carrots in gravy and pop out for a pie, and instead I munched in tasteless misery in front of the food channel. It's no fun at all eating veggies on their own, but Nigella baked a fantastic cake in front of me and I actually felt a bit better. It's really quite possible to feast on imaginary flavors if you put your mind to it.

By day two I was starving. I woke up at 4 am and couldn't sleep. I contemplated calling M&M for some conversation — something to take my mind off the munchy monster growling in my stomach — but of course that wouldn't have been wise. I finally blended a banana, an orange, a carrot and a kiwi, which did the trick. At the advice of my detox guru, who'd previously told me to call her at any hour of the day or night if I needed her (only in Dubai, eh?), I popped to the health shop before work the next day and bought some vitamin B6 and B12 capsules to calm my caffeine cravings and increase my metabolism. I think they might work actually — surprisingly, I haven't really missed my morning coffee(s) that much.

I had a few mood swings that day. I shouted at M&M. I scowled at the office cleaner as he smiled at me in far too friendly a fashion and threatened to sing again. I didn't have the headaches I'd been warned about, although day three and four at work were pretty tough. Stanley waved his bagel with goat's cheese and pesto in front of my face as I approached his desk. He told me to do something. I didn't even hear what it was; I was too busy watching the pendulum of his perfect lunch pass before my eyes. It was making my mouth water. I sat making crunching sounds with a Tupperware box of green pepper chunks, hoping my childish noises would bring an element of fun to the situation. No one likes a loud eater — especially not in the morgue. Nothing was satisfying my insatiable hunger though, and before I was forced to take a bite out of my keyboard, I raced home early and furiously steamed up some more broccoli.

Day five, and I actually felt pretty good. I might be imagining it, but I'm sure I have less of a bingo wing going on under my arm than before. I even survived M&M ordering chicken wings from Chili's to the flat, and ate my salad in skinny smugness while informing him of all the evils that were lurking in his calorific, fast food dinner.

So here I am, at the end of it all. I'm a survivor! I have managed a diet in Dubai — no mean feat indeed. I even got two cellulite-busting massages as part of the detox program, with a machine that feels a lot like having your arse and thighs sandpapered heavily by a lumberjack dressed as a Filipino. My cravings for red wine can never be silenced by the power of a vitamin pill (unlike the caffeine), but for a quick fix, I'd definitely do it again for a few days. Stacey says she's very proud of me, although I 'could have just gone to the gym' like her. M&M may have liked me for who I was, but I think he likes me even more than that, now I've lost a bit of the muffin-top that had started to bake above my jeans. I'm actually feeling pretty damn good about myself.

Nothing a good twelve-hour brunch won't sort out, I'm sure.

03/11

Lions and champers and beers, oh my!

Having turned down the mysterious invite for a rare, quiet night in, my newest friend Sash was without me as she tottered out of the cab outside the hotel and found a school bus waiting. 'Meet at the Hilton at 8.30 pm sharp,' the text had read. Sash had been intrigued. She'd glammed herself up to the max and cabbed it down there, not really knowing what to expect, other than that some other friends of hers would also be following the same instructions.

Sash is one of Dubai's most beautiful people — from Canada. I met her through a friend of a friend one day a few weeks ago, in a noodle bar. She does a spot of modelling on the side of her day job and has the kind of look and poise that turns heads in the mall when I'm next to her, making me feel a bit like one of Cinderella's ugly, fat sisters, in spite of my recent detox. She also has an excellent personality, is lots of fun, and doesn't really know exactly how gorgeous she is, which is even more annoying. But I like her a lot.

The others were waving at her from the bus steps, so she climbed on board to find roughly fifty other beautiful, dolled-up girls on board, and one guy. 'We're going to a party,' the guy informed them, grinning. And shrugging their shoulders they took a seat and chatted away merrily as the bus chugged away up the road.

They knew it would be safe — a friend of a friend had sent the text, although after an hour the girls discovered they were miles from their starting point, somewhere in Ajman (one of the seven emirates that make up the UAE). Not really knowing where they were going, they pressed their powdered noses to the glass in wonder as the darkness enveloped their party bus, and eventually pulled up at a grand, gated entrance, complete with security guards outside.

It was revealed they'd arrived at a sheikh's mansion. The driveway to this mansion was a mile long and as they giggled into their handbags the guy who'd shuttled them onto the bus informed

them that the sheikh in question owned the entire eight-acre plot
of land. He never revealed who he was, standing there looking
important, with some very expensive jewellery glinting from his
person in the night. He just said that they should all proceed to
have a nice time.

Like a troop of eager school children, the group were ushered
into the building, expecting hundreds more people to be waiting inside. There was no one. The place was relatively small, as
far as mansions go, and all on one level. It had a fully equipped
gym, two very large bedrooms and a lovely, modern fitted kitchen.
However, perhaps the most striking feature, as Sash recalls, was
the fully grown stuffed giraffe looming over the living room and
other taxidermy treats such as hawks, falcons and rabbits. Hunting
treasures, you might assume. Except, perhaps, the giraffe.

Surprisingly, when the group were led outside to the backyard,
there was no one there either, aside from a few dudes in dishdasha,
the local dress. They were all standing in wait around an entire
buffet of gourmet foods, which looked deliciously tempting in
the neon lights. The DJ was already spinning tunes in the corner
and as they were thrust into the spotlights, it became painfully obvious that the busload of beautiful people brought specially from
Dubai … were the party.

Still, determined to have a good time, Sash and the others
tucked straight into the food and took full advantage of the unlimited champagne flowing freely from shimmering bottles. And
as the strobe lights helped to blur their senses, a few of them even
took a turn on the catwalk, which had been installed conveniently
for the occasion. A few pondered a dip in the infinity pool, but they
hadn't actually been informed to bring their swimwear, so they
chose to admire it from afar and drink some more champagne instead, chatting to the guys about their lives, jobs and thoughts on

Dubai. The guys were allegedly all very nice, says Sash, and very interested in the girls' opinions.

Taking a shine to Sash (who wouldn't?) one of the sheikhs later drove her and a couple of others through some more of his property, and then proceeded to showcase his personal zoo. Adjusting their boob-tubes and treading carefully in their killer heels, the girls admired an adult male lion and two cubs, watching them with equal interest in the light of the moon. A little further on they were delighted to be shown a hippo in its own special pond area, a pen housing a rather sad-looking rhino, and two deer in their own little manmade forest. Swigging her champers, Sash asked if any of the animals could come and join the party, to which the sheikh smiled and said not today, but he usually let the lions out to roam the eight acres and occasionally the adult male could be found chilling out with them in the living room while they watched TV.

Overall, Sash informs me, it was an unbelievably awesome experience, which I would have loved, had I not been too hungover and lazy to leave my new flat. As they piled back onto the bus at around 4 am, the girls reflected on everything they'd seen. And while some were a little miffed that they had been purposefully gathered as ten girls to every guy, they all agreed that they'd been very privileged indeed to have witnessed the kind of private party that clearly happens all the time in these parts, behind closed doors. Minus a giraffe and lion or two.

Age and the-party-that-never-was ...

It's my twenty-eighth birthday in a matter of days. I know I'm getting old because HSBC sent me a birthday gift this morning. When your bank sends you hotel and dinner vouchers instead of a court summons, you're *definitely* an adult, aren't you? Mind you, this was from my bank in Dubai, with whom I do not yet have a credit card, overdraft or thousands of pounds of debt. It's another prime example of this city's current lack of communication skills. I know for a fact that if HSBC Dubai were in any form of contact with HSBC UK, they most certainly would not be sending me gifts.

I digress. I really should be happy about my birthday, because technically I'm sort of on track, right? I have a decent job, which kind of lets me have free rein over what I write — even if it's mostly about Brad and Angelina. I have a nice flat and no longer have to sleep on a concrete slab. I have beaches, brunches and the best karaoke bar in the world on my doorstep. I have blagging rights to pretty much every party in town, a lovely family and a host of nice friends. I'm not married, though. Nowhere near. Not that I want to be, of course (I'll leave that privilege to my boyfriend), but lots of my friends are getting married now. I knew it would happen as soon as I moved abroad, now that the flights are too expensive and I don't have enough holiday time to cover them all. Ah ... enough thinking. I'm having an awesome time here so far, and I have planned the party to end all parties.

It's a *Dynasty* theme night and it's set to take place on my fabulous rooftop around the swimming pool and bubbling Jacuzzi. I knew it would happen as soon as I saw it. Oh, there was a problem with the Jacuzzi that I may not have mentioned, but it's fixed now. Some rotten kids who were clearly taking advantage of their nanny sleeping on the job, decided it would be hilarious to fill the thing with bubble bath. I admit, actually, I did find it rather amusing watching giant bubbles floating over the balcony and drifting like mini rainbows over the Irish Village. If only there were little pots of gold at the end when they burst … that's an idea to sell to Nakheel, one of Dubai's biggest developers. They'd love it! Anyway, the security guards had palpitations as a spoilt woman threatened to get them fired unless it was sorted out, so they ran around for a while in a flap before scraping them all out by hand and refilling it with more water.

Everyone's invited to the party. Ewan has helped me organise it and we're even having a DJ up there, courtesy of a friend of a friend. I feel the need to make this event the biggest and best I've ever had, which of course goes along with Dubai's theme in general. But the more I think about it, it probably also goes back to my need to make up for the-party-that-never-was, which I think might have left me emotionally scarred.

To cut a long story short, when I was seventeen my mum arranged a surprise party for me, to take place upon my return from an exchange trip to the USA. I kind of cottoned on to it, though. The bowls of salted peanuts, streamers, and Mum in her finest attire and lipstick sort of gave the game away. As did my Jehovah's Witness friend Fran when she called to say she couldn't make it. (She always had some excuse.)

As the clock ticked past and no one showed up, it emerged that Mum had thought to tell my kindly boyfriend-of-the-time about her little surprise, in the hope that he would spread the word among my friends. Unbeknownst to her, my kindly boyfriend-of-the-time didn't actually know any of my friends. And the ones who did know him hated his guts because he was a cock. He never told anyone about my party. He probably forgot himself as soon as Mum walked away, checking out her arse as she went.

Of course, it's what every girl needs when she turns seventeen, isn't it — the slap-in-the-face realisation that her boyfriend really is a cock, all topped off with a feeling of total and utter unpopularity. Ever since then, I've really hated organising birthday things. And yes, I do want a fucking violin — this is a sensitive issue. Get playing.

To get in the birthday mood, I went for the all-you-can-eat-and-drink wine and cheese night at the Shangri-la last night with a few very nice people, including Stacey, Heidi, The Trader, Private Banker and Haaris, Stacey's kickboxing instructor, who came even though he doesn't drink. That, I thought, was really very nice of him.

M&M was late. He arrived on the way back from a business trip with a bag full of gifts, which he chose to give me in private before buzzing off again in his Porsche. I had a sneaky peek and realised it was lingerie! Expensive lingerie, I might add, of the smooth, silky black kind, complete with suspenders. No one's ever given me lingerie before — except Mum, when she bought me a rather sexy slip to go under a skirt, from Oxfam. I'll enjoy modelling it (when I'm drunk and all thoughts of my sagging arse are suitably blurred).

I thought it was very sweet of M&M to come, even though he clearly had to get home because it was late. But he knows about my 'party issues' so obviously didn't want me to think he'd forgotten, or didn't care. He also told me he's got a massive surprise for me, and I should keep next weekend completely free. Hmmm. It's all really very exciting at the moment! I'm starting to think the real party-that-never-was might just be about to start!

Ever seen a wheelchair float?

Oh, what treats for my birthday week! Today I got invited to an Aston Martin party, a free bra fitting, including a free bra of my choice (more lingerie — always handy), a laser show on the roof of a new building, and a shopping and Christmas carols evening in the Wafirooftop gardens (they're getting in early). Wafiis a great building by the way. It's a luxurious shopping mall shaped like a pyramid. Surprisingly there's hardly ever anyone in there, and I was told by a feng shui expert the other week at a press lunch that this is because a pyramid actually acts as a vortex and all the good energy gets sucked back out of the top. I'm not too sure what to think about that. I think the lack of custom probably has something more to do with the fact that everything inside costs about 100,000 dirhams.

There's also a dinner at the newly opened Raffles hotel coming up, and my second foray onto public radio — did I mention I spoke on a live show to support the launch of the website? Yes, Stanley made it happen, even though I'm supposed to be desk-bound. I just talked about celebs and stuff in the mid-morning spot and I really enjoyed it. And they asked me to come back. It's something I haven't had the chance to do since university, so I'm hoping I don't screw it up. I'm told it went OK the first time, anyway — M&M diligently tuned in and gave me some honest feedback when we met up later, even though Stanley failed to mention anything about it whatsoever when I got back to the morgue.

In spite of all this cool stuff, one of my particular favourite pieces of news this week comes in the form of a press release entitled 'Floating wheelchair canal race'. Open it up and it reads:

Ever seen a wheelchair float?

Little Wings Foundation, a project dedicated to assisting children with deformities and obtaining funding for the medical treatment, has teamed up with Reaching U's goal to bring awareness and acceptance of children with special needs to society. Teams of four will paddle it out to create awareness of children with disabilities. Free entertainment will be provided on the terrace.

I just think that's brilliant. I mean, it conjures up all kinds of things in one's imagination. As if it's not enough that the emirate's families might well be hooting and hurrahing at our disabled, disfigured friends as they paddle downstream for dear life, the organisers have promised even more 'free entertainment' on the terrace after the race. What joys! One can only hope it entails dragging each soggy participant out by their ears, sponging them off and then walking in circles around each one, judging them according to their disabilities and the amount of time it takes the ones who don't actually drown to complete the challenge. I can hardly wait.

Of course, I am aware that the press release might well have been written in a rather misleading fashion — as are so very many here. Perhaps the contestants that are encouraged to form these teams and float down a canal in a heavy, metal chair don't have to be disabled at all. Of course, they probably will be by the time they've attempted this race, but that's a whole other matter entirely.

I'm not sure I'll be attending this one, although I'll most certainly tell everyone else, via the website. It was so very nice of them to invite me. Keep the invites coming, I say!

The kebab cake, and other surprises ...

The birthday rooftop pool extravaganza was, in the end, super-vised by the building's two anal security guards, who spent the night picking up plastic cups and eyeing us all in annoyance like parents at a four-year-old's birthday party. It was rather irritating as they told us we could have the party and then on the night informed us we had to be off the roof by midnight. What party finishes at midnight, I ask you?

Still, it was shoulder pads galore and I felt super cool in my navy blue satin ball gown with matching zigzag eye makeup. The Trader showed up in a tux looking mighty dashing, and the DJ spun an excellent mix of retro tunes. I still have no idea where all the girls got their eighties and nineties dresses. There's a distinct lack of vintage or charity clothing stores in Dubai so I was really impressed with the amount of planning and effort everyone made. Sash wore a ball gown that, although an interesting shade of vomit pink and layered with ruffles, still enhanced her stunning figure in all the right places (cow!). It really was an awesome party.

The only person who didn't come was the Iranian inventor. He got in touch last week as he's been threatening to have Stacey and me back over for an Iranian feast ever since we moved out, so I thought I'd better do something nice in return and invite him to my party. Perhaps he didn't understand where it was when it came to the event. Perhaps he just couldn't have imagined anything worse, but neither of us has heard anything more from the other since then, so maybe that's all the niceties out of the way now and we can all move on.

Here I am cutting the scrumptious kebab cake on my birthday — a cake made entirely of meat. Naturally.

Once we were kicked off the roof, we all poured into a club round the corner at Century Village, a cluster of bars and restaurants within walking distance from our building in a lovely green setting, next to the stadium. Far too many more drinks were consumed and the champers was popped, followed by a screaming match in the street — my first ever extremely vocal disagreement with M&M, as I recall. More on that later.

Moving swiftly on … and Ewan was carted off to hospital, having been dropped on the floor like a rag doll by his friend during a run-and-jump, *Dirty Dancing*-type manoeuvre into his friend's arms. It was a tragic accident he'd like to forget, but one which made the night inevitably more memorable. The line of stitches kind of suits him, too. He's like a *Dynasty* war hero, only there was no jealous brother of his uncle's friend's pool-boy's cousin in the mix, unfortunately.

It was a classy affair indeed, and turning twenty-eight wasn't altogether awful. Plus, not many of us get to slice the world's first kebab cake. This very item — due to go in *The Guinness Book of Records* (category yet to be decided) — was cut by my very own hands last night in a lovely new restaurant called MerCURRIES in the Dubai Financial Centre. I was given the privilege because of it being my birthday week.

In case you're wondering, it tasted just like a kebab and the point was, quite simply, to prove that cake, birthday or otherwise, doesn't have to be sweet or served as a dessert. We also learned such things are great for Arab families too because you don't even have to be drunk to enjoy this type of kebab.

Dubai's outdone itself again. Happy birthday to me!

27/11

A weekend in South Africa …

I had a brush with Africa once before, when I won a safari holiday for two to Kenya. I wanted to take my boyfriend, as I could imagine nothing finer than sleeping under the stars, frolicking through the wilderness and befriending lions with my one true love. However, I didn't have a boyfriend. So I advertised for one on the Internet.

After dating my way round London for almost four months, weeding out the weirdos from the potential holiday partners, I decided to take my good friend Dani — only for us both to develop serious diarrhoea as a result of gorging on too much seafood. The illness lasted pretty much the whole trip.

Clearly, it wouldn't have been the most romantic of holidays had I taken a brand-new lover, so on reflection I was glad the boyfriend hunt didn't go to plan. But naturally, when M&M surprised me with a weekend trip to Cape Town, I was excited to make up for the last shitty (*ahem*) time I had visiting this magical continent.

You might be thinking South Africa is quite a long way from Dubai. And you'd be right. It's a whole eight hours on a plane, direct, and M&M went right ahead and booked us two nights in a luxury apartment and business class plane tickets to make up for missing the majority of my birthday shenanigans. By the time we left, it happened that we had some making up to do, thanks to the drunken explosion outside the club on my birthday. As I've mentioned in brief, that little episode saw us screaming on the darkened streets at 3 am — him in a tuxedo, me in an eighties puffy-sleeved blue ball gown. I'm certain it was quite a sight to behold. The catalyst was a combination of my own growing frustration at being number two in our relationship, and his uncontrollable jealousy over a lifestyle I refuse to give up in order to wait around for him. And alcohol.

Suffice to say we did an adequate amount of making up while we were away and Cape Town, as it happens, is probably one of the most beautiful places I've ever seen. It's the furthest away from

Dubai that M&M has ever taken me, and being out of the Emirates we could stroll carefree in a world that allowed lovers like us to embrace, kiss and hold hands in public. In spite of the endless rain and unpredictable temperatures, we definitely made the most of our freedom. In fact, I found myself falling in lust all over again.

Thank God my experience in South Africa was nothing like the one in the north. He's taken my nasty memories and made them all lovely and fabulous. Yup … being romanced like this is something I'll never get over, although it does mean I'm struggling to think of what to get M&M for Christmas. What's left of my wage every month would hardly cover a book about Cape Town, never mind a trip there. What exactly do you get for the married man who has it all?

29/11

A gay old time …

My friendship with Ewan has reached glorious heights since we met. And not only is a trip to Jaipur firmly in the diary, he's been introducing me to Dubai's happening gay scene, which, contrary to popular belief, is thriving. According to Ewan, thanks to a huge population of young professional expats, the scene is one of the most multicultural and diverse around. It's a whole new world of underground controversy including special catamaran trips, apparently. Anything goes out at sea, when there's no one around to catch you. Ahoy!

The CID (Criminal Investigation Division) is constantly doing the rounds, however. Consensual sodomy in Dubai is punishable by up to ten long years in prison. Imagine. Also, punishment can be even more severe if defendants are charged under Islamic law, rather than under the secular penal code.

Back in 2005, organisers at a popular haunt called The Diamond Club were silly enough not only to host a gay night featuring a transvestite DJ, but to scatter the whole of Dubai with flyers about it. *Doh!* 'Fluff Night' was sabotaged and the club was swiftly closed, but not before being made to issue a formal apology for 'violating Islamic laws and indulging in immoral activities' according to local English-language newspaper, the *Khaleej Times*.

Ewan tells me that a few years back there was also a raid at the Jules Club in Le Méridien Hotel, which happens to be just around the corner from our apartment block. We walked there the other night to check it out, which was when I loaded up on the gossip. It's known to be, and definitely was on our visit, brimming with homosexual hotties, all shaking their stuff in sleeveless tees to a relatively average live band. And totally ignoring me. I have to say, I found it quite refreshing not to be leered at by hammered guys in suits — although, obviously, buying my own drinks all night kind of sucked.

The band performing here on the night of the raid a few years ago were a group of fun-loving guys from the Philippines and a couple of them were arrested. Nothing very detailed was reported in the press, except that the people under arrest were being made to undergo treatment for their 'illness'.

I personally noticed the gaping void in *TimeOut Dubai* when I first got here — a magazine that in other cities is brimming with the latest gay and lesbian attractions, but here barely has its own page for theatre. In a country where the culture condones Indian men strolling around hand in hand, homosexuality is very much illegal and considered an offence punishable by God in the eyes of Islam.

You only have to stroll through the Mall of the Emirates with your Bluetooth switched on to see the kind of anonymous invites that float about, should you choose to participate in this risky underground game. The single gay man's best friend, however, is the Internet. In spite of government regulations placing blocks on sites like Gaydar, Manjam and Gayromeo (and my blog), there are always ways to get what you want — and who you want, for that matter.

Of course, no one dares to make a big deal out of anything happening on the gay scene. Not in public, anyway. But there are two very well-known nightclubs in Dubai that, while not openly advertised as gay clubs, are just that. Everyone knows about them. There are restrictions on touching, cuddling and canoodling, and strict door policies ensure they don't look at all suspicious on the outside. Once inside, you sure as heck can't take your shirt off, but apart from that, they're just like any other gay clubs you might find anywhere else in the world. And the 'after parties', usually held in villas or apartments following large music nights and famous DJ events, are known to be nothing but sex orgies at times.

Those in the secret circle are often invited to extravagant affairs after hours, many hosted by prominent locals. Sometimes they're even held in upmarket hotels and whole floors are rented out for free-for-all sexathons. A friend of a friend who attended one such event tells me, and I quote: 'Some local guys even arrive in drag, with an entourage of cute young things.' Others, he says, come from Arab royalty or rich families based in Saudi Arabia.

Many locals are openly gay (albeit behind the scenes) but to admit it to their families would see them shamed, blamed and ostracised. There are also many who have sex with men, but don't actually see themselves as gay. Some experiment with same-sex relations in their young adult life because they're deprived of sex with women before marriage. Many continue to have male sex, even after they're married.

Another mutual friend, who's actually straight, had just moved to Dubai from the UK when he was invited to a male-only party in the desert by his Emirati neighbour. Not really knowing what to expect, he went along to discover carloads of men just hanging out, with tents, lights … everything erected in the middle of the sand dunes. Booze and shisha were both free-flowing and for entertainment — a fleet of dancing boys. He says it was hard to tell at first that they were boys … but they'd been bussed in for the men's enjoyment and seemed to be having a good time also.

Ewan swears he's never done anything seedy, but he has just started seeing a guy called Sean, who caught his eye across a crowded buffet table. Sean still lives at home, but should they ever choose to live together in Dubai and get caught, it could well spell the end of their romance once and for all.

Being friends with Ewan is very interesting indeed. Not only is he now my partner in crime as far as freebie-blagging and social networking is concerned, but there's an element of law-breaking when he's out and about that tangles quite excitingly with our general debauchery. I never ever had that in a friend back home. I feel positively wicked.

02/12

Dishonesty pays …

Stanley shuffled over to my side like a hermit crab and ushered me outside for no apparent reason this morning. He made me wait there in a plume of his vile cigarette smoke, all the while wondering what I'd done wrong. Everyone seems to smoke in this place; the reason perhaps being a combination of boredom and the fact that ciggies are so cheap. Anyway, taking a giant puff he looked at me, and along with exhaling a curl of chemically laden fog he breathed the words: 'I'm giving you a written warning.' Right in my face like an ominous dragon. How charming.

I haven't been given a warning of any sort in any job since my friend called up McDonald's on my behalf when we were drunk and told them I'd died. I was eighteen and too far gone to make the breakfast shift. But Stanley has discovered my dirty little secret — the fact that I've been writing freelance to supplement my rubbish income.

Of course, placed on the spot, I denied it. I met his cloud of smoke defiantly with a flat-out lie. He couldn't prove it. I'd asked for a pseudonym. But Stanley said no, it was definitely my full name in the giant pink box above the article. It was also definitely my face grinning cheesily from the photo beside it. Error.

When they'd asked me for the photo, I half thought that they'd probably needed to check if I was hot enough to write for them — it happens in these parts with some jobs. I sent it off and forgot about it, along with my request for a pseudonym that they'd obviously ignored. No sooner had the lot been uploaded this morning than it caught the beady eye of cyber-scanner Stanley, who thinks my weekly article on Dubai life is in direct competition with the website I'm working on. I suppose it would be, if anyone actually read the website I'm working on. In actual fact, I think the other site is more popular.

But anyway, you can't have your kebab cake and eat it too, so in the face of his toxic billows I nodded my head and sloped back to my desk, having officially been warned. The actual letter came later this afternoon. He handed it over in an unmarked envelope, looking sort of sheepish, like a dodgy dealer giving me illegal drugs (if only) and I leaned it up against my monitor. It's still there. I'm refusing to open it. It gives me the Rage whenever I look at it.

Unfortunately, I'll have to quit writing the article for now. I can't very well carry on doing it under a different name, telling Stanley every week that no, it's definitely not me writing about exactly the same stuff, in the same style, on the same page.

Dammit. Stupid stupid stupid. I really liked that gig.

Thank God I still have a few other magazine jobs coming up. And the freelance for the dot com that M&M set me up with, featuring gift experiences and entertainment, is still going well, too. They now want me to write every month for a fixed amount, which all pushes the salary up out of the pittance category and into the realms of acceptable. Tax free, I'm actually not doing too badly these days. HBSC UK would be proud of me, paying off my debts instead of dodging them (albeit thanks to another loan).

Everybody freelances in Dubai. There's definitely an abundance of work here at the moment, what with a different new this and a bigger new that opening and launching every other week. The trick I suppose is not to let people like Stanley stop us branching out and making the most of it all, but to learn how to juggle it without getting caught.

07/12

The hills are alive with the sound of silence …

Yesterday I received a press release informing me a local dramatic arts group would soon be performing *The Sound of Music*. I practically peed my pants.

The most expensive tickets for this upcoming performance were going for 1000 dirhams each — that's more than 200 quid! And 300 were apparently reserved for children with special needs. The package also seemed to involve the all-you-can-eat-and-drink concept, which I'm not sure would have been a particularly wise gesture, given that no child, special needs or otherwise, should be encouraged to drink. But if that's the way they envisage people will stay to the end, then all power to them. I applied for some press tickets, knowing Heidi and definitely Ewan would be keen to check it out.

But alas, alack, this is all in the past tense, as tragedy has befallen our beloved show. I just heard back:

Dear Ma'am,

It would be a pleasure to have you over at the *The Sound of Music*. However, this is to bring to your notice that the event has unfortunately been postponed.

We have requested the venues as well as the performing artistes to give us new dates in a manner that we can retain the format of our event to the existing one and are now awaiting a confirmation for the same, before we convey the new dates to all concerned.

Regards,

Organisers

I'll admit the second part of that email deserves the award for most perplexing paragraph of the year, so far. As we've established, I get a lot like that. But the gist of it is that after building a day's worth of hope among theatre-starved expats, the hills of our peaceful emirate will not be alive with the sound of nuns or imported Austrian white kids after all. Gutted.

We must wait with bated breath instead, for a miniature version of 'The Nutcracker' at the Madinat. Gladly … on this occasion (probably having signed numerous forms) men are allowed
to wear tights.

Mulled whine …

Perhaps visions of sugar plums were dancing through my head
when I did it, but without really thinking, I posted a recipe for a
nice mulled wine on the website today, just to get people in the
mood for Christmas. Being in warmer climes, it's sort of snuck
up on me this year, so I was proud to finally jump on the festive
bandwagon. I found a recipe online that looked fairly easy to make
and photoshopped my own little image to go with it. Perfect. The
British expats will love it, I thought, basking in the joy I would
bring my fellow comrades.

Then I saw Stanley move from his chair. He appeared in slow
motion, shuffling on the carpet, head shaking, sleeves draping
over his hands in typical fashion. I minimised Facebook and my
chat window with M&M.

'You've put an alcoholic recipe on the website,' he said.

Oh, shit. 'Oh, well … yes, I know. But technically when you
mull wine, the wine sort of … well, it … you know, it's really not
like it's alcoholic at all … when it's mulling it's just like … grapes
… and cloves with a bit of …'

'Take it down.'

'Right'.

And off he shuffled out the door for a ciggie, which I've noticed he does after every single conversation that involves him having to leave his chair. I think I'm becoming the death of Stanley.

27/12

An orphan's Christmas ...

I uploaded photos of Stacey and me sliding down sand dunes onto Facebook, among a barrage of Merry Christmas emails today. Stacey and her visiting guy pal, plus M&M and I went camping in the desert a few nights ago and although the darkness got slightly chilly once our little fire had burned to the ground, it was nothing

Everyone should spend some time
with one of these guys.

compared with the Arctic climes of the traditional British winter. I don't miss that element of home at all.

On the whole, Christmas in Dubai turned out to be a drunken affair in Ewan's flat. After our camping adventure, Stacey jetted off home and M&M returned to his wife. The Orphans' Christmas, a collaboration of cooking efforts from roughly fifteen waifs and strays from work and various friendship circles, was the most fun I've had in ages — even though we managed to set fire to the dining table with a cracker and a scented candle.

To escape the smell of burnt fabric, we headed to the roof with our wine glasses and took some stupid photos, posing with our paper hats on and our feet in the Olympic-sized pool. We all agreed that this was something we'd have never thought we'd be doing this time last Christmas. This time last year, in fact, I didn't even know I'd be moving to Dubai.

It's a weird time here at the moment. There are the majority of expats, desperately clinging on one side to Christian traditions, trudging the food aisles of Marks & Spencer in search of anything to remind them of home. On the other side are the locals, carrying on as normal, patiently pushing their way past every Santa who throws a *ho ho ho* in the wrong direction and undoubtedly wishing it wouldn't be Christmas every day.

Heidi and I even went to see Santa in the Mall of the Emirates after we received an exciting free invite to the snow-play area in Ski Dubai. It was mostly full of kids, obviously, but we hugged ice-sculpted penguins and polar bears in our blue-and-red ski suits, screamed our way down a slope on rubber rings and then went for a glass of mulled wine in Après, the bar overlooking the ski slope. (Don't tell Stanley.)

It's pretty fascinating to see these worlds collide, although I can't say I feel as though I fit into any of it right now. Christmas has never been that much of an occasion in my household. In Dubai, the whole thing feels even more like a Hallmark-sponsored holiday, imported just to appease those of religious indifference, or those who don't really know any better. What is Christmas really? I hate to admit it, but this is the first year I've actually thought about it on a deeper level, other than which pub I might end up in, puking up the turkey.

M&M came over briefly on Christmas Eve and gave me a guitar. A brand-spanking-new Yamaha guitar, complete with ribbons and bows! I'm still amazed — it's an incredible present. As I've mentioned before, I didn't really know what to buy the man who seems to have it all, so I set about making a photo album of our trip to Cape Town. Stacey's watched my flurry of work over the course of the past two weeks with interest, always on hand with the scissors. The lounge has been like a little arts and crafts studio! I spent hours cutting out all the prints and making little love hearts out of pieces of the map, and sticking red tissue paper round our tickets to Robben Island. She was impressed. It didn't cost a lot, I'll admit, but it looks pretty neat and serves as a good reminder of our awesome weekend jaunt, seeing as we can never share photos online. He shed a little tear when I gave it to him. Thank God … I was so worried he would think it was shit.

In truth, M&M and I have been having a good few verbal scuffles lately, mainly because of his mounting jealousy over never really knowing who I'm with, when I'm not with him. This I can understand. When I'm not with him he can't know where I am, because he's with his wife and I'm not supposed to call him.

I've already established he's not entirely mine, but I'm starting to think M&M doesn't much like sharing me, either. I suppose his paranoia is heightened by the imminent arrival of The Irishman. I may have mentioned him briefly before, but he's a gorgeous guy I once had a fabulously romantic weekend with on a conference trip to Spain. We still speak on the phone sometimes. In Spain, after our work was done, we spent many an hour snogging under the stars and on our respective returns to London and Dublin, we sent texts back and forth. Just stupid things, you know, making each other laugh. A few weeks later, I got the job in Dubai.

The Irishman was the first guy I'd really liked in ages and one text from him lingers in my memory — one he sent late one night when I'd just got home from a party in London. He wrote *I adore you*, which put a stupid grin on my face for the whole of the next day. Just three simple English words leapt straight off that screen and into my heart. And even though deep down I knew distance meant nothing could ever happen between us, I kept them there.

The Irishman has now got a job in Dubai and is moving here very shortly. This worries M&M and in between assuring him that he has nothing to worry about at all, I wonder to myself whether that's the God's honest truth. I guess I'd be lying if I said the news hadn't stirred a few memories at least.

If Christmas is a time for reflection, I guess the truth of the matter is that since I got here, I've been well and truly swept away by this whole place and everyone in it! And M&M, although once a welcome part of a world so new and exciting, is also a powerful and somewhat overwhelming force that I'm now finding quite confusing, not to mention difficult to handle.

Hmmm. You know what … maybe I should just try not to think about it so much and have another imported mince pie.

01/01

A bad day ...

Oh crap. Today is a very bad day. A very, very bad day.

02/01

Happy New Year ...

Today I'm trying to adopt the popular expat holiday outlook and have a jolly good time. Starting with a haircut in Jumeirah. I've chosen a new place in a very posh hotel that backs onto the beach. They did Heidi's hair before Christmas and it's gorgeous. She sauntered into my apartment with brand-new highlights, looking like ... like she'd just stepped out of a salon, really.

I feel a bit bad because I usually go to another place, but I told the hairdresser there all about *him*, and I don't want to have to answer any of her questions. So, I'm letting the gay Lebanese guy at this new place work his magic, and I might even make up a whole new boyfriend while I sit in his chair — one who loves me and doesn't buy me a Christmas guitar and then dump me on New Year's Day.

Yes, you read that right.

The last five minutes have gone something like this:

9.45: I love him
9.46: I *HATE* him
9.47: I really fucking love him
9.48: I love him so, so, *so* much
9.49: I hate him

Suffice to say that just as I was pondering how far my affair with a paranoid, married, Muslim man could possibly go, M&M was thinking it too. He's decided to end things with me, so he can see how things go with his wife. I don't think I've ever felt like this before.

Oh dear. I can't believe I actually just wrote that. Sorry. I'm one of those people I despise. I'm a walking — or rather slouching quite pathetically in bed with a laptop — cliché. I'm a pitiful shadow of the woman I was last week, even though I'm exactly the same; just a man down, I suppose. A man who was never really mine, at that. A man who I was starting to think was more trouble than he was worth. Is it an ego thing, I wonder? No, no I'm actually pretty upset.

I thought I was going to be OK last night. I went to the cinema in Deira City Mall with Ewan, watched a bit of Will Smith, had a bit of a laugh. Another few clichéd thoughts passed through my mind, like, *I don't need a man, I'm fabulous on my own*, and then I came home and opened the fridge and saw two Flakes that he'd bought before, to sprinkle on our ice-cream. How thoughtful, I thought at the time. What a lovely gesture.

Only last night when I opened the door and saw them still there (we'd got too full for dessert), it was almost as if they shrank back in fear and muttered an apology, knowing that their innocent presence might well send me spinning right back into the depths of depression — which they did. Those two Cadbury Flakes suddenly stood for everything he'd just snatched away, everything I would never have again. His chocolatey skin, his smooth, sensual charm, his yellow T-shirt, his purple … T-shirt …

I suppose one of the reasons I'm so upset about the whole thing is because I sort of knew what I was getting myself into, and it didn't take a genius to see that it could only end in misery. I just went on with it anyway. But another reason, and clearly a thing of major annoyance, is that I just don't usually get dumped. I don't. I always do the dumping. Always. I was, until New Year's Day, a girl who had never been dumped.

Well, actually, that's a lie. I was dumped at university once, but I was eighteen and I didn't really care. Well … that's a lie, because I did care, but quite obviously those emotions have faded into oblivion, causing me to believe it was nowhere near as bad as this. Of course, I want to believe that my student-self felt nothing of this sort when my boyfriend dumped me, sitting on the top step of the stairs at his house party, drunk on cheap white wine, probably thinking he could do better than this skinny, spotty girl from Spalding, sobbing into the knees of her purple flares.

I want to believe that it wasn't anything like this. I need to believe that I'm the only girl in the world who's ever felt this pain — this tragic, awful pain. The woman I was just three days ago is spiralling into unknown territory, into battle with the girl he turned me into — a person who, just a few days ago, was actually getting a little pissed off with his snoring, a little irritated with his driving and more than angered by his jealousy. Am I now firing those cursed clichés out into an empty room? — *Who am I without him? How do I live without him?* — because I'm a woman who's been programmed to feel she should do this? How annoying it is, to analyse everything this way. I hate being a Scorpio.

But it was like this with my uni boyfriend, I suppose. Of course it was. I ran out of his house and onto the road without looking. I took the first train home to Lincolnshire and flung myself through the door, onto my dad. I couldn't eat for a week and I lost half a stone. Of course I felt like this. Time's just blurred it all nicely into nothing.

Right now — I love (well … lust) and hate M&M in equal measures and I can't go to work. My eyes are so puffy that I don't even think I could blame Stanley and his constant cloud of smoke. I can't roll to the other side of the bed because the pillow smells of him and he isn't there — even though, if he hadn't broken up with me he wouldn't be there anyway. He'd have driven off ages ago to his wife and I wouldn't have heard him go, because I'd have put my earplugs in to drown out that intolerable snoring.

Stacey's still not here, so after M&M left I called Heidi and got her to take me to the beach. This, I have to say, made me feel a bit better, though when she asked what had happened, I didn't really know what to say. We didn't exactly call it quits, or define a moment when we were no longer an item. We just sort of had a conversation about where we were going, and concluded that we weren't exactly sure. And after he kissed me at midnight under the fireworks, after we toasted the end of the year and the start of another with Veuve Clicquot and an endless buffet of the finest food, we danced on the grass till we couldn't keep our eyes open. We staggered back to my place and fell asleep, just like we'd done so many times before, only this time, when he woke up to leave before dawn, after he hugged me and told me he still loved me, he left.

It's a weird situation, really. It's not like he doesn't love me. But he wants to do the right thing. I can understand that. I don't want him to feel like a bad person, and I don't much want to be one anymore, either.

After sobbing the entire morning away in bed, stopping only to type, I plan to go up to the roof for a swim and have a sob in the Jacuzzi instead. Then, when I am done with that, I plan to sob for twenty sweaty minutes in the sauna. And then, when I realise what a spoilt little expat I've become, thinking my life is so tragic while mourning my losses in such a luxurious fashion, I am damn well going to go and get that haircut.

This is the start of a new me.

08/01

You can stand under my umbrella …

I stepped out of my building and practically fell on my arse. I cursed the cleaner under my breath and looked around for the CAUTION: WET FLOOR sign (he usually tells us when he mops — careless man!). But then I realised. The slippery slabs had nothing to do with Mohammed's thoughtless mopping. It was rain. It rained on my lunch break. And I missed it because I was inside eating leftover pita bread.

I haven't seen rain in months, except in Cape Town. I saw a lot of it there, of course, but never here. I could smell it all the way back to work, lingering in the air, reminding me of London. Dubai isn't built for rain, though. What few paths there are on my short commute to the office are now rendered impossible to walk on in my cheap flip-flops, because not only did it rain two days ago, it hasn't really stopped since. Dubai has officially entered panic mode, and most of it is now under water.

According to the officials, we've now been sloshed with a record rainfall of 110 millimetres since it started on Monday. Schools are closed, traffic is at a standstill on most main roads, and apparently some traffic lights aren't working. This is an absolutely terrifying thought, because people here in general can't drive very well when it's dry outside, let alone when their cars are resembling an army of submarines. It's mayhem out there! In fact, I wonder if the

Iranian's got the fleet-horse out. Now, there's a vehicle that could move in these conditions!

Poor Stacey wasn't looking forward to heading back to work as it was, especially after her Christmas break in the UK. And now she and Heidi are both pretty much stuck in their new office somewhere in the sludgy pond that used to be the building site/business district, Al Quoz. Last night, she saw people driving past in 4x4s, offering to help others stuck in smaller cars. Waiting in an impossible jam, she even saw some people get out of the van in front, wade to the shop nearby to get snacks, and then climb back in. And when other cars rushed past as fast as they could move, their own vehicle rocked about like a boat in the surf. Scary stuff.

I haven't really been affected because I can walk to work, so Stacey said it might be beneficial if I take a couple of Li-Los and the 'beer chair' we reserve for the swimming pool outside onto the street, where I might be able to cash in by offering life rafts. It's now painfully apparent that while the new buildings in Dubai are all very nice, a proper drainage system wasn't something that was really ever considered necessary.

I only hope my building is waterproof on the inside. I've heard that the sixteenth floor of a new tower block down on the waterfront (part of the Jumeirah Beach Residence) has started to leak. Not the first, or second, or even the fortieth. Just the sixteenth, which doesn't exactly speak volumes as to the quality of the building. So far, my apartment seems fine, but I've picked up all my shoes from the floor, just in case.

A couple of days ago, the heavens opening all of a sudden in the desert would have seemed a beautifully romantic metaphor for the state of my life since M&M left me. But I'm starting to see that every cloud has a silver lining. In this case, I've just heard the news that very soon *High School Musical* is going to be performed by the local drama group. I'm thrilled. A musical of Hollywood proportions, here in Dubai, with spoilt local expat kids all paying for a part in the line-up. This has made my day. Maybe even my week! Theatre, oh how I miss you. Let's pray the rain clears up so they don't all drown on their way to rehearsals.

10/01

What would you do with an island?

Two things have got me thinking today. The first is my encounter with The Irishman in a bar last night. I keep replaying it in my head. I haven't seen him since we parted in Spain after our conference last summer (the one that left me well and truly dazzled) and then, all of a sudden, he's grinning at me from a bar stool in Dubai, like a cheeky little leprechaun on a mushroom. It was surreal. It did funny things to my heart.

I knew he was coming, of course — he's starting his new job next week. But to bump into him like that kind of threw me and proved once and for all just how small Dubai is! We ended up drinking till the early hours with a host of people I'd never met before, which is why, in my hung-over state, I find myself dwelling on the second thing. Another press release. This one is to enlighten me as to yet another island being dredged from the sea. The world's first island devoted entirely to fashion, no less.

Apparently, the multimillion dollar Isla Moda, due to be started later this year, will combine a fashion resort, a multitude of themed residential villas, haute couture boutiques and luxury hospitality facilities. Fashion superman Karl Lagerfeld has signed a deal to design it, so who knows what it might entail, but I know a hundred ladies who can hardly wait to move to their lipstick-shaped desks, in their shoe-shaped offices (Jimmy Choo's, of course), in their towering mascara-wand-inspired architectural triumphs, into their own little corner of Wardrobe Lane. (I made that bit up, but it wouldn't surprise me.) Imaginations are going crazy.

As it stands, apparently, high-profile fashion designers from every continent (maybe not Antarctica) are getting involved by all designing different parts of the island.

The CEO of Dubai Holding believes: 'Isla Moda will cement Dubai's position as one of the top fashion and lifestyle destinations in the world.' How exciting! We already know that Brad and Ange have bought a slice of Nakheel's amazingly ridiculous project, The World. Justin Timberlake is allegedly not far away (in a secret location between Dubai and Abu Dhabi, so they say) but now this ... who's next? Kate Moss? Cindy Crawford? Cheryl Cole? It's like dangling a carrot in front of a thousand walking clothes horses. And we all know they can afford to sail there on their private yachts.

Isla Moda is set to play host to all sorts of exclusive international events, so says my press release, all of which will feature high-profile designers in the presence of the fashion world's top players. Fashion shows and limited-edition product launches will also be hosted on the island, once it's finished. Assumedly, those who aren't already loaded won't get to see these shows nor buy the clothes and accessories because not everyone's got a boat to get there. I suppose paddling up in a kayak might suffice, but it wouldn't be ideal for bringing all those shoes back in afterwards, really. I wonder if this is another thing they haven't thought through ...

Still, even if the houses don't look like wardrobes and the clubs aren't shaped like Burberry bags ... even if the bars don't drape us in Christian Dior and the cars aren't covered in diamonds as one would expect, I'm still going to be monitoring this development with intrigue through the lenses of my new designer Prada shades, darling. They're the most expensive accessory I've ever bought and let me tell you, whenever I wear them, my whole face is a fashion island in a sea of absolute envy.

14/01

Bush on the beat ...

As an icky, uncontrollable combo of rain and political misery washes down upon us, everyone will be confined to their homes for the day tomorrow. They just declared it a public holiday in light of George W. Bush's arrival. Of course, it's a widely accepted fact that he's a numpter and I think everyone wants a stern word. London and New York might section off a street or two, Sydney might offer up a private boat, Tokyo might even give him a few extra security guards with skills in martial arts should he show up on a whirlwind tour ... but Dubai is a city that takes no chances. So they've shut us all down.

How embarrassing.

Pretty much every road in the entire city is closing tomorrow to allow His Tex-ellency to travel in peace (even though he'll probably use a helicopter). Even the schools are locking the doors, but to be honest they had no choice. We don't even have the Metro here yet — if we can't travel by car, the only option is to fly or walk.

It's all go over here at the moment, though — the 'news room' is in a panic because no one really knows what's going on, or why,

and the *Gulf News* is out-scooping *Arabian Business* magazine
with what are probably just rumours. Stanley's going nuts, running around with his big suit all in a flap. Controversial!

'Democracy is the only form of government that brings peace
and stability and gives individuals the dignity they deserve,'
Bush drawled this morning, as a perfectly dignified emirate was
forced into hibernation, thanks to his questionable leadership
skills.

You've got to wonder how they told him, though. Did Sheikh
Mo take him aside as he stepped off the plane with a little whis-
per? Something like: 'Sorry, George, don't take it personally …
thanks for coming and everything, but … well, we actually think
you might cause some trouble, so we've evacuated the entire city.
Care for a doughnut?'

Poor guy — imagine if that was you. Imagine if you were so
shite at your job that an entire emirate was shitting bricks over
your arrival. I assume his arse is being well and truly kissed, and
he might well have some interesting things to say to add to his collection, but still — they know, he knows, we all know why they're
keeping us all locked in, out of harm's way.

Personally I don't mind in the slightest. I've still got *Heroes*:
Season 2 to finish, and a very nice duvet under which to snuggle.
Plus, The Irishman, Stacey and I have decided to go for food and
drinks once we're allowed back out again. And as his new place
isn't too far away by cab we thought it would be appropriate to his
arrival to go down to the Irish Village.

As this city gets more powerful, I can't help but wonder how
they'll deal with things like this in the future. It might be able to
build the world's tallest building, but it's looking like one of the
world's most ignorant men can still knock down an emirate.

The cleaning man who never was …

Our cleaner hasn't been round for almost three weeks now. He usually comes by every Thursday, but since the Great Floods we haven't heard a peep. Of course, we're hoping he hasn't been washed away, but more pressing on our selfish Western minds is the fact that our kitchen hasn't been cleaned for eighteen days and we're running out of plates.

It really is quite difficult at the moment, going home to a dirty apartment after such a hard day in the office, keeping the public informed of Jordan's latest breakdown and constantly correcting myself as to how many wax-based memorials are currently burning outside Heath Ledger's house. It's even worse for Stacey, when she has to go straight out to dinner in a five-star hotel or rush off to a party. The last thing we want to do is fold our clothes or take a hoover to our bathroom mats.

My mat, consequently, is the worst thing of all at the moment. Two Fridays ago I got quite hammered after an all-day cocktail session and bought myself the usual 3 am pie from 24/7 round the corner. Somehow, between finishing the pie and falling into bed, I managed to coat the bathroom rug in a fine layer of flaky pastry. Worryingly, the majority of flakes are at the top end, adjacent to the toilet. Now, I'd hate for anyone to judge me, or make any lewd, loo-based, meat-chewing assumptions, but every day since then I've been forced to re-trace those forgotten steps, drawing a frustrating blank every time. And it's not very nice.

Had the cleaner been round and sucked up my sins with the hoover, I'd have long since regained my dignity and probably had a few more late-night pies. But as it is, he's ruined it for me. And my rug looks fucking terrible.

Also annoying are the hairballs that have started floating down the corridor, between our bedrooms and the lounge. I'm not sure which are Stacey's and which are mine, but each delicate tumbleweed is a tragic reminder of how bad things could get if he doesn't come back at all. What if they all join up together in the corner of the living room and block the telly? What if one huge hairball collects beside the fridge and we accidentally cook it up with our dinner and choke, and wind up in hospital, and our parents have to fly over and identify our remains after the autopsies reveal nothing but intestines filled with our own matted hair?

Quite sadly, we don't have the cleaner's phone number. He was but a weekly blessing arranged for us by the previous tenant — a fairy in flip-flops with an enviable flair for cushion arrangements. We can't get in touch because although he's been cleaning apartments in our building for a while, nobody seems to know who he is or, indeed, where he comes from. The doorman did say he 'thought' he saw him after the floods, but he hasn't been back to our flat. Perhaps we offended him somehow, but we always tipped him extra. Perhaps we were just too disgusting for him, with our hairballs and sandy high heels and Marmite-covered plates. Perhaps he never existed at all and we've always been a pair of filth-wizards, just in denial. Perhaps we'll never know.

The doorman said he would arrange a new cleaner for us this morning, which took a load off our minds. Tension's been mounting and cutlery's running low. Neither of us can remember how to use a broom and we can't go out onto the balcony to fetch the mop because the floor is so disgusting out there now that our feet would turn black in the process.

I'm sure the new guy will do a marvellous job and we can resume our hard-earned existence in an equally pristine manner. But we'll always wonder what became of the cleaning man who never was.

09/02

An Indian adventure ...

Ewan and I, as well as a couple of girls from work, booked a trip from Dubai to Jaipur on the cheap-as-chips airline, Air Arabia. It's a bit like EasyJet, only swap the football hooligans for men in dishdasha. I didn't actually have a clue what was in Jaipur, aside from Indians, but it was bound to be an adventure no matter what, because we also planned to take the relatively short train journey from there to Agra to see the Taj Mahal. I've always wanted to see the Taj Mahal!

The Irishman was jealous when I told him where we were going. In a way, I sort of wish he could have come, but I didn't think it'd be quite right to invite him — I've been replying to messages from M&M again lately and his jealous streak just wouldn't have processed that information very well.

I know M&M dumped me in order to do the right thing, but it's obvious from his ongoing banter that he still wants to be involved. It's all a bit confusing ... but The Irishman hasn't really shown any signs of wanting to pick up where we left off in Spain, so it's not like I've got a distraction. And God knows I need a distraction, in the morgue that is my office. Instant messenger plus boredom equals bad behaviour. I even went so far as going home one night and posing for some rather kinky photos in the lingerie

M&M got me for my birthday. I knew as I added some essential photoshopping to the finished snaps that what I was doing was totally irresponsible, but it made me feel sexy, so I hit send anyway and waited smugly for his response. I'll show you who you shouldn't have dumped!

Anyway, I think the trip to Jaipur came just at the right time … when I really needed to take a step back. And now, looking at all my photos, it looks like we had a real adventure.

Actually, it's funny, but the fear I felt while gripping Ewan's arm as we raced past bicycles and herds of equally bewildered-looking animals is now almost completely overridden by awe — was I really there among such insane chaos? Me? Me, who now has manicures and pedicures and a cleaner (well, used to have a cleaner)? Was I just in a poverty-stricken city, holding my nose while snapping photos of dying dogs and grown men pissing in the middle of roundabouts with absolutely no shame whatsoever? I can hardly believe it.

To our Dubai-trained eyes, Jaipur was a smelly, filthy, rude city, whose train station doubles as a homeless shelter. Most of its people look diseased. With no road system to speak of, they drive without lights at night. They cycle on ancient bikes with barrels of hay and ladders strapped to the back, and they weave through traffic on motorbikes without a thought to maybe check their non-existent mirrors! Beggars approach your tuk-tuk when you stop and children play in pools of filthy water and walk barefoot where goats and cows crap freely. Pigs snuffle by the road in piles of rotting market leftovers. Wedding processions add an ill-fitting soundtrack to passing scenes of misery, and chatting women walk their toddlers in the middle of busy roads, absolutely oblivious to the dangers until they're forced to run and dodge a collision.

Most of the people we encountered viewed tourists as walking ATMs. We were ridiculed by passing strangers, scammed into paying more than necessary for meals in local restaurants and denied our trip to the Taj Mahal. Yup, we didn't make it there after all, even though it was only four and a half hours by train. We were involved in a bit of a scam — a greedy conductor tried to charge us 5,000 rupees for a journey that should have cost 250. When we refused to line his pocket he kicked us off the train in the middle of nowhere. Ewan was fuming. We all were. We're used to being rallied about at the whims of Dubai's crazy cab drivers, this way and the other without warning, but we never, ever get kicked out in the middle of nowhere. Don't they know who we are?

However, all that said, Jaipur had a perfect Kodak moment around every corner, even though it's swamped in agonising poverty. Embroidered saris all the colours of the rainbow blurred into roadside stalls of sparkling fresh fruit and vegetables. The inquisitive eyes of random animals hovered over wrinkled men making shoes, right next to piles of drying cowpats. After moaning at being charged ten times more than the locals to explore some of the forts we climbed, I must say they look even more impressive in the photos than they did at the time, set against the hazy outline of rolling hills. And the smiles of local children seem far brighter and far more innocent than our cynicism would allow them to be when we were actually there. I guess we were terrified of being out of our comfort zone, but that seems pretty stupid, now we're back in it.

A total contrast to Jaipur was Samode, our next stop and a 40-kilometre drive away in a luxurious Toyota! There we found the most beautiful garden imaginable — like something from a storybook. All around us, it was as though an apology was being offered for all we'd encountered so far — roses bloomed, chipmunks danced and ate from our hands, emerald parrots squawked. It was also a world away from Dubai, but a much-needed reminder of Mother Nature's existence. I'd actually forgotten how nice ancient trees are, how gorgeous grass feels when it's not thick and crunchy under a fierce desert sun.

Here, the birds sang without the fight to be heard over cranes and diggers. The dinners were served around a campfire on individual tables decorated with candles, and dare I say it, there were no ice sculptures necessary to make our lunchtime buffet on the lawn any more beautiful or decadent. The manager even gave us our room for an extra eleven hours free of charge, because we couldn't bear to go back to the city any sooner than we had to after check-out time. Such a nice man, with his rainbow-coloured turban and modern mobile phone. He liked us because we tipped everyone lots. We were just so grateful not to be in Jaipur.

I had another message from M&M while I was there, too, saying he wants to meet me when he's back from his latest business trip. The sexy snaps did the trick apparently (must have been the photoshopping on my thighs). Maybe because the garden was working a little bit of magic on me, I said OK. And when the nagging feeling of doubt kicked in I pushed it aside and concentrated on the smell of the flowers, the smog-free blue of the sky.

Trips like this make you think, I reckon: about yourself and your place on the planet, but other stuff, too. Back in the confines of safety, it's suddenly quite clear that life in these places, for all of its frightening poverty and awe-inspiring beauty, is real. Just a couple of hour's bargain flight away from Dubai's glitz and glamour lies the real world. While this trip hasn't exactly made me want to ditch the lifestyle I've now become accustomed to (don't be daft), I'm definitely a whole lot more appreciative of it now. I think I can say we all are.

13/02

Masters of The Universe ...

Back to life, back to reality (or Dubai's version of it, at least). No sooner has the cow poo from Jaipur dried on my trainers than master developers Nakheel have announced the next big thing soon to be constructed off our fine shores. They're knocking them out faster than we can all keep up. But personally, I like this one more than the fashion island. Oh yes. They might have created The World, but with all that money and enough creative genius to put any children's TV team to shame, they clearly woke up one morning thinking, 'It's just not enough, we need to do better.' And thus, they decided, 'We shall create The Universe.'

The Universe — a multibillion-dollar project consisting of 3,000 hectares of land — will take fifteen to twenty years to develop. It is set to be dredged up in quite a noisy, non-spiritual manner between Palm Jumeirah, Palm Deira and The World — three of the many weirdly shaped projects already polluting our view of the endless ocean, which God ironically created as part of 'The Real World'. Hello? Anyone remember that place?

Tons of celebs, so we're told, are already moving to The World. Brad and Ange will be living in Dubai's version of Ethiopia, so by the time The Universe is ready, they might even want a slice of the sun, too — to give to the kids they bought from other countries in 'The Real World'.

It's all a bit mental, isn't it?

If the rumours are true, this city won't even stop when it runs out of land and water to play with. I swear that not so long ago I heard whisperings of a floating city in the sky! It really has gone mad around here. Where do you invest in a property when the city limits are expanding by the hour? Which car do you buy when you might well have to upgrade to a solar-powered space pod in three years' time? Will buying an apartment in a building that looks like an iPod, be the equivalent of living in a rather embarrassing, battery-operated ghetto blaster when 2017 rolls around? These are things not even the developers can tell us. We've chosen to live in a city that constantly tries to outdo not only everyone else, but its own self. Maybe we should just embrace it. Right? Hmmm …

Unsure of what to think, I informed several of my friends at home on the matter and asked for their opinions for the website. I rather like this email from my lovely friend Sara on the subject:

Artificial = cool/desirable/nifty. Real life (whatever that is) = hackneyed/narrow-minded/pedestrian. Dubai will totally be like the Jetsons soon and Angelina can have little satellite bubbles to float her pick-n-mix kiddies in while she's having her aspirations rejuvenated in the life-justification salon.

I say, dredge up more of the sea for Angie! But why should she settle for The Universe when she could have a personally designed island in the exact relief of her genitalia, each grain of sand impregnated with her unique body odour, the glorious domed nerve-centre of which could be a planetarium-style arena where she could watch endoscopic journeys into her own body cavities in 360 degrees of egocentric intimacy? Benefiting, of course, from the complete privacy that comes with the remaining 10 metres of shallow water between her and Dubai's denigrated coastline (and Bruce Willis's new phallus island on the other side). Opportunity knocks!

Now there's a girl who needs to work for Nakheel.

Asking too many questions about all this stuff hurts my head. But I guess, when I'm standing on the outskirts of it all, scratching my head in confusion, at least I can look at the 'Real World's' tallest building from the boundaries of the Earth's crust and know that I'm living the dream.

15/02

Permission to launch ...

A small, goggle-wearing man in a full-body lycra swimsuit flapped past, goldfish-style in a huge bowl of water as I turned to The Irishman and informed him that this was quite possibly the most impressive hotel launch party I'd ever had the fortune to attend in Dubai. At that point in the proceedings, we hadn't yet witnessed the troupe of equally versatile acrobats throwing themselves around the lobby above us on a series of trapezes, and climbing up and down the walls like genetically mutated spiders carrying roses in their teeth. Neither had we experienced the limitless free champagne or helped ourselves to a plate of free sushi from the buffet, or accepted an offering from the carvery station in the very spot that would, some twenty-four hours later, actually become the hotel's new reception.

The glistening new Monarch Dubai acquires the coveted address of Number One Sheikh Zayed Road and looms over the adjacent Fairmont like a threatening schoolyard bully. We've watched it being built for months and naturally Dubai's media elite was out in force for the launch the other night, with their army of plus-ones.

The Irishman has seen a fair few things that have shocked him so far. I've watched his eyes widen in wonder on many occasions, just as Stacey's and mine had when we first arrived. I feel like some sort of guru at times, here to ease the exasperations of a new and nervous boy–child; to turn this new beginning into an adventure instead of a struggle. At times I feel like I'm seeing the things I've started to take for granted all over again, through a brand-new pair of eyes. I guess it's easy to forget the craziness that to us is now commonplace, but is still completely mind-boggling to other people!

We've been hanging out a lot, and while I can't exactly say I've forgotten about our wonderful weekend in Spain, when we kissed in the starlight and confided in each other our dreams, I can definitely report that we're inching into friendship territory now. The Irishman knows about my dalliances with M&M too. He doesn't approve — not that many people do. I can't tell if it's because he still 'adores me', as he wrote in the text message I'll never forget, or if it's because he's concerned his new 'friend' will get hurt, but with so much going on in his new life at the same time, I think it's an unspoken understanding that we're better joining forces as mates anyway. God knows this place is weird enough without adding any further complications.

As such, The Irishman has integrated quite swiftly into my friendship circle and adds his Irish charm to nights on the town. Getting to know him properly has been a lot of fun actually. I find it kind of strange how certain people come in and out of your life the way they do. When we first clapped eyes on each other in Spain, he'd travelled from Dublin and I'd travelled from London. And now here we were, not even a year later, watching a man perform bizarre acrobatics in a bowl full of water in Dubai.

Back to my meeting request from M&M. I obliged. It was a reunion of sorts, having both established that we've missed each other since he dumped me for his wife. He came over the other day to talk and one thing led to another, and now … *ugh*. OK, I'd be lying if I said the pain of losing my married, jealous, somewhat possessive boyfriend hadn't started to subside by the time we actually met up again, but there's something about him.

M&M is so powerful and commanding; so passionate about everything; so passionate about me! It's not like I need him, but when he takes an interest in me, when he listens, when he sends those sweet declarations directly to my inbox … well, it's hard to resist going back. It's hard not to respond to his messages at work when everyone else in the morgue at work is just so goddamn dull and quiet, too. I flirt with him and thus with potential disaster every time I hit reply — and I hate that I love the attention. M&M to me is like a magnetic force and I'm the weaker object of his affections.

He hasn't exactly done anything about becoming single in the time we've spent apart. But … he's whisking me away for a two-day mini-break in the Maldives, which is so exciting, and this will give us a couple of days to be alone again and talk. I've never been whisked anywhere quite so exotic in my life. I thought Cape Town was pretty extravagant, but taking me to one of a collection of idyllic islands in the crystal-clear Indian Ocean, just a four-hour flight from Dubai, probably tops his growing list of grand gestures. OK, so it's rainy season, but I'm not going to be picky.

In accordance with Dubai's almighty plan for self-improvement, every event in my life at the moment seems to be bigger and better than the last thing. Did I mention that I even met Céline Dion the other day? Well, OK, I didn't actually meet her, but I sat in the same room as her with my laptop open and tapped everything she said into a Word document as she politely read her spiel into a microphone at the new and celeb-attracting InterContinental hotel down in Festival City. I was even given a press pass to the concert, which I'll flash with pride if I can face the torturous traffic jam that I'm sure will exist between us on the actual night.

It feels like every day is a launch party for the next, and perhaps a little bit of Dubai's winning spirit is rubbing off. I have to say, although I haven't forgotten the lessons I learned in poverty-stricken Jaipur, in the fake world I now call home, it feels like there's a lot more to look forward to.

18/02

Endings and beginnings ...

Uh oh. Perhaps I spoke too soon. Two major events have coincided this week to put a serious spanner in the works. Not only did Stanley shuffle over the other day, take me aside and announce that he was 'letting me go', but Stacey has informed us that she's leaving Dubai. I'm still in shock.

On the former ... well, things haven't quite been perfect in the morgue for a while, have they? I've been toying with the idea of quitting the job anyway, and the night before the firing I felt the inexplicable need to gather every pair of shoes that had been collecting under my desk and take them home; something I still find quite spooky. I showed up with my arms full just as Stacey was getting back from the gym, and couldn't even explain the sudden spring clean. It's not like we've done the same with the flat since the cleaner went AWOL.

I was planning on sticking it out another couple of months, perhaps, and I've been keeping my beady eyes on other media jobs on offer for a while — ones that offer similar perks, of course.

I suppose it's been pretty obvious from the start that this one wasn't ever going to live up to expectations. Even after months of running the website alone, bugging Stanley for more resources, I wasn't any closer to getting any help on my last day than I was on my first, in spite of constant promises to expand the team and create more structure going forward. In fact, instead of hiring me an intern, Stanley hired another person to work above me a few weeks ago, which went against everything he'd promised me from the start. One day, without warning, I was told to report to a woman I'd never seen before, and had to spend about a week telling her how to operate the computer system. I felt quite sorry for her actually. She clearly couldn't believe the state of the place, or the soul-destroying silence of the morgue.

I've hardly seen anything at all of Hazel or the magazine team, aside from Ewan, obviously. The awesome camaraderie I envisaged only ever existed in my head, and the site is like a completely separate entity to the magazine; something that no one really cares much about, apart from me. I actually think Hazel and her crew were annoyed at the website, and me, for taking some of the attention away from them and their precious magazine.

And now for the spanner. Allegedly, Stanley says I said something derogatory about the job during my last radio broadcast.

Now, this is what upsets me more than being fired. I may have sounded a little hung over, as the broadcast in question was made the morning after a rather heavy night out involving Harry Ghatto's (as usual), but I'm pretty sure I'd never slate my own company live on air. I ran over the entire hour's broadcast in my head, racking my brains. I'd maybe felt a little peeved at being ignored for so long when there was so much left to be done with the site, but as for blurting something bad about my own company or job on the radio, to the whole of Dubai … not on purpose. Not ever!

I happen to think Stanley was just getting a little bit sick of me trying to press the issue of improving things; a little weary of having to assure me daily that things would change when he knew they never would. He was probably sick of being told by his own boss that he, as my boss, couldn't give me what I needed in order to succeed. This inkling was in fact confirmed when he took me into the little conference room for 'the chat' and said, almost wearily, almost like he'd given up weeks ago, like he'd written me off as a lost cause, 'You're too ambitious.'

I looked at him, flabbergasted, and a little laugh escaped my lips as he shuffled in his seat, clearly anxious about following the orders of whoever had instructed him to let me go.

'How can I be too ambitious?' I demanded.

I wanted to know how he as a manager could call a member of his department 'too ambitious' when he'd hired me to launch and run an entire website single-handedly, and still not bothered to find me any help. Had I not been too ambitious he would have had one site update a day, and probably a cut-and-paste job from another badly written press release at that, seeing as he'd long ago told me not to go out and meet anyone interesting in order to source more content.

He didn't have an answer. He just played with his sleeve and mentioned the mulled wine incident, and the freelancing, which served as a backup to his decision. Fair enough, I suppose. But he couldn't play me a recording of the offending broadcast in question — not because it would have made a difference to his decision if I sat there defending it, it seems, but because he didn't have it, and he hadn't even heard it himself anyway.

Yes. He had never heard it. He'd been on holiday you see, and heard about it on his return. It appears that Stanley was instructed to fire me over something he didn't even bother to check out himself. I shot him another look, which I think burned straight through to his very soul because he shuffled in his seat again, quite uncomfortably. Even if he didn't give two shits about letting me go, you would have thought in the long run he'd have quite liked to arm himself with a vaguely incriminating piece of evidence on the off-chance that I might have something to say about it.

'You didn't hear it?'

'No.'

'Well who did?'

'I can't say.'

'Right.'

Stanley said I could stay the rest of the day but when I left the room, fuming, he appeared to get a little nervous and asked me to leave immediately. I assume he'd guessed my plan to email the entire company and my list of contacts (which I'd already stashed elsewhere, along with my shoe collection) and tell them what had happened. M&M says it looks as though they just wanted me out for combined reasons and then made up an excuse, knowing I'd never have a leg to stand on in light of Dubai's non-existent employee rights.

Of course, I marched straight back to the flat, grabbed my laptop and headed down to the coffee shop, whereupon I contacted a recruitment agent who lined me up two interviews by 5.30 pm. Thank God Dubai's still desperate for anyone with a modicum of skill in the English language department — even if they do shoot offensive, imaginary comments out to the masses on public radio.

On the latter subject of Stacey leaving Dubai, I think it's a combination of her commute to work being a hellish hour-long process there and back, mostly stuck in traffic, and also feeling a bit like she never really gave London a go. Well, she had just graduated uni when she moved here with me. Thanks to her time at the travel publishers she's got a lot more experience under her Prada belt now, so I can't really blame her. It's just all happened really quickly and I'm really sad. In fact, I'm totally in denial that she is leaving me now, what with all this stuff going on.

We've gone from sharing a room on the landing of the Iransion, sleeping side by side in biscuit beds, befriending half of Dubai over tragic renditions of Bonnie Tyler in the karaoke bar, to growing up quite suddenly and going to the gym. Well, Stacey's been going to the gym. I'm still convincing myself that the Jacuzzi beats the flab if you spend long enough with your arse pressed up against the jets.

I think it's always going to be hard to say goodbye to someone that you've spent pretty much every second of your life with for so long. It's definitely been an adventure, but now everything's going pear-shaped, it feels like Dubai's even more of a challenge than ever (*sigh*).

In spite of the interviews at a couple of advertising agencies both going well (they're looking for creative copywriters and the pay is so much better than in publishing!), I'm taking a month's work placement at a new international media company. Ewan has just started working for them, too.

It all sounds quite exciting actually, especially for Ewan, because he's been taken on permanently. The company specialises in out-door advertising, and the CEO has been developing a media arm of the company that will boast two new consumer titles to go with the radio stations they already have. Like much of Dubai, it appears to have popped up out of nowhere but it works for me — I need a job! I'll be editing a health and beauty trade publication, while Ewan acts all important as the section editor across two men's titles. After that … well, I guess I'll just see what turns up. Maybe some copywriting, maybe some work for the media company. Or, per-haps, the Iranian still needs help with the fleet-horse (*sigh*).

Ewan is going to move into the flat for a bit and then we'll look for a new place together. The timing worked out well on that front at least, although spiralling rental costs makes this particular task even more daunting than before. Still, most media-based companies are positioned at the other end of town near the aptly named Media City, so it does seem pretty pointless for us both to stay here … even though we have this amazing pool and Jacuzzi and … oh, I forgot to say, we found our cleaner. He didn't drown in the floods after all. He had some family problems back in India so had to go home for a bit, without telling anyone. Still, at least we have closure on that front, too. Poor sausage.

It's all about endings and beginnings lately. In a strange way, although it's slightly nerve-racking, I'm kind of excited! And I'm looking forward even more to the Maldives with M&M now. No matter how wrong it might be, I bloody well need some time out.

22/02

Theatrical flashbacks …

Last night was *High School Musical* night. I think I mentioned previously how excited I was about its brief upcoming fling with DUCTAC — the theatre in the Mall of the Emirates — so I was even more excited that Ewan took me along as his plus-one with some press tickets. We're all so theatrically starved in this place, he could have chosen anyone from a list of deprived culture vultures, but I think he knew I've been needing a bit of cheering up since Stacey re-packed her rucksack and headed back to the big smoke, leaving me jobless and alone (*violins again please*).

It happened so quickly — she just upped and went. No point hanging about, I suppose, but after a drunken, cocktail-laden affair at the Madinat, no sooner had my hangover subsided than her room was empty, and she was texting me from the airport. Everything's changing.

Naturally, we were the oldest people in the audience at *High School Musical* who didn't have children with them, but I was suitably impressed from the word go. In spite of a few dubious notes in the key of amateur, the atmosphere was amazing. *Go Dubai and your completely underestimated theatre scene*, I thought, munching on another fizzy cola bottle for added sugar-fuelled enthusiasm.

I almost wished I'd auditioned myself, but then the kids involved were all pampered expats whose parents had been expected to pay an arm and a leg in order for their precious offspring to take part. I wasn't sure that calling Mum and Dad and asking for some pocket money would have gone down too well at the age of twenty-eight, but I've always thought that a life on the stage was my silent calling, you know. OK, so I dance like I'm having an electric shock and my vocal ability stops somewhere between Harry Ghatto's and the shower, but there's always been something magnetic about the theatre for me. I remember my parents saying that my teachers told them I was wasted at a normal school. Mum said they thought I should have gone to drama school.

Looking back I think my teachers might have meant that the kid who carried a stuffed tiger round the playground, talking to it like her only friend, was probably special in another sort of way. But I never forgot that.

Last night, the dud notes were practically drowned out, thanks to what sounded like the entire room singing along. Everybody knew the words. Even the mum in front of me was mouthing the lyrics as her daughter clapped her hands in the air and sang, 'We're aaaaaall in this togeeeeeether.' Quite fitting for Dubai, I felt.

We gate-crashed the after-party that was held at a restaurant near Ski Dubai. They had curtained off a section and filled it with ice-cream, popcorn, candy-floss, mini beef burgers and, surprisingly, beer. I think the little starlets were as high as me on e-numbers by the time we got there, but I watched them jumping up and down in their glad rags, still singing songs from the show to each other, and remembered feeling the same after we'd wrapped the opening night of *The Dracula Spectacular* back in my home town when I was twelve. I was a proud and just-ashyperactive member of SADOS. It stood for Spalding Amateur Dramatics Society (still not sure what the O stood for), but as Ewan pointed out last night, some sixteen years too late, the rest of town probably called it 'saddos'.

I think we all have our own *High School Musical* moments, when we realise that the world doesn't really look the same as it used to. It's an up and down rollercoaster of a ride in Dubai, all of a sudden. But I guess we can choose how we deal with these things. At the end of the day, we can either let progression make us feel like a saddo, or be the bigger person and learn the new words.

27/02

Playing away by the rules ...

I know that M&M is bad for me, but every time he jets me off somewhere *uber-romantic* like this I get so completely overwhelmed that I momentarily forget how wrong we are for each other. The cracks don't show — or at least they're covered with a fuzzy blanket of lust and admiration for this man who has it all and is more than happy to share it. I'm starting to think I'm sounding as shallow as some of the other people already milking the madness of everything Dubai has to offer. I know, and my friends know, I should never really have gone back, should never have succumbed to those magnetic forces, but his promises, his declarations of love, his seemingly hopeless devotion ... they're all added extras in a very persuasive man who's difficult to refuse. And you should have seen our room in the Maldives.

We stayed at the most luxurious resort — a perfect circle of an island with an infinity pool looking out to the endless twinkling ocean. Our room even had an outdoor bath with his'n'hers back rests in it! There were two sinks with a bathrobe and his'n'hers slippers for each of us. It made me think of a place Stacey stayed in once, which was so posh that they actually embroidered her initials on her pillowcases, just so she could sleep in personalized peace.

M&M and I toasted such idyllic charms with our champagne glasses, got a little naughty on the day bed by the plunge pool and feasted on seafood overlooking the crashing waves at the resort's ultra-posh gourmet restaurant, which sat perched on a wooden jetty. The portions looked more like miniature art exhibitions than meals — it was almost scandalous to eat them. But suffice to say it was amazing. The room even had its own iPod, complete with sexy songs — ooh la la! A bit of Morcheeba's 'The Sea' is enough to get anyone in the mood, in such a fitting location.

Oh ... and while lounging in a hammock, we had a bit of an argument over the fact that I've been spending so much time with The Irishman lately. M&M doesn't like it. Of course, he's always been a little wary of his presence in my life because I made the serious faux pas of telling him about our weekend of snogs in Spain. But seeing that M&M has been in and out of my world so sporadically since we met, I didn't really think that my friendship with another guy — former fling or not — would be any cause for major concern. Perhaps I was being a tad naive.

As it is, The Irishman and I have made a very good job of becoming firm friends in light of Dubai's amusing melodramatics and, I suppose, the dramas involving M&M himself. The Irishman is good with advice, you see. I can't help but tell him things. He's one of those people, and we all know one, who's always got time to listen. He's a bit of a calming influence. Always offers a fair word — plus, he's always up for a night on the town getting pissed when M&M is home with his wife.

Whereas M&M and I appreciate the finer things in life (thanks to his no-expense-spared attitude), I'm learning that it's people like The Irishman who help me find the humour in it all. He's one of the few people here that I can always count on to take a step back with me, to acknowledge the fact that some of the things we get to do because we live in Dubai are actually so far removed from our normal lives that they're rendering us spoilt, overindulged and spoon-fed.

In fact, this reminds me … just the other day when we were sitting in his living room, he accidentally spilled his can of Coke over the side of the sofa. He tutted and stared at the fizzy wet patch creeping across the floor before looking at his flatmate and asking: 'When's the cleaner coming?' I almost peed my pants laughing. He was joking, of course (I think), but I can't remember the last time I cleaned anything for myself either. Thank God our cleaning fairy reappeared.

As we sipped cocktails from coconut shells, M&M made it very clear that he doesn't like me spending time with The Irishman. This still stings a bit, if I'm honest. But there's something about him that scares me slightly — something that makes me shut up and close off in the face of adversity. I really can't explain that. Don't get me wrong, I wouldn't be with someone if they really scared me … and most of the time he's fantastic. I've never been with anyone so attentive. It's just that every now and then he gets this hardened look on his face and a distance in his eyes, like he's imagining the ultimate betrayal happening behind his back. This makes me shy away from telling him anything more, even if it's something entirely innocent. This makes the wall grow bigger.

I guess I don't want to provoke his imaginings. I'm happy most of the time. I'm adapting to my sheltered bubble — or at least I was before it started to burst. Perhaps he imagines my betrayal because he knows that he's doing exactly that. Perhaps because he's cheating, it's easy to envision how someone else might eventually do the same to him.

Is that what happens to people who cheat, I wonder? Do they then become cynical and cautious, knowing what to look for, expecting similar signs from the people they dare to trust themselves? Does guilt make you see things that aren't there in other people because you measure them against yourself? I'm not really sure, but to save an argument or making him upset in such a perfect place on such a perfect, aquamarine-coloured date, I found myself agreeing not to see The Irishman as much when we got back to Dubai.

28/02

The end of the affair …

They say bad things happen in threes. First the job, then Stacey leaves, then M&M gets busted for being a play-away hubby. Seriously. His wife knows everything. I feel terrible.

After an otherwise magical Maldivian weekend, imagine my surprise to receive a text from my jet-setting lover, informing me that he's leaving the country again, with his wife. She found out about our affair. I'm still not sure how.

I know for a fact he didn't tell her straight out. He can't have. He's too nice to have been able to face hurting her up to this point. I feel so bad for her, whoever she is. And I feel pretty disgusted with myself for thinking that we could bask in the exquisite splendour of that island, tangle ourselves in Egyptian cotton and not expect karma to fly right in through those floor-to-ceiling windows. I'm positive he was going to tell her eventually, though. Or … hmmm. Is that what all mistresses think?

I was out in the mall, still high from the mini-break, shopping for some outfits for my new temp magazine job and trying not to call The Irishman when I got the text. My blood ran cold. I read it a million times, praying for the horrid words to re-form themselves and spell out something happy. I had to sit quietly in Starbucks for a while and stare at the floor. Then I cabbed it back to the apartment and locked myself in my room. I'm still having visions of a mad Arab man, some cousin of a brother of an older relative or something, coming to get the filthy mistress who dared to seduce the perfect husband. A thousand scenes from non-existent movies are still hurtling through my mind: doors slamming, fists pounding, screaming in Arabic disturbing my entire apartment building in the dead of night. Perhaps there'll even be a murder (*gulp*).

As I hide from forces unknown, trembling pathetically beneath my duvet with my laptop, my phone and a very strong vodka and Coke at my side, the thought that a major event is unfolding, just as it did before, is playing on my mind. Around New Year's Eve, as I was trying not to think that M&M's attentiveness may have actually been verging on possessiveness, and just as I was wondering whether it was all too much to handle, he dumped me. And now this. After telling me I shouldn't see The Irishman, our relationship has exploded into something I really wasn't looking to be involved in. Jesus! Has fate stepped in again to reconfirm how absolutely fucking wrong this all is?

I'm sleeping with the doors bolted, and Ewan's promised to keep a knife on his bedside table. He won't get arrested for possessing a weapon if there's a raid — he'll get arrested for living with a girl he's not married to. This place is crazy.

15/03

A shock to the system ...

In a shock visit from something approaching good news, word came in today that Dubai's new Metro is probably going to be finished ahead of schedule. Yup. Parts of the world's largest automated Metro project are wrapping up early. My London-trained ears pricked up immediately and the cynicism set in. The word 'Metro' or indeed 'train' simply doesn't co-exist harmoniously with the line 'ahead of schedule', does it?

For a moment, I was thrown. They're calling the operation 999, because apparently the first line will start moving on September 9, 2009; exactly when they said it would, when first they laid these 15.5-billion dirham plans.

Someone official, called Mohammed (naturally) said: 'We are right on schedule and have achieved a number of milestones ahead of time … people in Dubai will see the trains running on the test track on Sheikh Zayed Road by the end of April.'

Mohammed is definitely not making it up because, come to think of it, M&M said a few weeks back that the trains are already arriving — he's seen them from his office window. They're ugly, eighties-throwback carriages with blue-and-white squiggles all over them. I was actually a little disappointed to learn this. I was half expecting some sort of multi-leveled, futuristic, silver-bubble-style thing that would essentially hover above the track and drop only at each station to allow the people on and off. I was also expecting further news of a duty-free service on board, the opportunity to make a five-star hotel or restaurant reservation while in motion, or perhaps the option of travelling in a private chamber dripping in gold and sponsored by local jewelers. But so far it's just looking like a regular train service. How boring.

I know Dubai has money and everything, but seriously, London needs to pay attention. [*Begin rant:*] If I may just say, the amount of times my days back home were ruined by impromptu work on random tube lines was unbelievable, as well as unacceptable, considering the cost of a travel card. Plus, even after all this 'work', London's travelling homeless shelters don't even have air-con, or wireless Internet, or women-only carriages (a serious boon in light of some people's obnoxious body odors). How shit is that?

If Dubai can dig a tunnel under a creek and get 25,000 laborers working round the clock to cause as little disruption as possible, and still get it all done ahead of schedule, I think there's something very wrong with how the Big Smoke has thus far sorted out its transport issues. [*End rant*].

The frog and the impossible flat hunt ...

The hunt for a new apartment is not going well. In the past week, Ewan and I have viewed all manner of two-bedroom places in the Marina and Barsha areas, and have so far walked away with nothing but fading hope.

I've been slightly spoilt with accommodation in Dubai so far (aside from the Iransion, obviously). Back in East London, my idea of luxury living was having a front door that wasn't kicked in every three months by hooligans wearing hooded jumpers. Once, Lucy got egged on the way home by a bunch of kids in the council-owned block next door, and a few weeks prior to that, a kid no older than twelve snatched her mobile phone right out of her hand as it was pressed to her ear. She'd been talking to a friend at the time and never did get to finish the conversation she'd been having ... about the growing number of intimidating hooligans watching her on her way home.

The other day, however, while inspecting an indoor pool in a newly opened apartment block in the Marina, Ewan asked the agent where exactly we were supposed to sunbathe. I thought he had a valid point. The fact that the elevator hadn't been connected yet and was still operating manually, leaving us and our estate agent stranded on the fifteenth floor for half an hour, wasn't half as important as the fact that we might have to move somewhere without a suitable space for catching rays.

In my opinion, the best place we've seen so far was a pad behind the Mall of the Emirates in Barsha. It was like something out of a Tim Burton movie. The entrance to the building was bathed in neon green and purple lights, and the lobby was decorated with an enchanted forest scene. Pixies, fairies and giant trees with grinning faces greeted us as we walked in.

The gym was host to a family of Egyptian sculptures. Tutankhamun beamed at us from the end of the corridor, and the rooftop pool with no view was guarded by a humongous concrete frog. I liked it. It would have been a bit like moving into a youth club — a colourful escape from our 'young professional' labels in the real world and everything else that's been going down. Ewan wasn't impressed at all, however, and insisted we keep looking. Shame.

We're seeing a couple more tonight. It's funny but these places all look the same after a while. They're just tiny, empty, expensive spaces, mostly overlooking a construction site. But with rent going up by the week, it's important to choose the right one, and find it quickly. I wish we could snap up a waterfront property like The Trader's and wake up to the ocean or the Marina every morning. Our budget would have bought us that, five years ago. Now, however, it only gets us a sniff at those buildings in the shadows — the ones that lost the views to something bigger and better, and are now ultimately unsuitable for people like us.

We've both started our new jobs at the media company, which are keeping us pretty busy, so everything's happening at once. At the weekend I'm moving to the maid's room in my friend Margot's spacious villa in Satwa. Ewan is moving in with another friend until we find somewhere together, which I guess will save us a bit of time and money. Margot's villa is actually in the same compound as The Irishman's, which wouldn't impress M&M at all, if he were here. It's a great place, everyone's friendly, and it doesn't even matter that I'll be showering every morning in a foot-wide tiled square with no curtain, right next to the washing machine. I'll be sleeping in a room that's still bigger than the one I rented on Hooligan Lane in London.

Renting and ranting ...

Last night I went for dinner at Sash's friend's apartment. I knew it would make me jealous, seeing that Ewan and I could never afford to live in such a glamorous place, but I was intrigued. The apartment's in one of the original Emaar towers (another big developer in the UAE) in the Marina, and has been filled to the max with art and trinkets and the kind of expensive furniture people like me can only dream about.

I absolutely long for a home that's filled with the essence of me and not cheap tat from a catalogue shop. I'm sure we all do. But I guess this generation rarely has it because we all move around so much these days. Personally, I haven't been in one place for more than two years since I was eighteen. And before that, of course, I was living at home with Mum and Dad, getting my laundry done, getting my plates washed, getting driven around by ... er ... OK, much like I do here, but you get my point.

Anyway, everyone around me seems to be moving house lately, including Ewan and me. And, of course, if buying a luxury pad isn't an option, you're forced to fling yourself full throttle into the rental market. If you're a citizen of Dubai at the moment, there is little else on everyone's lips. The competition is fierce. It's much worse than I remember it being in London. Or New York, for that matter.

With this in mind, I decided to do a little research. If we can really live anywhere these days, how does Dubai compare to other cities? Well, most decent double rooms here now cost between 4,000 and 5,000 dirhams a month. That's roughly 760 pounds a month at current exchange rates. If I lived in London, judging by a popular rental property website (gumtree.com), I could have my pick of locations for that money right now. And I definitely wouldn't be slumming it. I could have a room in Greenwich overlooking the Thames, for 523 per month, all-inclusive. For five quid more a month than I'm paying here, I could live five minutes from Marble Arch. When did this unfinished, dusty, Middle Eastern city become as desirable/overpriced (depending on how you look at it) as central London?

If I moved to New York, based on what I'm expected to pay here, I'd have 1,388 dollars to spend on a place per month. Looking at their biggest community website (craigslist.com) I could have a double room, sharing with two other girls on the Upper East Side (East 70s and 2nd Avenue — Carrie Bradshaw-style!) for 1,250 US dollars. If I wanted to 'slum it' and live ten minutes away from Manhattan in North Brooklyn, I could live five minutes' walk from the subway in a double room, in a nice, fully furnished apartment for 800 bucks. I wouldn't have a swimming pool or gym in London or New York, of course. And I wouldn't have a maid. But I would be able to cross the street without dodging a bulldozer, wading through sand or hailing a cab that may or may not get me there in one piece.

I'm not entirely sure why this brand-new city of shopping malls and moderate interest from tourists has suddenly grown just as expensive as two of the busiest, most popular city destinations on the planet. But as we dined on barbecued prawns and rocket salad in the luxury of Sash's friend's apartment I decided I'd have to lump it. It's an unfortunate fact, I suppose, that until I feel the need to settle and invest, there's really no choice but to suck it up and pay the rental costs of living like the modern somewhat spoilt gypsy that I am.

Home sweet home, number three ...

M&M called me the other day. We spoke on the phone and he didn't sound too hot. In fact, he sounded exhausted and emotionally drained. I think he's had several earfuls and a whole load of threats from angry family members, but he's confirmed that they don't know who I am, so I'm not about to be killed in the night, which is nice. He's apologised profusely for scaring me, but to be honest, I really was more concerned for him. I remember what The Trader told me ages ago, about the views on infidelity in Muslim culture.

As a result of him getting busted, M&M's wife has decided to move elsewhere and he's moved to a new apartment on his own. He snapped it up at lightning speed, with very little hassle. Money helps a lot, I'm guessing.

The apartment Ewan and I just signed up to live in, however, was the biggest and most decent place we could find for the budget we'd set aside. Although, while we may have achieved the quantity part, the quality of our new surroundings leaves a lot to be desired. It was never quite my dream to live on a building site.

Our new two-bedroom apartment sits on a main road, in an area called TECOM, which is still very much under construction. Our living room balcony overlooks a vast expanse of sand, which appears to have a racing track for camels on it. The fact that our block has only been open for a few months, the swimming pool isn't ready yet, the gym has no equipment in it and the building is completely surrounded by forklift trucks and metal fencing bearing hazard signs for builders, made it a relative bargain.

We're soon to be residing in the unfinished ugly sister of a neighbourhood called The Greens. No taxis will know how to find us when we call them, and there's no local shop within walking distance from which to buy our supplies — not that we could walk anyway, because there aren't any pavements either.

The Irishman finds this all very amusing. We've been spending a lot of time around the compound's swimming pool these past few days and it's fun having him as a neighbour while I'm staying in Margot's maid's room. I kind of forgot I wasn't supposed to be seeing him — oops!

He's got it all set up, living here. I tried to find a room in the same compound but they're few and far between — because it's so great, no one ever wants to move out.

The good thing about our new place, I suppose, is that it's closer to M&M's new apartment. I haven't seen very much of him since he got back. He's been sorting out his life, but surprisingly he's calling me a lot and appears to be even keener on me than ever. I wake up to text messages from him almost every morning, asking how I am before I've even opened my eyes. I know it's him when I hear the beep. I'm not too sure what to make of it all, if I'm honest. The first night I stayed over in his new place, he sort of acted a bit funny, too, like he didn't really know what to make of the fact that we could spend an entire night together without having to leave Dubai, without him having to run off back to another bed. His reaction freaked me out a bit. I did have quite a scare, imagining an angry Arab was out to kill me, and I feel genuinely terrible for his wife, who now has to deal with moving away, as well as with the fact that her trusted and beloved hubby has been sneaking around behind her back.

I've never had to put a face to her name, or hear her voice. I never knew anything about her, which I guess made it easier to forget that what M&M and I were doing was paving the way to another woman's heartbreak. Not knowing her at all was how I allowed him to charm me, whisk me away and grow increasingly besotted with what he technically shouldn't have been able to have. But now for some reason I can really picture her clearly. Someone out there, quite justifiably, hates my guts. Someone out there is a wreck, partly because of me. Ugh.

I can hardly put the phone down, though, can I … tell him not to call me because I feel shitty about the whole thing and think we should call it a day. What about him? It sounds a bit like he needs me more than ever. Or maybe he just thinks he does.

Anyway, in other news, the temp job at the media company is going quite well, thus far, in spite of the whole place reeking of organised chaos. I'm getting quite a few nice freebies lined up as a result of editing the health and beauty trade publication. Ewan loves work too — he's a stylist for two different fashion sections in different mags. He's running a team and has way more blagging power than he used to have in the old place.

Also quite exciting is that some of us are keen to book a trip to Nepal in the next few months, including The Irishman, Sash and a few others. It's dirt cheap if we fly from Dubai to Kathmandu. It'll also give us the chance to spot tigers from the backs of elephants!

I'm not planning to tell M&M just yet that The Irishman is set to come along. It was arranged while he was AWOL, while I needed to make some happy plans, and while I wasn't really sure if I would ever see him again. He wouldn't like it very much at all if he knew that The Irishman and I were still talking, let alone arranging to go away together. OK, so we're not going by ourselves but I just don't want to upset him. He's got enough going on, without imagining another betrayal. For now I'm concentrating fully on my move into the new apartment. If it all goes well, Ewan and

I might even adopt a kitten. How domestic would that be? Home sweet home number three, with a pet. Maybe we really are moving up in the world.

29/03

It'll be all-white...

Only in Dubai could the words 'dental' and 'spa' sing together in glorious harmony. Previous to my teeth-whitening session at Dubai's Dental Spa the other day, no amount of trickling water over shiny stones or leafy plants in terracotta pots could have persuaded this dentophobe that behind the fancy charade there wasn't a torturous session just waiting to unfold. But believe it or not, a trip to the dentist can be fun, if you live in Dubai. Revitalising even. In Dubai, if you work for a health and beauty magazine and talk to the right people politely with a red-winestained smile, the dentist is your friend.

'Friends' is a bit of a buzzword here, actually. As I was lowered in an adjustable chair in my feng-shui-style room, my treatment specialist, Hilary, switched on the plasma TV screen attached to the ceiling and asked if I wanted to watch pretty fish swimming about in oceanic bliss, or ' ... the one where Rachel, Ross and Phoebe get set for a wedding'. Obviously I chose the latter — proving that this show gets through every crack in the system. As I opened wide and rivaled the canned laughter with the obligatory *aaah* sound, I was left wondering whether any human being on the entire planet will ever live a life free from this bloody American sitcom. I think I may have mentioned how it's blasted across the nail salon every time I get my acrylics done, too.

My treatment was the 'plasma power whitening treatment', available for anyone like me who feels a sudden urge to fool the world she hasn't spent the past ten years drinking cheap merlot and indulging in blue slush puppies at every cinema viewing. I didn't want to go too white, of course. No one wants a set like Simon Cowell's. You can almost spot the little tooth fairies hard at work, scrubbing them with magic paste during commercial breaks on *The X Factor*. I wanted something that wasn't blinding, but not the yellowy beige my destructive lifestyle had turned them into either.

The Dental Spa, like much of Dubai, tries to add a dose of glamour to everyday routine. And had Hilary known the hell I've just endured, what with the flat hunt, the job loss, the married-boyfriend bust-up and the departure of Stacey, she'd have no doubt been delighted with her newly appointed role as therapist and dentist all in one. Thankfully, my mouth was at her mercy so I couldn't fill her in.

As soothing music filled the air and the chair lovingly massaged my back, Hilary set to work on my teeth. Why don't all dentists' chairs do this? Of course, I won't lie. Dentistry is never going to be a truly spa-like procedure. There are lights, loud noises and machines that suck and buzz and hiss. There are pastes and funny tastes and that gentle trickle of drool that always escapes from the corner of your mouth onto the nurse's glove, making you feel like a helpless baby. *Friends* helps a bit. Fish take your mind off it all for a while and a chair massage is very nice, but it's still the dentist, after all, isn't it? Dubai never fails to confuse me. I don't know what's real and what's not anymore.

When all was said and done and I wiped my face in the mirror to reveal a smile that now lit up the room, I couldn't help but feel as though a little bit of Dubai magic had just taken place. I even got a kit to take home, so in three to six months I can refresh my pearly whites at no extra cost. How good is that? It doesn't mean I can go straight back to the colored goods, though — no red wine, cola or other teeth-staining concoctions are allowed for three days. Jesus, it's like the detox all over again.

But then, she didn't say anything about white wine.

01/04

Selfish help ...

Sean, Ewan's boyfriend, has offered to help us look for furniture to fill our new flat on the building site, which is a very nice gesture indeed. It's quite a big place actually, and we're expected to buy absolutely everything for it, except the kitchen appliances — unlike the Iransion and our last luxury abode, this one comes as empty as the expanse of desert that constitutes our new 'view'.

Our weekend journey took us back to the road where Stacey and I used to work for the publishing company all those months ago; a never-ending strip of furniture stores and car parks featuring tiny shops that don't sell tampons. As Ewan and I don't have cars and haven't driven for years, I thought Sean might have offered to hire a van so we could drive from store to store, collecting bedroom sets and sofas. Ewan predicted that he would almost certainly make this lovely offer, being the caring, considerate boyfriend that he is.

We would have offered to pay for the van, of course, but having Sean's help would have saved all manner of hassle, flagging cabs that never stop on a main road, juggling essentials like plasma TVs and organizing deliveries left, right and centre.

So imagine our surprise when Sean rocked up in his two-seater 'selfish car', boom box pumping where the back seats should have been, and offered to follow us wherever we might care to go in our cab. We looked at each other in disappointment as he waved cheerily from behind the wheel, fiddling lovingly with the knobs in his sparkling Honda S2000. He was clearly oblivious to the fact that his offer might possibly be seen as slightly pointless, not to mention annoying.

Obviously, Ewan can hardly blame Sean for wanting the sexy sports car with its high-performance, high-winding inline four-cylinder engine, superbly balanced chassis, minimalist cockpit comforts and racetrack-ready suspension ... but when it comes to 'helping' us move, an engine that loves to rev, an ideal 49/51 weight distribution and a super-slick six-speed gearbox isn't going to shift a three-piece suite from one end of Dubai to the other. Evidently, Sean was seeing not an opportunity to help his wonderful boyfriend and his flatmate, but the chance to parade his brand-new toy up and down a busy road in broad daylight.

'He's just *so* Dubai these days,' Ewan whispered in my ear as Sean zealously revved the engine, practically drowning out a nearby digger. I can see what he means.

Reluctantly, we rang for cab number one and spent the majority of the day jumping out of cars, traipsing round furniture stores and arranging various deliveries that might or might not be delivered, judging by previous customer-service experiences in this city. Fair enough, Sean was quite helpful whenever he managed to find a parking space and join us in our shopping ventures. But in between stores, Ewan and I stood wiping our sweaty foreheads in frustration by the roadside, trying to hail the next cab as Sean raced merrily round the block in his man-mobile, calling at sporadic intervals to see if we had caught a ride yet.

Later that night, as we sat on the floor in our dusty, empty flat, Sean leaned back against the wall where the sofa should have been and took a swig from his beer bottle. 'Maybe I can help you get your new kitten,' he offered, having heard about our grand new plan to become pet owners. Ewan scowled and I flashed my new, shiny white smile in Sean's direction. 'Let's see how it goes, shall we,' I told him, making a mental note to ask M&M instead. M&M might have a selfish car too, but at least he knows how to use it properly.

04/04

Return of the Iranian inventor ...

It seems like ages ago that Stacey and I moved into the Iransion. New to Dubai we really didn't have a clue how to handle the mad inventor with his weird horse-powered contraption on the driveway, or what to do when he tried to convince us to help him take his invention to America, where he'd become a megastar eco-warrior.

Of course, we just wanted to go out and get pissed. He was a freak — a man with a twisted vision; one who would probably spend all eternity in his villa in Jumeirah inventing things, making art and shagging the maid.

Well, who'd have thought it? The Iranian's gone and done it. He's now a frickin' media star! He called me up, wanting me to rewrite his website. Being the picky fellow he is, he published only elements of what I wrote, choosing to believe that his basic

English could fill in the gaps. The result is somewhat interesting. I'm not so sure we work together. We have different … styles. Still, the press caught on. The fleet-horse is everywhere. Everyone wants a slice of it … well, everyone in Dubai, at least.

I met him yesterday on the street outside the office. He pulled up in a flashy red car and crossed the road, grinning from behind mammoth designer shades with a smile almost as shiny as mine. He slipped me some cash for my help and told me I must have been regretting my decision not to join him in his venture all those months ago. He then told me, sorry, he had to run because he was late for another newspaper interview.

He's really changed.

Today the local rag *7Days* printed the interview, only quite unfortunately it doesn't really quote him at all. Instead, it recounts the opinion of a veterinarian, who pronounced his horse-powered contraption 'sick'. I just received a text from the inventor. He asked me:

Hi Backy (yes Backy, not Becky), *Pls read the page 2 of 7days and kindly do let me know the article is against me or not. Regards.*

I am now, apparently, his translator.

I didn't really know what to say. I kind of felt sorry for him. The dude has been asked to exhibit his invention in America, where they actually do think it's kind of cool — perhaps even useful. Maybe he wasn't so crazy after all. Maybe he was just in the wrong place. Maybe America, the land of opportunity, with all its wacky, freaky people clinging to their dreams, will welcome him with open arms. Maybe he can find some new, impressionable yet slightly less cynical ladies to live on his mansion landing. Maybe he and the maid will find success and happiness across the pond, inventing more … er … inventions and living happily ever after in a house filled with real Iranian children. And horses. Who am I to destroy his dream?

In the end I told him: 'I think you should call them.'

The paper can deal with him now. I had enough of it last year, and quite frankly, I'm scarred.

15/04

Going international …

To me, advertising always sounded like such a glamorous career. And I appear to have blindly walked into a time when there are jobs galore and a burning desire for English copywriters. It's my current understanding that if you're living in the Middle East and possess the ability to string a sentence together, you're more than welcome to apply.

Let's keep in mind that I knocked on their doors with no more of a portfolio than a few online articles about Britney from a trash magazine and website. I was incredulous to the point of rude with the girl from the job agency to start with: 'What? They want to see me?' But yes. Yes they did. Could I make it in half an hour?

Now, had I knocked on the door of this particular ad agency in London (or New York), flashing my new white smile, I know for a fact that some bespectacled man in a T-shirt with a crazy logo on it, and perhaps a hat and mismatching shoes, would have looked me up and down with contempt and slammed the door in my face. Even if I'd knocked again, adopting a pleading voice and wielding my stunning portfolio full to the brim with witty phrases, catchy punch lines, award-winning double-page ads and stripy-legged creatures of my own creation as huge and internationally worry-ing as Ronald McDonald, he still would have told me to email him and then never replied. He probably wouldn't have even opened it, forgetting my existence as soon as his boss's son (the lucky unpaid intern) wheeled in on a scooter with his Starbucks skinny latte.

I'm not selling myself short but neither am I bigging up my copywriting skills. As far as I'm concerned, the first person to walk in claiming knowledge of the alphabet would have qualified, and so it seems that I have quite unwittingly landed myself another full-time job.

As I may have mentioned before, the money for copywriting here (and probably everywhere else, for that matter) is better than magazines and to be honest I reckon I'm in for a lucky break. I mean, when I was working for Stanley, I was expected to write paragraphs, conduct research and speak to members of the public (during valuable Facebook admin time). On top of all that, I was often subjected to a senior's cruel slashing of 'things you just can't say about Dubai'. With advertising, at least, I'll be cutting it short. One-liners, maybe a thirty-second radio script here and there, but nothing too draining. No editors, no ridiculous publishing hierarchy or impromptu page cuts after spending hours slaving over, for example, how not to make it seem like Lindsay Lohan's relationship with a woman was … well … a relationship with a woman.

As we've established, working for a gossip source when you're not allowed to mention drink, drugs, sex or gay and lesbian ex-ploits is not the easiest of tasks. It takes a certain special creativity to write for a trash site that has no room for trash. It's a creativ-ity that goes completely unnoticed, because when people want the real story and the real degrading filth, they'll just go to Borders and buy one of the magazine imports that are still allowed in. Some might say this is quite ridiculous — I mean, why ban these things from your own media circuit if you're just going to sell them from elsewhere? Well, calm yourself down. Don't worry. There's no 'filth' slipping through the cracks at all. Not in Dubai.

Someone, somewhere, goes through every single page and crosses out the rude stuff with a black marker pen before it's allowed on the shelf. Exposed thighs, thrusting cleavages, naughty winking nipples — they're all zapped. Rumour has it they get the prisoners to do this, although it's never been confirmed. It wouldn't be surprising. It must be a good way to keep them quiet (coupled with a box of Kleenex).

Anyway, the articles I penned during my full-time publishing work were left somewhat lacking as a result of all these cuts. To mention that Emiratis throw alcohol-fuelled parties in the desert in houses adorned with stuffed giraffes and lions and pens of rhinos in the garden was a no-no, even as part of an informative, innocent local piece about the joy of pets in the household. Something like that might give Dubai a bad reputation.

After dealing with Stanley for so long, I'd learned not to argue the point that in no way could something so cool make Dubai look bad, let alone how amazing it would be for tourism. I mean, I for one would fly from afar just to see such things — Dubai's closer to the UK than Africa and way more interesting than a trip to Bedfordshire's Whipsnade Safari Park.

People are getting really strict about this lately, by the way. Not only can we not write about animals, sex, or the gay and lesbian affairs of Hollywood, we can't write anything about the issues Dubai is facing lately either. It's evident that something's afoot — including the introduction of sneaky taxes left, right and centre, like road tolls. We're now expected to pay a fare, or *salik*, when we cross certain bridges and drive certain routes that we never had to pay for previously. Some aren't even new — and that's saying something in these parts.

When I moaned about this particular issue to M&M, he told me that Abu Dhabi has a lot to do with it. Apparently they're lending quite a lot of money to Dubai at the moment, and if it wasn't for them, Dubai would be bust already. Shocking. It's all hushed up, of course. No one's supposed to know. But basically, because Abu Dhabi are even more conservative and restrictive, and because they're investing a lot in fixing up their silly little neighbour's mistakes, media laws have been introduced to save 'journos' like me damaging Dubai's reputation and economy. To the outside world, Dubai's a force to be reckoned with — a city of dreams that's growing stronger by the day. Yet mentioning that no normal citizen can afford to live anywhere other than on a building site, well, that would be in bad taste.

There comes a point where acceptance just makes for a more peaceful life and I'm thinking that if I can't write the paragraphs I really want for Dubai's biased magazine and website features, I'll write one-liners for its biased advertisements instead. Simple. Timesaving. And far less stressful.

The health and beauty magazine job has given me some great perks, but I'm really looking forward to getting out of the loud, crowded office and sitting quietly on a beanbag all day, twiddling my pencil (that's what they do, isn't it?). I'm also looking forward to racking up the freelance I'll now be able to do on the side without Stanley looking over my shoulder. The gift experiences and entertainments dot com I've been working for is still keeping me busy. Lifestyle magazine stuff should keep the perks rolling in and having more money means I might even be able to do some more travelling. I absolutely do think I may be on to a winner this time!

The pirated treasures of Dubai ...

It's late at night. Ewan and I are lounging on the sofa watching another episode of *Will & Grace* from the box set Sean kindly lent us. We haven't yet had our TV connected, having spent all our cash on a 42-inch screen, so since we've moved to the building site, our evenings consist mostly of a wholesome meal, courtesy of Wagamama's home delivery service (once they've managed to find us), and three episodes of a DVD series before bedtime.

Anyway, we're enjoying one of these luxurious evenings when the doorbell goes. Well, it's more like a knock on the door because we haven't had our doorbell fixed yet either. Nothing really works at the new place: the swimming pool is still empty and they've just started to expand the road in front of the building so now we can't even use the front entrance without falling down a hole or over a digger. I digress ... we look at each other in confusion, each willing the other to de-wedge from the sofa cushions and make the treacherous voyage over the pouffe, beyond the crumpled IKEA rug and across the pile of sandy shoes, to the door. One of us wins. The other opens the door, and the Dee-Wee-Dee Man steps inside.

'I have Dee-Wee-Dee moo-wees,' he says, thrusting forth his bag of goods like a proud school kid before his mother. He won't move beyond the crumpled rug, and heaven forbid he bless the pouffe with his pirated treasures. His eyes dart nervously around the room. He sniffs the air for what might linger beneath the scent of chicken udon. He knows he's doing something naughty, and he knows that we know he's doing something naughty, and he knows that we know that the authorities might know he's doing something naughty, but it doesn't stop him knocking. And it doesn't stop us looking either.

Well, we always want what we shouldn't really have, don't we? It's human nature. If someone says no you can't have something, a little voice screams, *Yes, yes, yes I can!* and that voice continues in my flat as the Dee-Wee-Dee Man unloads another pack of classics. And before we can say 'the new Indiana Jones in Russian', the entire crumpled rug is heaving with foreign-subtitled Chinese versions of Indian-Italian-Hollywood-Bollywood classics, all with indistinguishable celebrity photos grinning from behind cheap, vacuum-sealed polythene sleeves. It's just too much to resist.

The other day, Dee-Wee-Dee Man even asked Ewan if he wanted 'special moo-wee'. It didn't take a language barrier the size of the Burj Dubai to understand what that meant. I was actually quite impressed that he waited till I wasn't home, before hitting my flatmate with the offer. Perhaps he got a whiff of the fact that I wouldn't approve (along with the chicken udon). Perhaps he sensed in me a lady who would never permit a stranger to lay before her any filth, on a filthy rug, in her own home (*ahem*).

Gladly, Ewan refused and we wound up with a jumpy copy of *PoultryGeist* instead — a cheap student horror film about bloodthirsty chickens. I kid you not. I guess it beats a *Will & Grace* repeat, anyway. For a night, at least.

26/04

Cabs, cats and little gifts on mats ...

We were so looking forward to having a little friend in the house. The furniture's all here, we've managed to figure out how to get home each night among the ever-changing construction sites constituting our neighbourhood, so we thought it was the perfect time to become pet owners. Kitten people, if you will. Luckily, a mutual friend rescued a pregnant mother-cat after she'd been abandoned a few weeks ago. She took care of her, helped her after the birth and made sure all the kittens got their jabs. It was the perfect adoption scenario — from one loving home to another. We didn't even have to ask Sean or M&M to help us move her in — she was hand-delivered to our door. Yesterday was a bit of a nightmare, though. We went to Carrefour to get all the gear, but they were surprisingly low on kitten food. We cabbed it round the corner to the pet shop on the way home, but as we hopped out of the car, leaving all our shopping bags in the boot, the driver refused to wait five minutes while we went inside and proceeded to speed off in anger with all our shopping. After we'd made an automated service call to the police — yes, automated, as in 'Dial 1 if you're being raped' (shocking!) — he zoomed up with a furious screech, dumped our eight bulging carrier bags on the ground and sped off all over again, just for effect. Ewan suggested maybe we had made him miss a prayer. I think he was hungry.

Preparing for our feline friend's arrival was traumatic indeed, but never mind, we thought. We'll brush it off. It would all be worth it once we had our little baby in the nest, chasing cotton, purring lullabies and kissing us both with her tiny wet nose. Pets make everything better. We've called her Gizmo because of her large, Gremlin-like ears. Although, I've only seen her for a total of ten minutes because she's currently lost. Yup. On day two of living in our care, Gizmo's gone AWOL. Ewan just called me. He took the day off work to cat-sit (too early in the job for me to bunk off, too) and apparently, he can hear her, but can't see her. His last email implied she might have got stuck in a drain, which is slightly worrying.

I know she was around last night because she kept me awake. She's only twelve weeks old and yesterday her whole life changed. For the better, of course — she gets to live with two of the most fun, stylish and sassy people in Dubai; people who'll offer her endless kitty-cat snacks and soft-toy amusement. Ewan even donated his favourite grey cushion for her to use as a throne, and as we placed the carrier on the kitchen floor and peered inside at her tiny, tabby-coated frame, we promised to worship her in return for her total devotion … as long as she stayed cute and didn't fuck up the sofa.

But how did she reward us? Well, the ungrateful ball of fluff rewarded us with a strangled symphony of sorrow that lasted all night, as well as some door scratching thrown in for good measure. She also abandoned the litter tray and left a nice, moist shit

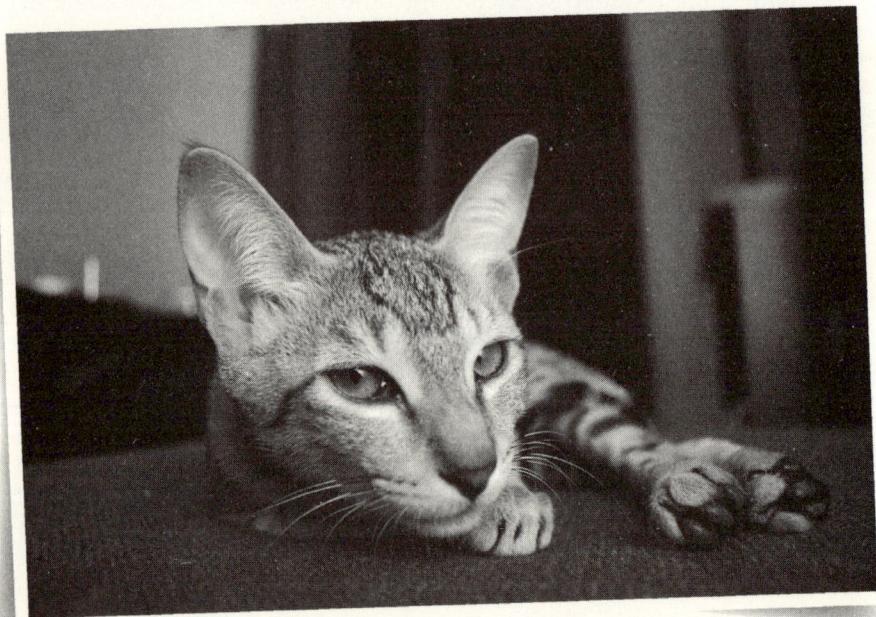

Gizmo: the beast from Satan's cattery. Can't you feel the evil seeping through this page? (shudder)

on my bathroom mat. It made me gag when my alarm went off this morning. And the feather in the cap is that she's turned into the invisible, shrieking monster.

I always thought that if I could be any animal on Earth, I'd be a cat. Graceful, proud, intelligent, clean, composed and elegant — just like me. They hold their heads high through every situation, like royalty in the animal kingdom, which is precisely why Ewan and I decided to adopt one. No whinging, sniffling, needy dogs for us, we thought. And besides, I think Arab women are afraid of dogs. I once saw a lady jump and literally run to hide behind a chair when she saw a little terrier walk past in Century Village. I think they're considered dirty, and anyway, there's nowhere for anyone to walk a dog in Dubai, really. There's hardly anywhere for people to walk.

It's just a shame that after all our effort, our very own, long-awaited kitty cat appears to be a bigger diva than Mariah Carey. Maybe that's just what Dubai cats are like, though. She's a breed called a Desert Mau, which is funny because the *mau* is exactly what's coming out of her mouth at impossible volume. I think she's a bit of a mongrel — large ears, long limbs, long tail. As I type, I've just had another email. Ewan has found her, shrunk into the back of the fridge. She hissed when he attempted to pick her up with an oven glove. Bitch.

04/05

THE EGO has landed ...

I've dealt with egos before. Magazines are full of them. Dubai is full of them; people who think they're better than they are. But every now and then you come across one that just blows everything else out the window; one major force that reigns supreme. Someone whose name you feel forced to place in capital letters, just to get the point across to those who may not quite understand the power you're dealing with.

Stanley wasn't so much an ego — more a lost soldier at war on a corporate battlefield. He struggled to do the right thing by everyone, even when he didn't really want to. People like Stanley are different, in that they spend their days fumbling around in the dark, afraid of losing the position they know they probably didn't really do much to earn in the first place. However, egos genuinely don't give a toss about doing the right thing by anyone. Their way is the only way and if someone doesn't agree, well, their own stupidity is bound to catch up with them sooner or later.

My new boss, EGO The Great, lives in the permanent guise of a 'creative'. 'Creatives' are fascinating people who demand more respect than any other set of employees in any other industry I've ever dabbled in. I've found others in the agency also calling me a 'creative'. It's a label I'm still struggling with, if I'm honest. I'm not entirely sure I like to be summed up in such a way. Seeing as I kind of fell into all this by accident, I'm now, I suppose, a little like Stanley, fumbling about in the dark.

I certainly didn't earn this, like many others who've knocked on similar doors clutching perfect portfolios and sporting very funky designer glasses. Something about it makes me feel quite uncomfortable, as though a certain brilliance is expected of me that I can't actually deliver.

Quite often I'll be sitting casually on a beanbag, chewing my fake nails while watching the desert try its best to reclaim Dubai outside the window, when all eyes will turn to me, eagerly anticipating a groundbreaking idea to fall out of my arse. They'll stare, wide-eyed, waiting for the next award-winning stroke of excellence that'll shoot us all collectively to Cannes, which appears to be the key to unlocking the ultimate door in the world of advertising in general — the meaning of everyone's existence.

They'll gaze at me until I'm forced to say the first thing that comes to my mind, just to make them happy, just to make them think I'm actually pondering the brief at hand, instead of what I'm going to order in for dinner. Nine times out of ten, of course, what comes out is utter shite. But because I'm a 'creative', they'll nod, write it down and look at each other like I might just be a genius. Because I'm a 'creative', my idea, however crap they secretly think it is, must be digested, discussed and analysed. It holds worth and merit, even though no one really understands why.

I'm living a lie, basically. And so is everyone else around me. I'm a hundred per cent sure that if my fellow 'creatives' really thought about it, really looked beyond my new title, they wouldn't see why I'm here any more than I do. EGO The Great sees through me, however. It's his job.

EGO The Great is a man who eats only apples, bananas and chocolate — in the workplace at least. And the girl who was here before me said that in all of her five years with the company, she'd never seen him eat anything else. He never leaves at lunchtime, never unwraps a sneaky sandwich, never goes down to the canteen for so much as a Diet Coke. That would be deemed as too 'normal', I assume. On his desk at all times is a bar of organic dark chocolate, the luxury kind from France. If we're summoned to his room for a discussion he will sit there breaking pieces off, sliding them into his mouth in front of us like a sexual tease from a candy commercial, but will rarely offer any.

He doesn't own a mobile phone — they're more a hindrance than a help. When we need him, we must simply wait for him to grace us with his presence. Yet we need him all the time, for it is his final word, his valued opinion on which we hang. We cannot do anything without him. Should we think of something good, he must first twist, alter, condescend and re-invent so that it becomes his own. And then we must set to work once more, towards gaining approval for hopefully, finally matching the inexplicable visions in his head, while he organises his music on iTunes.

He's worked very, very hard to get this far, so I'm told, to get to the point where he doesn't have to do anything at all for people to think they can't live without him. Occasionally, he will call me on my work phone (although he can clearly see me from his room, three metres away), and ask me how to spell a word in English. I feel very important when he asks this of me — such is his power. Knowing that someone like him needs someone like me makes me feel a sense of achievement I never found with Stanley. And, like everyone else here, I'm not even sure why.

Sometimes, I think he's a wizard, casting a magic spell over us all. A dark-chocolate-eating, Converse-wearing wizard. Whatever he is, this fascinating entity is certainly making life interesting as I scramble my way, Stanley-style, through this weird new world.

13/05

Risky business ...

M&M wants to take me to Yemen next month. Despite warnings from absolutely everyone I know about potential kidnappings and men who carry AK47s to breakfast, I'm intrigued. I quite like the thought of going somewhere considered so dodgy to the rest of the world, with my married Muslim boyfriend. Call me a drama queen, but it would be fantastic if we were kidnapped for a while.

I hear they only murder people sometimes, and the majority get to live quite comfortably in little houses made of stone, being fed cake and Arabic tea by bearded men and women, eager to know all about you — what you do for a living, where you go, what you carry in your bag.

I love telling people all about myself. And so does M&M. It would be awesome. I wouldn't have to lie awake at night listening to a wailing cat, or wake up early thanks to a rumbling digger. The mountainous regions in Yemen are very peaceful. And also, maybe if my face was in the papers I'd have a valid excuse for quitting the agency when I got back. I could throw one of EGO's chocolate bars back in his face when next he made a request: 'I'm a tortured kidnapee!' I could shout. 'I have issues, I almost died out there, and no, I cannot spell the word "antagonistic" for you today — I have to go to therapy!'

I'm starting to think I'll go anywhere to get away from Gizmo's screeching. Ewan and I cannot for the life of us think what her problem is. She's acting like a spoilt princess. She shredded an entire four-pack of loo roll the other day too; it was like a white Christmas had blessed the living room when I got home from work. She stared at me from the doorway as I went about the mess with a dustpan and brush. I'm sure I saw her smirking. Ewan has taken to calling her The Thing.

Ewan's been a little grouchy lately, to be fair. Since I left the media company, he says the office we were all rammed into has become even more crowded and disorganised, and his last pay cheque came in two weeks late. He's not a happy bunny at all, seeing as they promised him the world when he first started.

Not only this, but the editor-at-large is a guy who's quite well known for his womanising antics around Dubai and Ewan is finding himself the shoulder that many girls are coming to cry on.

Apparently, this guy — let's call him Heathcliff just for fun — is working his way around the sales and marketing team, and is halfway through conquering the girls in editorial. He swans around town as a VIP at every party, schmoozing, boozing and using as a result of his power in the glossy magazine world. I always thought he was gay when I was working there, but apparently not.

Anyway, word on Heathcliff's treatment of women in the company is spreading like wildfire, even among those who don't work there. I'm so glad I left when I did. There might not be an excess of juicy gossip in the advertising agency (they speak in Arabic most of the time anyway), but at least I'm not expected to run about for sleaze balls for no money. And I'm not so grouchy when I come home to a bog-roll blizzard in the living room.

Gizmo has started to creep into the living room when we're watching Dee-Wee-Dees now. She pokes her little nose round the corner to see what we're up to, then darts back behind the fridge to add her own lonesome soundtrack when she spots that we've seen her. We end up having to shut the door so we can't hear her, which is kind of sad. We imagined we'd be fighting over whose lap she'd sit on by now, who would get to stroke her lovely silky fur as we watched another episode of *Will & Grace* or *Poultry Geist 2*. Perhaps the dream was not to be. In light of everything, a risky trip to dangerous Yemen sounds heavenly right about now.

21/06

A truly shit time ...

A girl at the ad agency called Nina has been arriving at the office later and later every day lately. I asked her what was up this morning as she yanked her swivel chair out from under her desk with a vengeance and flung herself down in it hard, looking thoroughly pissed off.

'Fucking International Shitty!' was her reply.

Now, funnily enough, I know what she means. It's been in the news a lot lately. International City — now renamed by its residents — is in a lot of trouble. Nina didn't want to move out there in the first place, but like Ewan and me she was forced to move somewhere totally inconvenient owing to spiralling rental costs in the city. And now, after months of clamping both her nostrils and her windows shut against an offensive stench, Nina spends her mornings squelching her tyres through a marshland of shit, which is now spilling out from the nearby sewage plant.

International City is another resort-style residential area, miles away in the Al Warsan region of Dubai, along the road to Hatta. Along with a few businesses and soon-to-be tourist attractions, its colourful housing blocks are themed on architecture you'd usually find in Italy, Spain, Morocco, Persia, Greece, China, Indonesia, England, Russia, Thailand and France.

Nina lives in England. She hates it. It is quite literally, shit. A few months ago, the smell started drifting first through her bedroom window every morning and into her dreams, and then through the air vents in her car as she drove to work. But now, her entire block is flooded with raw sewage. She's having to watch families with kids try and dodge things like condoms and tampons drifting down the street. Last night, she says there was even more shit on the streets surrounding her building.

The air-con in her flat doesn't take the smell away. She can't open any windows because the stench is so bad that it makes her want to puke, and she's afraid that if she does open them the mosquitoes will get in. She has bites on her arms. 'Who knows what those fuckers are carrying?' she complained this morning, slapping her hand on her desk so hard it must have stung. 'I'm probably diseased!'

I'm keeping my distance, even though I feel sorry for her. Living on a construction site surrounded by diggers and dealing with a possessed kitten is bad enough, but I can't imagine what I'd do if my flat stank of a soiled toilet twenty-four hours a day and my street looked like a turd that wouldn't flush. Roads and pavements are completely submerged in her area and the shit is even bubbling up, swamp-style, from the drains. Blog sites are going crazy as people complain and plan letters to the authorities about their disgusting dilemma. But to be honest, it's looking largely like the authorities don't really give ... well, a shit.

All this actually makes me think about the state of the sea here at the moment. A couple of weeks ago, I saw a pile of dead fish washed up on the beach. I almost stood on one as I walked along the shore. Apparently, it's been happening quite a lot on all of Dubai's public beaches lately and the general consensus is that all this digging and dredging out at sea is killing the wildlife.

Also, because Dubai is growing so fast, the sewage facilities are working overtime and there are now so many disposal trucks waiting to dump their loads (*ahem*) that the drivers are having to queue in the blazing, stinking heat for up to sixteen hours at a time. Well, of course, they just can't be bothered, so in some cases these tired, bored, frustrated people, deluded by the monotonous stench of their day jobs, are drilling open manholes and dumping their untreated sewage straight into them, whereupon it then flows straight into the sea (and International Shitty, by the looks of it).

Nina's still looking mightily pissed off at her desk. I'm planning to avoid her for a while. She doesn't smell bad or anything — the stench has yet to pollute her actual person, but the people walking past her with their fingers clamped over their nostrils aren't doing much to help her crappy mood.

24/06

A fairytale called Yemen ...

Upon landing in Sana'a, it was obvious that we were somewhere, let's say ... special. Sweaty, organised chaos at the airport meant it took an hour for M&M and me to get our visas and to shuffle through immigration, but we were soon collected in a clapped-out taxi with mismatching doors and a hole in the floor behind the driver's seat. We were told that this was one of the city's most modern cars, supplied by the hotel we'd been booked into. M&M's face was a picture. I could tell he was dreaming of his Porsche.

Fearing for my life, I sat down, trying not to touch more than I was meant to. I clung to what was left of the doorframe as we were driven to our hotel. I know I've mentioned previously how terrified I am in cars at the best of times, but I've never exactly had to watch the road whiz past underneath my feet as I've been travelling along before. I tried to look out the window, so as not to puke.

Driving through the old city I felt my eyeballs bulging at the view. Fruit and veg stalls spilled from the sidewalks, floating balloons bounced on strings in the breeze, and hollering streetside shoemakers waved their arms animatedly in every direction as we whizzed past. It was a bit like Jaipur but cleaner, and I didn't feel as though there were any kidnappers out there at all, actually. Everyone was smiling.

I felt like our little car was a time machine, chugging along through the rainbow, although none of the colour came from the people. M&M warned me against wearing my latest flowing dress purchase — bright blue and covered in flowers. Most women and tourists in Yemen stay concealed beneath black scarves and abayas. It's advisable to go with it, out of respect. You'll stand out like a muppet if you don't. This is, after all, a strict Muslim country — even stricter than Dubai. While children ran free in a kaleidoscope of coloured clothing, we rarely saw a woman who wasn't covering everything but her eyeballs.

Our hotel was called the Sana'a Nights Tourist Hotel. Our driver pointed it out as we approached and I did my best to look impressed at the somewhat dilapidated, slightly lopsided construction ahead, which was made of gingerbread. Well, it wasn't actually made of gingerbread, clearly, but its sandy-brown colour and white-lined windows made it look positively edible, and definitely crumbly. Apparently, the people of Yemen like to confirm their hotels are for tourists by putting this status into the names. Tourists stand out, not only for their milky skin and protruding telephoto lenses (I'm guilty of that one) but also for their wide-eyed stares and flapping guppy mouths. This is probably because Sana'a is a pretty awesome scene to see. M&M was gripping my hand in the car. I wondered if he was allowed.

Sana'a, if you've never cared to google it (I definitely hadn't until it came to booking the ticket), sits within a mountain range and thus endures the temperamental forces of Mother Nature. One minute the sky is sapphire blue, the next it's showering hailstones the size of marbles on your head. It's a city forgotten by time, yet time has taken its toll. It dates back to the Kingdom of Saba which lasted from about the eighth century bce to the sixth century bce and its multi-storey buildings of tawny brown clay line cobbled streets that should by all rights be hosting Dickens' characters. I noticed after a while that every building looked like a gingerbread house, not just our hotel. Icing-sugar paint outlined every tiny window. I couldn't put my camera down. I think M&M was annoyed.

The city has been inhabited for more than 2,500 years and wandering its streets with M&M behind our guide, Ahmed, I whispered that I felt as though we were exploring a living fairytale. It took me right back to when I first sat on Dad's knee, behind a storybook. The characters are all here too. Hansel and Gretel wearing dungarees and smiles caked in grime run at you from doorways, scattering clucking chickens and scaring donkeys in their path. The creepy grandma sits huddled over piles of ripe tomatoes, her face, what can be seen of it, contorted with a cheek full of *khat* — a leaf that acts as a stimulant and is said to have an effect like caffeine. (I tried it. It tastes like ... well ... leaves.) But what's probably the most fascinating thing about the place is that when other ancient civilisations were battling it out with stones, these people here were building and living in these amazing, multi-storey houses.

M&M chatted in Arabic with Ahmed, who was actually the father of the guy who ran the hotel. He told us he often takes people out to the mountains. At first I wondered if he was going to kidnap us. Even though he seemed pretty friendly, you can never be too sure. But apparently Ahmed had no intention of locking us up in a little house, or feeding us chewy leaves. He just wanted to show us the amazing Yemen. And as we left bustling Sana'a in his rickety four-wheel drive, the pages of our fairytale kept turning. We wound our way along perilous mountain roads like a modern Jack climbing his beanstalk into the sky, and stopped to take pictures of entire villages cast into mountainsides.

The ancient walls out here look as though they might fall at any moment, yet children still race among ruins, squishing up against the bricks, chasing bedraggled goats, tugging the hands of weary mothers from shop front to food stall, never once fearing their world might suddenly crumble.

One of the most impressive sights was most definitely the Dar al-Hajar, or the Rock Palace. Perched on top of a humongous boulder, like a curious giant plucked it from the ground and put it there, this amazing building was once the summer haunt of the powerful Imam Yahya during the 1930s. It's a bit of a favourite destination for Yemeni families, as well as tourists, although the local kids followed us around up there like we were famous members of a pop group (Yemen's great for the ego). 'Surrah, surrah!' they shouted. 'Take a picture, take a photo!' So I took about 800 more.

At this point, I found myself thinking how The Irishman would have loved it in Yemen. We've become photography buddies, and he's almost as addicted to his camera as I am. Of course, I didn't tell this to M&M, who may or may not have traded me in for a milking cow in response.

It was the people who really made this weekend adventure for us. I've never encountered such amazing hospitality. I wish I could speak Arabic, then I could have learned more. I got the impression that M&M had a much more fulfilling experience, being able to converse with the locals.

At the hotel we were treated to a private dance performance featuring daggers and dishdasha swirling on a bright red carpet. At the end of the trip, Ahmed took us to his house to sample tea and his wife's homemade cake. I could tell M&M felt pretty humbled sitting in that house. So did I. It was so basic, but homely and filled with such impossible love. I felt guilty for imagining we might have been kidnapped.

Ahmed told us he wished more people would come to Yemen, to see how beautiful it is, and how safe it is, and how friendly and hospitable the people are. I felt like telling everyone that no matter what might happen in the future, or what's happened in the past, at that very moment in time, Yemen was the most incredible, warm and interesting place on earth.

Although … you can never be too careful. We definitely saw a few AK47s at breakfast.

27/06

Not pet people …

Ewan and I have reached the end of our tether with little Gizmo. It's just not working out. Since we got her, the screeching hasn't stopped and even though she now lets us pick her up with our hands rather than with an oven glove, we feel the time has come to go our separate ways. Ewan was fuming when I got back from Yemen. Not only did she keep him awake every night scratching at my door while I was away, he says her intolerable bawling all but destroyed his romantic movie marathon with Sean. Even the Dee-Wee-Dee Man is knocking less and less frequently these days. Apparently, not even Ewan's weekly promise that next time he'll buy from his 'special' collection makes up for the fact that we're murderers, secretly torturing hysterical toddlers behind closed doors.

I've placed an ad on the community message board with a collection of six adorable kitten photos, taken in our candlelit living room for extra cute and cuddly effect. It seems like the quickest way to get rid of her.

I was determined to mask her inner demons as best I could. Should any hint of evil shine through, we'd be screwed. Thus, my note says something along the lines of:

I'm devastated to have to find a new home for my darling kitty, but I'm leaving Dubai and can't take her with me. I really want my beautiful sweet baby to go to a good home, which is why she's free to the first person offering her the love she so deserves.

We'll see how it goes. I just hope it works. She's been so vile lately that I've actually resorted to cruelty. The other day she was shrieking so loudly on my bed as I was drying my hair that I pointed my hairdryer at her like a weapon, making her bolt for the door. She paid me back by shitting on the sofa. Fair's fair, I suppose.

01/07

Social networking ...

I appear to have fallen out with M&M again. He sounded rather upset when he called — someone sent him a photo I posted on Facebook of The Irishman holding a falafel. It's clear I took the photo, and only a few days ago too, which is why he's mad. He sounded positively distraught, actually. Of course, I'm aware of how stupid this sounds, but you have no idea how much he despises him, simply because we once shared that damn Spanish snog.

It was all quite innocent really. Honestly. Inspired by Yemen, The Irishman and I went down to Dubai Creek with our cameras to take some photos. In the late afternoon, the golden light on the dhows and around the dusty old souks is really pretty and The Irishman has recently bought himself a super-snazzy new Nikon camera, which is even better than mine.

We were experimenting with shutter speeds, ISO, all the camera settings that we thought would sound impressive as we walked along the creek, trying to outdo each other with our shots. It was an awesome afternoon. We stopped for a falafel and a drink from a coconut shell at a stall near the water, and took some silly photos of each other. I loaded them up on Facebook when I got back, secretly hoping I'd snapped some better shots than him. I didn't even think it might have been a bad idea. It didn't even cross my mind that M&M might care to look, let alone be affected. The call came shortly after. He ranted and he raved, he almost cried. What was I doing out with The Irishman?

I slammed the phone down on him, so repulsed by his actions and too angry at his insulting questions to even bother explaining. I'm starting to realise M&M never sees anything the way it really is when it comes to my male friends. With The Irishman, he seems to see what he thinks is happening, and then convinces himself I'm out to destroy him or something! You know, I think his separation has made him even more possessive than he was before. I'm actually getting sick of it. We just had a fabulous time in Yemen, too … I don't think I've ever found a trait so unattractive in a man.

Of course, it's embarrassing to have to tell The Irishman that I'm not supposed to see him. He thinks M&M's an idiot. He thinks I'm out of my depth and that things are just going to get messier. I feel he might be right, but every time I try to distance myself, it feels like M&M fights even harder for control. And if a creekside photography trip is enough to tip him over the edge, what would he think if he knew we had plans for Nepal? Ugh.

A beachfront balls-up ...

Last night, in order to escape Gizmo's wailing and Ewan's ensuing fury over his shitty job, I went out with M&M to 'talk'. We headed to JBR Walk — Jumeirah Beach Residence — a long stretch of dining establishments, mostly fast-food joints, along the beach near Dubai Marina. This strip of outdoor fun is fast becoming the place to be at the newer end of town and forms the base of a large row of ugly, beige-coloured residential towers that appear to have been built in a day.

Many apartments in these blocks have amazing ocean views. Back before they were built, residents were lured into buying off the plan, thanks to promises of luxury pads, a private, exclusive beach club and beach park, and free access to several gyms. More than a year down the line there are still no gyms, the beach club isn't open yet and the private beach park is a free-for-all, accessible to everyone (in spite of residents paying a service charge for the privilege). To top it off, the balconies protruding from most of these apartments have been constructed using so much concrete and cheap dark paint that they block all natural light from the rooms, making each one feel more like a jail cell than a luxury pad. I've been to several house parties in the towers. They're all the same. They all emit the same depressing vibe, no matter what colour the living room's been painted. And at every party you can guarantee that someone, somewhere, will accidentally pull a door handle off.

There are several swimming pools dotted about the complex, which has thirty-six buildings stretching over 1.7 kilometres. Unfortunately, the towers surrounding these pools loom so high into the sky that their shadows render sunbathing impossible, without picking up your towel every half an hour and relocating to the next patch of light. Sash is a resident and she calls this process the Pool Crawl. She's constantly moving from one illuminated strip to the next in search of a tan. She'd love to go to the beach of course, but the dead fish keep putting her off. Sash has also spoken of rats scurrying about in the suspended ceiling; no doubt a result of questionable sanitary conditions during the construction process.

Allegedly, a rich local bought a couple of these towers at the start and deliberately kept them vacant, so as to make the most of rising rental costs at the peak of the property boom. However, it's looking like the cunning plan backfired. More people are moving out than in to JBR as the word 'recession' lingers on everyone's lips. Those who can afford it are now moving into better quality properties, which are now going at a far cheaper rate. The case for living in JBR isn't much supported by the fact that everything inside it keeps breaking, either. You might be able to build a castle on sand in Dubai, but it doesn't mean it won't fall down.

Rather like skateboarders might congregate along London's South Bank (minus the plastic bottles of cider and homeless people), residents of the complex and Dubai's local youths gather to eat and puff shisha on the streets of JBR Walk. They stroll along the stretch in awe of imported palm trees, spouting fountains and a view of the manmade palm island in the distance, just a few hops and skips away from the crumbling wreck of an old hotel, currently being bulldozed to the ground in slow motion to make way for something more modern. The whole area, in true Dubai form, is up and coming — and coming down — all at the same time.

The restaurant M&M and I chose to 'talk' in last night had us witnessing some of the chaos JBR residents evidently endure on a daily basis — perhaps to a lesser extent and exaggerated by my spoilt Western opinions on how things should be, but infuriating nonetheless. To start with, they brought the wrong order. I know. Terrible. But not just the wrong order, mind — M&M's spaghetti turned up on the same plate as my grilled salmon! Now, in some places, like Italian restaurants frequented by dogs in Disney movies, diners may eat from the same plate, but one would hope not here, in the real world, if Dubai can be classed as such. And I was still mad at M&M. I didn't much fancy eating off the same plate. Realising their mistake, they shuffled it off to the kitchen and eventually reappeared with two plates, but my salmon was still missing an essential item.

'Where is my baked potato?'

'Sorry, ma'am, we changed menu. The salmon doesn't come with potato now, just vegetables.' [*Note: The salmon costs a whopping 68 dirhams, by the way.*]

'But your menu says "baked potato".'

'We changed it.'

'Then why isn't it crossed off? Why didn't someone tell me when I ordered?'

[*Blank stare.*] 'Sorry, ma'am.'

[*Look of expectation from me.*]

'We'll make you one.'

'But it's too lat — oh ... OK, fine!'

Fifteen minutes later, when I'd almost finished my salmon and M&M's spaghetti was all but a few cold strings coated in tomato sauce, a semi-cooked, sliced baked potato arrived at my side. Recognising that we were close to becoming unsatisfied customers, a member of staff kindly offered us complimentary coffee for the wait. Sighing and thinking what a decent gesture that was, I sucked it up, thanked him and ordered a latte. And then waited. For an hour.

'Excuse me, we're still waiting for a complimentary coffee.'

'Oh ... er ...'

'Your colleague offered it free [*because of the shit service*].'

'Oh ... right ... um ... I'll get it.'

Twenty minutes later, still no coffee. But magically, the bill arrived without us even having to ask for it — a hint, perhaps, that we'd outstayed our welcome?

Fuming and deliberating using my past status as restaurant reviewer/freeloading event-attendee as backup, we called the manager and explained our dilemma, dealing with what seemed like resentment until he was forced to acknowledge that yes, his staff were perhaps a little ... misinformed. As we were chatting, the waiter who had initially offered us the free coffee came over and flat-out denied to his manager that we had ordered anything at all. Lovely.

We were offered the coffee again, plus a complimentary dessert, but it was late, we were tired and quite clearly unwilling to sit there a second longer. After paying the full bill (yes, the whole lot — suckers!) we reached the end of our ordeal a little wiser and sloped off into the night, dejected and still angry at each other, thanks to everything else around us going tits-up.

I can't help but think the JBR complex, labelled as finished but clearly only halfway there in oh-so-many ways, is a disaster area in general. One that looks relatively decent, in a freshly painted, council-estate sort of way, but in actuality is a magnet for inefficiency and angry, whinging snobs, like me.

The sound of freedom ...

A spontaneous thunderstorm was brewing in the sky as the phone rang. A friendly sounding Emirati gentleman had seen my ad and was calling to see whether Gizmo was still searching for a new home.

'Oh, my baby ... er, yes of course,' I told him, shutting myself in the kitchen so he couldn't hear her screeching like the Exorcist in the bedroom. 'You can come and take her now, if you like. I'll get her things ready.'

Feeling only marginally guilty, I gathered her litter tray, toys and what was left of her food into a bag and went about shoving her wriggling body into the carry case. Of course, she screamed throughout the entire process and even tried to bite my fingers when I went to stroke her pointy ears through the bars. Bitch. I called Ewan, who was out with Sean. I told him our fluffy demon was about to be taken away forever into the unknown, just as she'd begun to trust us ... just as she'd begun to live a life in front of the fridge instead of behind it. 'Thank fuck,' he replied. 'Oh, don't forget we need tea bags if you're going out.'

Worrying that she'd yelp and cry and give the game away in front of her new owner, I shushed her with the most soothing voice I could muster as I closed the apartment door behind us and made my way downstairs in the lift. But as the 4 4 pulled up outside, the heavens opened. I looked up into the rain and whispered my heartfelt thanks to God, hardly believing my luck. It was as though the Almighty Himself was blessing this shameful handover, telling me it was OK to pass the baton of evil to this poor, unsuspecting gentleman, who probably hailed from a quiet home and thought his life was about to improve with the addition of a beautiful, loving pet of perfect temperament.

'She's a bit scared of the weather,' I told the man in dishdasha, as a lightning bolt flashed across the sky and a roar of thunder almost managed to mask Gizmo's antagonised screech from within the carry case. He took her from me quickly and looked through the bars as the rain hammered down.

'She does seem a bit upset,' he said, scratching his beard with his other hand.

I threw my best forlorn gaze in his direction. 'Yeah, um. We've grown so close … and she doesn't go outside much.' I pretended to wipe a little tear, which luckily looked real thanks to the downpour we were now standing in.

'Ah. Do not worry, I take very good care of her,' he assured me with a kindly smile. 'What is her name?'

I told him. He frowned. Something told me he'd never seen Gremlins.

Before she had a chance to scream above the storm in protest, Gizmo was bundled into the car along with her few belongings. I threw her an apologetic glance through the window and I swear I saw her mouthing vile insults in a language only Satan's creatures understand. With another flash of lightning she was gone, speeding down the road towards a brand-new life. As I write, she's probably out there somewhere, irritating even more innocent eardrums and ruining the nights of many more, unsuspecting souls.

Me? I'm just glad to watch my Dee-Wee-Dees in peace for once.

Sex on the beach ...

Michelle and Vince. Most of us in Dubai now equate these names to the likes of Romeo and Juliet, Tony and Maria ... Posh and Becks. These names are certain to go down in Middle Eastern history as the epitome of love doomed. Of course, there are no daggers, men in tights or musical numbers crooned from rooftops involved here, but this post-brunch tale of woe is one that every person in Dubai is watching unfold with bated breath as we go about our wholesome and restrained daily lives (*ahem*).

What happened was this ... Michelle met Vince. Vince met Michelle. Their eyes met across a crowded restaurant and once they'd managed to focus on each other through their individual booze clouds, they decided that a bit of after-dinner nookie might well be a nice dessert. This is fair enough, you might be thinking. This is how the game is played by many horny youngsters today. However, Vince and Michelle, their values a little fuzzy thanks to an all-you-can-eat-and-drink bender, chose to do it (so to speak) on a sun lounge. On a beach. In front of an embarrassed Muslim security guard. He warned them not once but twice that it might be a good idea to stop; at which point, allegedly, Michelle chucked her shoe in his face. Game over, sister. They're still behind bars.

It's been a few weeks now since the story first unfolded. And thanks to our couple's careless shenanigans, not a Brit in the city has been left unscathed by this brazen confirmation of a stereotype. The sordid affair began with an all-day champagne-fuelled blowout at the infamous Yalumba in Garhoud, so I'm told, and ended on a beach, very badly. But the pages are still turning, the tears are no doubt still falling, and Michelle's unfortunate sponsors are still reeling in shock and shame.

We're all sitting here wondering what the long-term effects of Michelle and Vince's actions will be. M&M reckons they'll be imprisoned for a very long time and thinks they deserve it. I do too, but then again, M&M and I have broken a few rules ourselves in a very strict country that has no tolerance whatsoever for misbehaviour. Ewan, while understanding what they did was wrong, feels sorry for them both being banged up in prison like shameful convicts. He, after all, is gay and worse would happen to him if he threw this fact in anyone's face, with or without his shoe.

While they await their fate, which could include up to six months in the slammer, deportation and an inevitable future filled with total humiliation, it's looking like the rest of us here have to suffer as a result of their behaviour. We're now being watched everywhere we go. There are police cars outside every bar! Not even Harry Ghatto's is safe and that's on the second floor of a hotel tower block. It's only a matter of time before one of us walks the wrong way out of a shopping mall, stinking of booze. They're probably ordering in the extra prison food as we speak.

15/07

Catamarans and kisses ...

I thought that spending the day on the catamaran would be an ideal location to set the plans for our trip to Nepal in motion. The Irishman and I have been talking about it for a while now. The flights are still cheap and we've got four other people interested in coming, only the guys involved are notoriously bad at allowing

A typical weekend in Dubai (spoilt, moi?)

us girls to pin them down for dates. There's nowhere to run when you're out at sea.

'Naaaat the frickin' catamaran agaaaain …' The Irishman moaned when I suggested it. 'I was only on it last week, I was!' I fear he may be starting to take his new lifestyle for granted. Once we were all on board, of course, we threw a couple of dates out there for Nepal and then got down to drinking. Watching him laugh and chat to randoms, and swig Corona after Corona, I was glad to see The Irishman didn't really seem to mind being back on the catamaran so soon after his last voyage.

The live and loud DJ and the open bar with drinks all included in the price of the ticket mean this five-hour party on the ocean is a pretty regular occurrence in Dubai. It leaves every weekend from its spot in the Marina, chock full of sun-kissed boys and bikini-clad girls and winds up some five or six hours later at Barasti, at which point everyone clambers from the decks, drunk, obliviously sunburnt and ready to carry on partying. It's the brunch equivalent for those who don't much care for the food part.

On this occasion, the sky was a clear blue instead of its usual dusty grey. It was one of those days you never want to end — good vibes, good people, the feeling that your life is absolutely perfect and you wouldn't change a thing.

Of course, it's moments like these when an overly analytical mind follows such thoughts with: *Well, maybe I would change a few things …* It made me think back to all the petty arguments I've been having with M&M lately, who unfortunately has been getting more and more possessive. Of course, he didn't know that at that moment I was out on a catamaran with The Irishman — his self-appointed arch-enemy.

I'm well aware that I'm kind of daft for getting myself into a position where I feel like I can't tell my married boyfriend where I'm going in case he gets angry. But the blow up after my photography outing was enough to silence me. In fact, there have been so many petty fights lately, I just don't like to rock the boat, so to speak. I'm asking myself on a daily basis whether we're still together or not. We seem to fall out so much that I wake up in the morning not entirely sure. It's a big pressure, feeling like I'm replacing his wife. I mean, a few months back I wasn't even allowed to call him for fear of someone finding out I existed. He seems so fragile, though. I don't even know how to bring this up without causing a serious problem.

After M&M pretty much forbade me to spend time with The Irishman on our Maldives trip, I have, of course, continued to see him without letting on. My consequential secrecy is probably contributing to his suspicion and jealousy. I've been weaving quite a tangled web, I suppose, but telling M&M I'm still seeing him would upset him, and not seeing The Irishman would upset me. And Stacey, who's seen it all unfold from the start, says I shouldn't let anyone order me around. She's bloody right, I reckon. Married or not, it's a pretty harsh sentence when your boyfriend tells you not to do something you really enjoy doing. Unfortunately, a character flaw of my own is that when I'm told not to do something, I do it anyway, on purpose, a lot. It's a Scorpio trait. An astrological prerequisite. Not my fault at all (*ahem*).

I let the ocean carry my thoughts away as I watched the surf slap the sides of the boat. As we sailed around the Palm, a man in the know, who sounded like he worked in property development, pointed at one of the branches dotted with beige-coloured villas. He told us that although they've been designed for families wanting private beach space for playing and paddling, people have been warned not to swim. I've never thought about it before, but apparently there's no natural gradient from the beach out into the water. This could take a while to develop. A mother and her nervous child can walk a certain distance from the shoreline at a pleasant slope, before dropping off completely into the middle of the sea!

The muggy afternoon crept into evening. We were all deposited at Barasti on the wrong side of sober and before I knew it, Heidi, The Irishman and I were at the property developer's house in Barsha, which was buzzing in the midst of a sweaty party. It was so hot and there were so many people crammed into the villa that the air-con had long since given up. People were perspiring so profusely, it looked as though they'd all been swimming in their clothes, and that's just what happened next. One by one, they all started jumping into the pool, whether they had swimwear on or not, creating a sexy, sweaty soup of sunburnt limbs and Li-Los.

The Irishman and I watched all this unfold in amusement from our spot on the lawn. We'd been chatting all day and most of the night, and by this point we were pretty hammered and more than halfway through a bottle of vodka. Looking at the girls in the pool, he laughed, flashed his impish grin and told me how fun it is getting naughty in the water. Staring at his profile under the stars, something inside me felt suddenly sick ... you know when a giant wave of icky-ness just washes over you and you can't speak? He implied he'd had a recent experience with a girl ... one I didn't know about, and once the wave had passed and I could breathe, I exploded into tears, right there on the lawn, at someone else's house.

Everything came pouring out (apart from sick, thank God), about how M&M was being so controlling, and how I didn't really know how to stop what I had started ... and how The Irishman telling me about this other girl set the Rage inside me, at him, at myself for getting so lost somehow. Looking back, it must have appeared a little bit like one of those scenes from a Californian teen drama — one that has a melancholy tune playing in the background, as the semi-naked partygoers rock out in slow motion, oblivious to the world crashing down around a broken delinquent; a poor little rich kid who's just lost everything, everyone, and her pride. I expected him to laugh like he usually does when I act like an idiot and slur a drunken rant in his direction. I thought he'd call me an emotional moron and tell me I should just dump M&M, as he has done many times, along with most of my friends. But before I could gather my emotions back together and prepare for his tactless Irish attack, he kissed me, right there on the lawn, at someone else's house.

Something started back in Spain, back at that conference, back when we first sat on the grass in the starlight and spilled our souls to each other along with a different bottle of vodka — something that was never finished. I've pushed it out of my head. I've been telling M&M his suspicions are stupid, just so I can remain the girl he wants me to be. In order to please this powerful, generous man, I've been acting the part of the adoring girl who can't wait to spend forever trying to replace the wife she's just helped to boot out of the picture. What an idiot! I really don't know what to do.

I've never been one to ignore destiny when it knocks on the door, even though this time, I probably should, right? The thing is, I really don't think it's ever knocked so hard and so persistently as it's knocking right now.

20/07

To be or not to be in a relationship ...

I have an inkling that a suspicious M&M read a few text messages between The Irishman and me the other night, when my back was turned. It was nothing too revealing, thank God. I can't prove it, of course, but on 'hearing' proof from 'someone he knows' that we'd been at the same party, he flew into a tearful rage and acted like the world had ended. It scared me, to be honest. I had a feeling he'd react in an extremely emotional way and I really didn't want to deal with it. His tirade, right there in his Porsche as he screeched to a halt outside my house, was riddled with sentences like 'I gave up everything for you', which he didn't, because he was busted, and 'You've broken me this time', which I probably hadn't, because I'm pretty sure he'd taken it upon himself to invade my privacy when he'd seen my phone lying around on his sofa. So I finished things.

Having seen us locking lips at the party, Heidi pulled me aside and told me I should end it with M&M and hook up with The Irishman once and for all. She reckons we belong together. But although I felt a flight of long-pent-up butterflies as we shared our drunken kiss, the thought of losing The Irishman as a friend actually worries me.

In a crisis Skype conversation, Stacey asked whether I feel the need to be with The Irishman because I'm secretly in love with him, or because I feel the overwhelming and childish need to disobey a powerful, married man who keeps telling me not to see him? I'm still not really sure how to answer. I just feel like utter shite.

Even though things have been rocky since I felt the need to start keeping my friendship with The Irishman a secret, I'm now plagued with this terrible, all-consuming guilt for cheating on the man who first cheated on his wife to be with me … even though I'm not entirely sure I cheated, as I never really know if we're an item or not. What a mess. How does a mistress begin to cheat on her man anyway, when he's cheating on someone else to be with her? What strange force comes into play, when the cheater turns into the cheated, and the new cheater doesn't have the guts to admit it? Christ! Where's Jerry Springer when you need him?

I can't imagine what M&M would do if he found out about my kiss with The Irishman. I finished things with M&M without telling him what had happened, which is something I'm not particularly proud of, but I'd really rather he didn't know the details. He'd torment himself over it, and me, if he knew.

I know it's more difficult for Muslims when it comes to the issue of infidelity. They can't just take the stage on a daytime TV show and battle it out in front of a live audience. There are rules and obligations to uphold, a different set of laws to abide by, involving all sorts of stuff I've personally never really been involved in. M&M's always kept that side of things to himself, probably so as not to freak me out, and I never did find out what really went on while he was AWOL with his wife. I never asked.

I've booked my place on the Nepal trip — a fact I did admit to M&M. As predicted, he doesn't like it one little bit that I'll be heading to a forest with his arch-enemy in just a few months, riding elephants and chasing the tiger trail. But I'm single now, so I suppose it shouldn't matter, right?

05/08

Paving the way to Pammy Land ...

As we know, both Justin Timberlake and Brad Pitt have already announced their architectural plans for improvement on our shores, but no one really anticipated the flock of Hollywood A-listers would ever include a bleach-blonde ex-Baywatch star, who's previously awarded her major assets only to the likes of quadruple-page spreads in *Playboy*. The world is most definitely a-changing. News came in via The Irishman today, who really has his finger on the pulse, and later, a forwarded press release, that Pamela Anderson is currently designing an eco-friendly hotel in Abu Dhabi.

With this in mind, I have to wonder who else will be banging on our doors, begging for a piece of the action. OK, so she's doing a bit of good with her hotel — it's set to be built using minimum fossil fuel emissions and will be run (probably not by her at all) in an environmentally friendly way ... yada yada yada ... but if we're letting any old American model/actress/author/daughter of a furnace repairman in with a blueprint and bikini, what's next?

Who is the UAE catering for now anyway? We're told it's tourists, but few people I know can afford the hotel rates, and the new hotels are being built with millionaire visitors in mind. It's not as if your average Joe from Scunthorpe is going to ditch the holiday caravan park for a trip with Shaz and the kids to the Playboy Mansion, no matter how 'green' it claims to be.

We're all wondering exactly what Pam laid on the table for the chance to get involved (oh, stop it), but apparently it was actually Abu Dhabi royalty who asked her to become a hotelier. Obviously, her potential has been recognised from afar.

She told the press: 'I'm building a hotel there. It is environmentally friendly. I went there with the Make a Wish Foundation and met some great people. The royal family was really friendly … It's built with no fossil fuels at all in Abu Dhabi, where they have all that oil,' she tells us. At least she's done her research.

With this influx of celebrity investors, it looks as though the UAE is well on the way to becoming the glamorous destination it wants the world to perceive it as. The thing is, celebrities have invested in a lot of other places over the years, and it hasn't changed the fortune of any one city yet. Mind you … stick up a building in the shape of Pamela herself and I'm sure the punters would be flocking.

10/08

The Lebanese mafia …

Now that I'm at the agency, I feel I need to devote some space to the people who form the basis of my working week. And as

I may have mentioned, the ad industry in Dubai is powered by the Lebanese — a group of people I had absolutely nothing to do with before stumbling into this position.

They pretty much rule the roost these days, thanks to the civil war forcing them all to flee to new territory. As much as 70 per cent of Dubai's management in top advertising and media companies hails from Lebanon and (don't tell them) some people refer to this takeover as the city being hit by the 'Lebanese mafia'.

Beirut's loss was Dubai's gain. They're an interesting breed and I'd be lying if I said they haven't taught me a lot. I observe them in action with the same sense of awe as I would a group of preening monkeys in a zoo.

The Lebanese are all very beautiful. This goes for men and women alike. The men are mostly tall, well groomed and shiny of shoe. Out of the office they're big fans of shirts — designer ones mostly. They also like blazers a lot. Looking at them out on the scene, they group together like herds of schoolboys, visible in darkened corners only by the shimmer of their hair gel. They usually order liquor by the bottle and being a friendly bunch, will happily offer anyone a glass, providing they're female.

The women have long and unimaginably thick hair. It's their pride and joy. When walking anywhere, they swish and swirl their locks about like models in a permanent shampoo commercial. Even when nobody else is around, they will twirl and flick like mermaids flirting with an invisible sailor. They also wear make-up all the time, to the point where you can just imagine them setting a 3 am alarm for a re-touch, just so they wake up fresh. They're glossy, tanned and pearly of tooth. I'm not making any accusations here, but allegedly you can get a no-questions-asked plastic-surgery loan in Lebanon.

There's a campaign I'd love to work on. 'Lips, tits and she-dicks from $19.99 a month' is way more catchy than 'Get the car you've been wanting with no interest rate', but sadly, as yet I've not had the chance to show how I can help with such things.

The Lebanese are very proud people. My colleagues send emails constantly with stories from their country and not a day goes by when someone isn't jetting off 'back to Beirut to see the family'. Consequently, I don't think I've ever met anyone who isn't from Beirut, so either Beirut is a city designated especially to my colleagues and their families, or this is a huge, all encompassing statement meaning: 'I'm from somewhere in Lebanon you won't have heard of, and I can't be arsed to explain.'

I don't blame them, if this is the case. Mentioning I grew up in a humble hamlet called Pode Hole surrounded by combine harvesters isn't half as exciting as claiming England's capital as my birthplace. London is close enough and I don't have to explain about inbreeds, marshland or the real meaning of the word dyke (which is actually a river or stream, contrary to popular belief). To the Lebanese, the words 'I have family in Beirut' encourage gasps from people like me and let's face it, everyone loves a bit of drama.

Sometimes I think the Lebanese almost bask in the absolute torture they have each 'personally endured', which is why it's a little confusing how most Lebanese patriotism swings from support of Lebanon to France, where they all seem to wish they were from.

At lunchtime, our work canteen is stocked with Lebanese food, which is pretty much the same every day and costs 25 dirhams a plate (about four quid). There's usually a green salad, a plate of hummus, dry bread and a few hot trays containing chicken or lamb with rice and copious amounts of garlic and lemon juice.

A Lebanese foodie fave of mine is cheese manakich. I usually like to eat this in the early hours, fresh from the bakery on the way home from a night spent boozing. It's the equivalent of stopping for a kebab. You still wake up swimming in oil with bits of indistinguishable meat (which could also be floor sweepings) on your T-shirt, but unlike a kebab, you would also order it in the middle of the day, perhaps as an accompaniment to some healthy grilled fish or chicken. Never one to turn down a free meal, I now take it for breakfast and eat it in its cold, sodden format every Thursday, when it's cycled in free for employees.

I mostly take my food and dine *al desko*. I never eat in the work canteen, in the same way as I never really socialise with my Lebanese co-workers outside of the building. It's not that we don't get along, or that they're not lovely people, which they are, it's just that the Lebanese in Dubai speak their own special language, comprising Arabic, English and French. At liberty they switch between the three mid-sentence, leaving you wondering whether you've misheard the start of a conversation, or whether something went wrong in your eardrum.

Sitting round a dining table, trying to engage in lunchtime conversation can be a bit like listening to Shakespeare for the first time — you know it makes sense, but you just don't understand it. You think about it for a bit, translate it, process the meaning, only to discover the next part is even more confusing than the last. And to top it all off, the man you're listening to is only talking about the possibility of singing a ditty later, or in the case of the Lebanese, flying home to nurse his mother after her boob job.

Pour a few drinks into the mix and the situation is heightened. In an effort to make sense in your company, the Lebanese slur between languages as you stare at them blankly, wondering when it's appropriate to go home and watch people you understand on BBC Lifestyle. Not to be rude, but it can get tiring after a very short amount of time. It makes you miss the good old days, when you could cartwheel round the conference room, so confident

216

were you in a place where everybody knew you. (Fact: I have cart-wheeled around a conference room.)

So far, thanks to this new cultural integration, I've managed to pick up the fabulous word *khallas*! The first syllable is pronounced a little like a phlegmy cough. This word is fired around every room in the agency like a BB gun, loaded with passion. It means 'I've finished', 'I'm done', 'that's that', or words to that effect.

As you can probably imagine, I use this one a lot in Dubai.

17/08

One man and his empire …

The Irishman has moved to a villa on the Palm. You should see it. It's bloody awesome. It's the kind of place you might visit in your dreams occasionally, but as with the luck of dreams, you'd probably wake up as soon as you dipped your big toe into the infinity pool.

The Irishman is actually living in the maid's room, which is small but still a decent size for one man. He might sleep with the washing machine outside his door but at least he gets an en-suite bathroom. And when he wakes up in the morning, he can see the sea. The ocean view was the main pull for moving out of the amazing villa compound in Satwa. His reasoning was, 'If oi'm only garna live in Dubai once, oi may as well live somewhere amazing, to be sure.'

I'm so jealous. He's like a modern-day Gilligan. He says he's taken to jogging along his 'private beach' in the mornings and his flatmate has a kayak, which he sometimes uses as a fishing boat. He's got one of the fish he caught in the freezer, which he's saving for a barbecue. He's really proud of it. I'm not even sure what kind of fish it is, but it's huge and nothing like the little ones that have been washing up on the beaches lately. I guess there is still some life out there, somewhere. When he took me out in the kayak, a man with a megaphone told us off. They're dredging up land for The World and The Universe and Fashion Island, and whatever else they're constructing from nothingness in the vicinity and the security guards don't want anyone to die — this would look bad for Dubai. When you ignore the fact that you're paddling round a manmade island in the middle of the Gulf, in the middle of some of the planet's most ridiculously ambitious construction projects, it's really quite cool.

Since our kiss, things haven't exactly been weird between The Irishman and me, but I think we're both aware that a line's been crossed. Like I said, I really don't want to lose him as a friend, so I've been making a conscious effort to remain just that … a friend. To be honest, I think we've both brushed it under the carpet. I reckon The Irishman views my association with M&M as a bit of a mess, and something he can't be arsed to get involved with at all. He probably doesn't want to get beaten up by a jealous Arab for a start, but when I think about it, the fact that he's had to listen to me talk about things going absolutely tits-up with a married man ever since he got here, has probably killed any romantic thoughts he ever had for me while sober. No one likes a home-wrecking whinger, after all.

I went to visit him on the Palm the other day with my new friend, Svana. She's a lovely girl who works in PR and has lived in Dubai her whole life. I met her at an event I was covering in a hotel and while our emails started out as one might email a work colleague, we seem to have developed a proper friendship and I've been integrating her into my circle. It's really nice having another

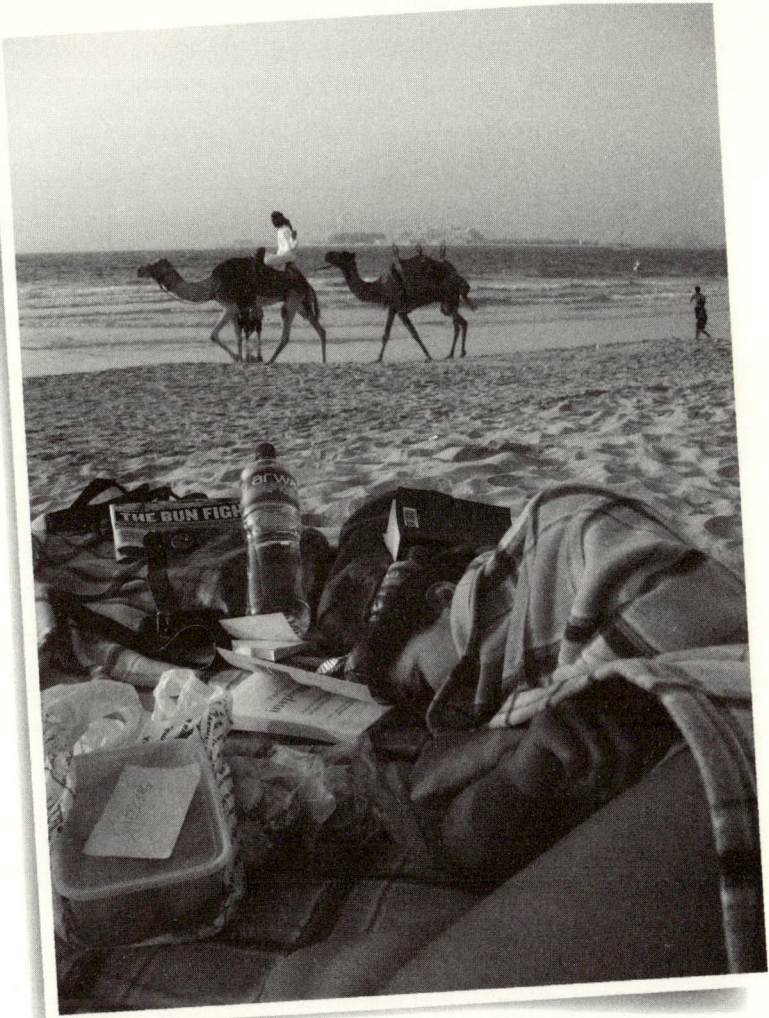

*You never know what you might miss if
you fall asleep in the wrong place.*

close girlfriend after Stacey, and she's even planning to come to Nepal with us, which is cool.

Anyway, we rocked up at The Irishman's with some wine and an impromptu mini beach party ensued. His new flatmate — the British guy with the lease for the villa — proceeded to regale us with tales of his entrepreneurial success while lounging on a beach towel and sipping a beer. Interestingly, he has a variety of get-rich-quick schemes on the go.

We were particularly intrigued to hear about the painting in the garage. Apparently, he keeps it there on an easel to show people at random on the off-chance that they might want to buy it, even though it's shit. He reckons there are so many stupid people with money and no sense in Dubai, that it's only a matter of time before he sweet-talks someone into buying what's essentially a worthless canvas splattered in paint. The guy might well be a genius.

It sort of reminds me of a friend of a friend here, a sweet young Australian girl called Rochelle, who's just twenty-one and models to make a bit of money while she's living with her boyfriend. About a year ago, the pretty Rochelle took on what she thought was a more permanent role as personal assistant to a rich business-man, the CEO of a national bank. She basically met him in a bar and he offered her a job. This guy was paying her 10,000 dirhams a month to be at his beck and call, only ... he never called. On about three occasions, Rochelle was asked to deliver envelopes for him to various points around the city and once she had to collect his dry cleaning, but she never went to his office, never saw him face to face, and never really did anything in the way of work.

The money kept hitting her account every month, though. She lounged about on Jumeirah beach, dined in fancy restaurants and hit the spa for hours on end during the day, waiting for an assign-ment that never came. She even bought a chihuahua. Eventually, after about three months, she started to feel bad. When she called him up at work to ask what was going on, a lady answered the phone. Rochelle asked for the man who'd 'hired' her, the CEO. But it emerged that the man behind the name wasn't the CEO at all. He was actually — according to the shell-shocked receptionist — just a random employee at the bank. Granted, he was on an exceptional salary, but he had no need for a PA whatsoever. No one else had one.

This arrogant man, who'd spied the gorgeous part-time model in a bar, had basically offered Rochelle 10,000 dirhams of his own salary every month to have her run around after him, whenever he might need a little boost.

There are some amazing characters in Dubai, as we know. But The Irishman's new flatmate hits the top on the scale of eccentric, now that the Iranian's out of the picture. The new island-dwelling, kind-of-confusing Irishman with his vast, expansive, expensive villa, infinity pool and private beach is most definitely another.

27/08

The imaginary ability ...

The other day, EGO The Great asked me to write a musical. I was just swivelling away in my chair, repeatedly pressing the inbox button on Facebook, when up he swaggered and stood behind me as I frantically minimised my sins.

I hesitated for a second, without turning around. What an amazing request. As he perched his little bum in non-committal fashion on the very corner of my desk, he explained he wanted a little score, or song, to place over a car commercial. Well, of course, I imagined Elton John's first thoughts when approached to compose *The Lion King* — 'This is my chance!'

Just as my imagination was saying 'OK, that sounds great, let me get right on it', what actually came out was a spluttering induced by a sudden reality check: 'A musical? I ... I ... I'm not Andrew Lloyd Webber!'

'Pretend you are,' he said.

If only to please and impress my wizardly mentor, I would have loved nothing more than to have stood up, skipped with gracious joy to the nearest grand piano and spontaneously produced not only a sudden ability to play, but a musical score of such significance and beauty that no car commercial would be deemed worthy of my talents. The truth is, however, I am not Andrew Lloyd Webber and no amount of pretending will ever bring me close to being the same flamboyant baldy who's changed the face of Broadway — even though I love and respect his work (clearly). So I said: 'How can I pretend to be Andrew?'

He frowned at me. 'Use your imagination.'

I nodded and smiled weakly. I've learned not to continue these futile conversations with 'creatives'. I told him yes, of course I would use my imagination and yes, yes of course I would pull a musical score out of my arsehole (I didn't say that bit) as soon as I'd finished with Facebook (I didn't say that bit either).

A few hours later, I still couldn't imagine being a composer. I mean, don't get me wrong, I did have the opportunity to become one, once. Having dismissed my instructor when I was fifteen on the premise of him obstructing my creativity, after about four lessons I composed a few absolute gems of originality; pure lyrical genius they were. To give you an example of how I stretched and challenged my teenage mind, one line went: *You gave me a broken heart and you're tearing me apart.* I know. Amazing.

When I was sixteen, however, I gave it all up after learning 'Wonderwall'. It was all I ever needed to impress the boys. I wouldn't even have to get to the chorus before my miniscule cleavage and caterpillar eyebrows were forgotten, so wrapped up were they all in a cloud of awe. A chick who plays guitar is always hot — something that has been confirmed by several people as

I've grown up — although admittedly, it's hotter if you're younger. As it turns out, there's only so far you can go with lyrics like *You gave me a broken heart and you're tearing me apart* before it stops being an amazing talent from someone so young, and turns into a pathetic, attention-seeking attempt from someone who, quite frankly, needs to get a life.

Understandably, I may have denied the world some sort of rights as far as halting the evolution of my talents is concerned, but getting back to the present, I doubt very much that this 100-year-old business with a global reputation at stake would lay it all down for a song called 'The Nice Car' in the key of G Major. I doubt they would do this, even if EGO The Great told them it was indeed composed by an emerging yet wasted talent who made it up while pretending to be Andrew Lloyd Webber.

In the end, I produced some sentences that rhymed and hoped it would be enough.

06/09

England, Dubai and the theory of pie ...

Even though Ewan and I have been promised a shop in our building site of a neighbourhood ever since we moved in, there still isn't anything for the residents in the vicinity except even more half-built apartment blocks and towers of unoccupied units. Surprisingly it seems rent is actually going down in Dubai now. People are moving into nicer areas for less money as the 'recession' takes hold.

Obviously, no one wants to admit we're in a recession. Dubai is flat-out denying it, even though some of its projects are being

223

halted and rumours of employee culls are rife, especially in project development and real estate. There have been a few whispers around the agency, although I'm not too worried (probably because I don't care enough), but judging by the way things are going at his work, poor Ewan's right to be getting more and more freaked out. The media company sounds to me like it's falling apart at the seams!

The roving, randy Heathcliff is still choosing to ignore his emails about overdue pay cheques, and in person, when he's cornered, he insists he's sorting it all out. Then inevitably he swans off to another glitzy event, leaving everyone else, including Ewan, in chaos. The other week, Heathcliff decided it might be a good idea to get an attractive member of his staff, who fancies herself as a singer, to record a CD to give away with the magazine. As disaster unfolded in the office, he and the warbling object of his affection spent hours in a studio somewhere, having fun, making music that never actually saw the light of day.

Also, after promising Ewan he could hire his own assistants (something Ewan was looking forward to doing immensely), Heathcliff has taken the liberty of doing it for him. Ewan's new fashion assistant has no skills whatsoever in writing or styling and is seriously making life difficult. She does have killer tits, though, which probably explains Heathcliff's decision. The whole office is pissed off now, quite rightly.

In an attempt to chill him out, I suggested we head to a new pub called Nelson's in the Media Rotana across the road. We've been watching them build this new hotel for months. It stands in a rather out-of-the-way location near the camel racetrack, which we can see from our living room window. This suggestion cheered Ewan up immensely — he'd heard rumours that the pies at Nelson's were spectacular. I was also excited, because the idea of walking to the pub was one I thought I'd left at home in the UK. As we know, there aren't many pavements near our building.

Now, I don't mean to whinge. It's very nice that we have a pub at all here in Dubai, let alone one in walking distance from our flat. But I'll tell you now, Nelson's is a very confusing place, housing some very confused people. Let me set the scene. When Ewan and I arrived, it was slap bang in the middle of happy hour and every male English expat over the age of thirty seemed to have taken on the obligatory propping up of the bar. The place was loud. The smoke was so thick you could barely smell the fresh paint and cheap perfume. The DJ was spinning 'everything that us crazy Brits just love', which of course includes Westlife, Phil Collins and the Bee Gees. Grateful wives who hadn't been for a bevvy in months gyrated in the corner as the DJ beamed in delight. Bemused hotel guests watched from the sidelines, wondering when Dubai started building places that should, by all rights, be sitting on wind-savaged streets next to train stations, littered with homeless people.

The dark mahogany-panelled booths, reminiscent of train carriages from the forties, were simply calling out for a pub quiz huddle. A girl in a hat read a romance novel and sipped a Guinness between the gaps in her teeth. A frazzled waiter knocked my chair in his hurry to deliver what was probably a plate of very late, lukewarm food.

When it came to service, I was ignored for about ten minutes at the bar. Finally, after questioning several other members of staff on my behalf, the barman still had no idea if they served white beer or not (FYI: they don't). Ewan and I sat in a booth with a table for eating our food, although no one cared to offer us a drink, menus or cutlery until we asked. After ordering, our waiter forgot us. We asked again. Our drinks never appeared. A waitress approached. We ordered again. No drinks arrived. We ordered again. She brought my wine and asked, for the fourth time, what Ewan had ordered as ... oh ferfuckssake, she'd forgotten. I thought he was going to explode.

Thankfully, you'll be pleased to hear the food is excellent. Being nestled at the bottom of a world-class five-star hotel, it bloody well should be. Shame that the concept of a pie has been so tragically misunderstood, though. When it finally arrived, I was presented with a mini casserole dish full of pie filling. Not a pastry flake in sight. No sides, no top, no nothing. It tasted good. Absolutely awesome, in fact, but still, that is not a frickin' pie, is it? Calling it a pie is dangerous. There are people who would travel further for such a promise. People with issues.

The funny thing is, I'm not entirely sure whether this strange new world of incompetence, ignorance and mayhem is offensive beyond all comprehension, or thrilling in its English authenticity. The service in English pubs is supposed to be terrible, isn't it? The entertainment is supposed to make you cringe and the crowd are expected to kill all serenity usually associated with having a quiet drink away from home. When you're not being ignored by a skinhead called Clive with a tattoo the size of Putney on his forearm, you're getting your bum pinched by an eighteen-year old wobbling about with a jelly-shot, or serenaded by an eager karaoke DJ, who's set up the popular weekly 'Songs with John' because no reality TV talent show, record label or even cruise ship dared to trust him with a microphone anywhere else.

Ewan was bubbling with the Rage as the incompetence unfolded. It did nothing to improve his mood, but he did enjoy his pie, which made the trip somewhat worthwhile. Nelson's is one of those places that could definitely claim to be unique, at least in Dubai, but will probably never bother. I have a feeling that it might keep luring me in until I can actually figure out how I feel about it — at least until they grasp the real meaning of 'pie'.

11/09

Tales of a Middle Eastern earthquake …

It just happened! It's the most exciting thing to occur in Dubai since the infamous sex scandal. A natural disaster just struck, right here, with its epicentre seemingly right around my very office. I shit you not. Everyone was evacuated. People were standing on the streets, wondering what it was they didn't feel, looking at the trees that weren't even damaged, observing all the cars that weren't flipped over onto their roofs, engulfed in balls of flames.

Only I wasn't here. As the earthquake, measuring 6.2 on the Richter scale caused tremors around Media City (and at least one pen to fall off someone's desk), I was in a recording studio about two miles away, making a radio commercial. As the world was shaken, I was listening to an American talk about credit cards.

I have never been so annoyed. I didn't feel a thing. The pesky quake didn't even think to include me. Me! A survivor of many natural disasters. I would have known what to do. I was in New York on 9/11. Granted, that wasn't a very natural disaster but I was still a part of it. I helped find a place that still delivered pizza, and I called up to book tickets for *RENT* when no one else really felt like it. I have always been there to offer support. Always. Until today.

Imagine my disappointment. I feel so very useless. People in my office are traumatised. I don't think they'll ever get over it. A guy who sits opposite me even said, 'I didn't bother going outside.'

'What? WHY?!?' I screamed, thinking he was so shocked, so mortified, so terrified of imminent doom and destruction that the poor thing had just crawled under his desk and started praying. Apparently, though, he saw it as an ideal time to use the Internet, seeing as it's so goddamn slow when everyone else is on it.

There wasn't even any looting. I was informed of the tragedy while still at the studio and fully expected to come back and find my apple, box of Nature Valley Crunchy Granola Bars, and condom-on-a-lollypop-stick gone, stolen, pilfered. But nope. Nothing. Even my computer's still here, flashing up all the work I have to do before the end of the week/world.

Seriously, this has to have been the most boring natural disaster ever. It started in Iran — in the southwest of the Iranian port city of Bandar Abbas, to be precise. I think three people were killed there, which is terrible of course. For us, though … nothing. Most of Dubai already looks like its been involved in an earthquake, anyway. I very much doubt most people would have blinked if another pile of rubble were to appear on the side of the road.

13/09

It's a decency thing …

I've booked a spontaneous trip to New York to celebrate my birthday in November, which appears to be springing up on me rather quickly — it feels like I only just had the last one. New York is a whopping fourteen-hour flight from here — direct — but I feel the need to go because it's kind of a second home to me. I lived there for a couple of years after uni and then Lucy moved over too. It was so much fun, such an overwhelming experience that I think it might have left my feet with this permanent itch to see and experience even more. It definitely made us want to move in together when we both got back to London ... New York changes you, in a way. We clung to our past life in Manhattan together, feeling like it made us kind of special.

Anyway, you can't book a trip to New York without planning what you're going to wear when you get there. I thought it was time to check out what was up in the fashion stakes ... or Dubai's version, at least. I went to the Mall of the Emirates.

This should have been a normal kind of day trip, you might think: a pleasant stroll through one's thoughts, perhaps accompanied by an iPod, perhaps with a view to staying for coffee while pondering the purchase of a new bag. However, when I got there and let the shopping commence, I suddenly realised I might be breaking the law. I started to sweat. I fidgeted. I developed an overwhelming sense of paranoia that everyone was looking at me and I couldn't get out of there fast enough.

Now, before you say it ... no, I wasn't shoplifting. No, I wasn't dancing in the aisles high on Red Bull and I wasn't carrying out my make-up and beauty regime courtesy of The Body Shop (highly recommended — they really don't mind). I was, however, wearing a rather short skirt.

I know. Stupid.

According to new 'decency' rules set in place by the city last week, my little skirt was no longer welcome in such a public place. It hasn't really been welcome for a while, actually. All these lunches and brunches mean that in spite of the odd detox, my legs perhaps aren't as lithe and twig-like as they used to be. But here in Dubai, I'm likely to come across a lot worse than the fashion police if someone picks up on a personal wardrobe malfunction.

So what are the new Things We Must Not Do? Well, playing loud music, dancing, nudity, kissing and holding hands in public are all now considered inappropriate behaviour. I even heard a rumour about whistling being unacceptable. If you're lucky enough to still have a job round here, God forbid you hum a happy tune or a high-ho as it's off to work you go …

Pants (I take it this means trousers and not knickers) and skirts have to be of appropriate length, and outside clothing should not expose body parts indecently and should not be transparent. So basically, gymnasts, teenage bogans and cheerleaders are not welcome.

Most interestingly is the ban on hand-holding for unmarried couples. They don't say exactly how they're hoping to differentiate between couples who are married and couples who aren't. Perhaps we'll all soon be instructed to wear a sign on our foreheads when we're out and about. Perhaps they're planning to employ some sort of Relationship Surveyor to peruse the malls in search of wedding rings (or lack thereof) on all entwined fingers. This could be interesting to watch.

[*Enter stage left*] Love-struck couple, strolling hand-in-hand through the Apple Store, looking for a new laptop to host their naughty threesome photos.

[*Enter stage right*] Man with frown who asks if they're legally married.

Her: He hasn't bothered to ask me yet.

Him: But I was going to, I swear!

Her: When?

Relationship Surveyor: Yes, when?

Him: Errrr … will you marry me, honey? Maybe, sometime in the future? Maybe … I mean, oh God, don't arrest us, will you marry me now? No pressure.

Personally, I've seen plenty of Indian men holding hands in Dubai, engaged not to each other, but in a lovely stroll along the open beach. I'm pretty sure they're not all married, although to date, and to my knowledge, no one of authority has ever said a word. They've definitely made sure to eye me up and down as they've passed, though — perhaps looking for a wedding ring?

I'm wondering who would get into more trouble if caught touching limbs in a shopping mall — me and my boyfriend (well, ex-boyfriend now, I suppose, who's technically still married, just not to me) or them? I hope I never find out. Not long ago, two women from Lebanon and Bulgaria indulged in a little smooch on the beach and landed themselves in jail for a month, where they probably got a whole lot more than that. Ouch.

I suppose I have an excuse for finally retiring the mini-skirts, without laying the blame on my shamefully un-toned pins — it's Dubai's fault, not mine. Actually, perhaps that's part of their master plan — the thought behind the plea for women to dress respectfully. It's 'Cover it up, love; we don't want to look at it'.

Hmmmm. It seems Dubai knows what the haggard wishful thinkers of Britain quite embarrassingly fail to comprehend — that mutton dressed as lamb just isn't all that tasty. Luckily, whatever I can't wear here, I can most definitely wear, without a doubt, in New York. As I remember rightly, in the Big Apple, anything goes.

20/09

The killer villa crisis ...

A new set of rules, recently introduced, is angering people all over the emirate. They state that unless you're a family, you can no longer share accommodation in one of Dubai's many villas. I would have quite liked to live in another villa — but maybe with arrangements that didn't involve sleeping on a concrete bed on a landing under a Twister towel, feeling the evil stares of orphaned children boring into my skull and threatening to invade my dreams. Thanks to these new instructions, it's not to be.

Dubai Municipality appears to be acting rather like heartless swines about the whole thing. Some people in Karama and parts of Umm Suqeim are currently surviving like squatters, having had their electricity cut off as a warning. All manner of people, from every colour, culture and occupation, have written to the press about how they'll soon be forced to live on the streets once they're ushered out of their homes. The papers are screaming with furious soon-tobe refugees. But does the Dubai Municipality care? Quite simply, no.

I am fortunate enough, like many others, to live in a nice home and muse about the petty troubles Dubai sometimes brings me, like jealous married boyfriends, a difficult detox or a missing cleaner, but the people who are laying the foundations — the builders, the bakers, the pedicure-makers — have long been forced out, thanks to all manner of silly new rules like this. As one of the more fortunate expats of the UAE, it saddens me greatly to think of how this city might treat me, should I cease to have a salary and lifestyle that's thought to contribute in greater measures to its bigger, gold-encrusted dream. Inner-city dwellers have spent years building a life here, and they're now being forced to leave thanks to nothing more than greed.

The municipality has informed us that evacuating people sharing villas is essential, because they're straining our public resources and causing health and safety issues. No one can argue with that, I suppose. However, expats living in villas, in one room per person, paying all the bills and living in perfect safety have also been given their marching orders. So everyone's wondering how unsafe or unhealthy it really is, and how much do they really just want us all out and relocated into expensive and unoccupied high-rise apartment buildings?

In the long run, I'm not exactly sure what all this means for Dubai. If it's an aim to make us invest and stay longer as the bubble bursts around us, it's a bit of a funny way of going about it.

27/09

The ethics of endings ...

Ewan's having a very bad week. He's broken up with Sean. I've noticed them spending less and less time together lately, but apparently things came to a head the other night when Sean wanted Ewan to go out and get drunk with him and his friends, and Ewan just wanted to stay home and zone out in front of the TV. A common discussion in any household, you might be thinking, only it's understandable here because Ewan's having a totally shit time in his disastrous job and doesn't have any money.

He's still working diligently, every hour under the sun to get everything done in the face of total incompetence from everyone else around him, and I guess Sean's got everything quite cushy really. He's still living at home with his expat parents who wash, iron and cook for him daily. He's still speeding around in a very fast, very expensive 'selfish car' and wanting Ewan to accompany him to bars, brunches and parties, just like they used to. It's no one's fault the dynamics have shifted. They're just different people. Different people who've been drifting slowly but surely like the sands in a gentle Dubai breeze.

I didn't even hear them arguing in Ewan's room. I was lying on the sofa watching *Gossip Girl* when Sean sauntered in solo and gave me a nod as he approached the TV cabinet. I thought he was going to join me on the sofa — Ewan's been known to kick the poor guy out of his bedroom while he finishes up his day's workload. But Sean picked up the pirated *Will & Grace* box set from the shelf, flashing me a rather apologetic look as he rested it under his arm. Alarm bells sounded in my head. I sat up. I knew then that it was over. He loaned it to us ages ago and has never, ever asked for it back.

Later that night when Ewan ventured into the kitchen, he looked remarkably dry-eyed around the detoxifying white face-mask he'd applied. He said he was fine and sighed as he poured boiling water over a green tea bag. He really did look fine. I asked him whether he'd done the right thing and he frowned at me over his teacup — a look that said 'Duh, of course I have'.

I guess sometimes you just know when something's not working out. But then again, you're lucky if you're the kind of person to actually trust your heart and let it go. Some of us try to fight it when we know something's not working out. We let things drag on unnecessarily and we don't even know why we put up with it. We analyse the fact that we don't know why we put up with it; when we realise we don't know, we experience even more self-loathing for being weak and stupid. Slowly but surely we spiral into a vortex of misery and self-deprecating torture — everything gets messier and more complicated and even dirtier. But we still can't find the strength to walk away.

I wish I could be more like Ewan. He seems perfectly happy in the knowledge that he and Sean made a clean break before the chance for any real heartache emerged. Now he can get on with his shitty job and come home to his shitty flat on a building site without being nagged about going to the Irish Village every five minutes.

This clean break — so sudden, so uncluttered and simple — makes me feel even more like a tool for faltering when M&M called me the other day. He's heard about my birthday plans to visit New York and he wants to come too, which I'm sure is a very bad idea, seeing as we are most definitely not together anymore. When I told him 'this is a very bad idea, seeing as we're most definitely not together anymore', he said he's taking a business trip to London and can simply tag NYC on to the end of it before flying back to Dubai. He said he would stay in a hotel so I wouldn't have to see him if I didn't want to, as I'm staying with my friend Todd in Brooklyn.

I didn't even bother pointing out that NYC is fourteen hours from Dubai, whereas London's about seven. 'Tagging it on' is hardly the term for such an extravagant addition to a business trip. That's just the way he is. I didn't even bother asking why he would fly all the way to New York to be with someone who quite possibly wouldn't want to see him. That's just the way he is.

I said he could come, if only to get him off the phone. When he, or anyone for that matter, calls me at work, I have no choice but to pace the corridor as I talk and hope EGO The Great doesn't stroll past and see me slacking off. Of course, EGO spends all day slacking off himself, but he's earned that privilege and I haven't.

I also said yes because Stacey's coming too. She's flying straight from London to meet me there, which will be awesome!

Perhaps it won't be too difficult, M&M being there as a friend … if indeed we can attempt to be friends. I don't actually know what he wants from me, you know. Although we had a break, it wasn't exactly clean. Certainly not like Ewan and Sean's. They've now committed the final act in severing whatever ties may have bound them. Whatever inkling of hope may have shone for the future has been snuffed out for good. It's official. They've deleted each other on Facebook.

Even more sex on the beach ...

Well, we've been watching the headlines since it happened and it was just confirmed, thanks to less-than-dignified medical testing, that our lust-struck heroes, Vince and Michelle, *did* actually have sex on the beach after their inebriated cocktail afternoon back in July. Having vehemently denied this previously, we're all still sitting here wondering how much more trouble they can actually stir.

Vince has apologised profusely for his actions on the front page of local rag *7Days*, while his mates back in the UK rag to the press about what a ladies' man he is and how they're not really surprised he got his horn on in Dubai. (You call yourselves 'friends'?) Meanwhile, Michelle was charged a few days ago with indecency in a public place, consuming alcohol and having an illicit affair with businessman and visiting holidaymaker Vince.

The majority of people who move to Dubai respect the culture and obey the rules based in sharia law that are enforced by the ruling Maktoum family of the city, so writes one commentator on the UK's *Times Online*. 'Dubai is very accommodating to us Westerners ... those of us who have normal moral values live very comfortably here.' Ouch.

I guess the commentator is correct. Canoodling on the beach, filling cracks with sand in an encounter we may or may not remember the next day has long been a delightful way to spend an evening … in Ibiza. Here, as has been demonstrated many times over with many different issues (including mulled wine) the code of conduct reads differently. We may not have a copy saved on our computers or pasted to the walls, but we don't need one. We're not supposed to need one, anyway. It's ingrained in each of us, from the moment we arrive. It's common sense. It's self-control. It just … is.

As I think I said before, since this couple's cheeky encounter, topped off with a shoe-flinging and flurry of racial abuse, the police have been out in force, checking up on bars and loitering outside popular drinking establishments. We can't blame them, I suppose. Dubai is a five-star city being mauled in the media for acts that Ibiza has long been taking in its stride.

It is true, perhaps, that in seeking to attract all these Westerners to boost the flailing economy, Dubai is also reaching out to those with opposing values. The Emiratis aren't so perfect themselves behind closed doors, but heaven forbid they show it — or show their city to be too lenient with troublemakers.

As we know, public displays of affection have long been met with scowls and disapproving looks. Those of us who act without thinking quite often retract in embarrassed shame at momentarily forgetting the rules. It happens sometimes. You do forget where you are. You forget to keep your instincts in check. Some things are hard to get used to, but we do our best to try. These are the things we accept, I suppose, as fair trade for the sunny weather and (so far) tax-free salaries.

We can only hope that people will side with Dubai when it comes to the views on imposing strict rules of conduct. I know I'm being a bit of a hypocrite but most of us move here for a change of scene, not to bring the same unsightly scenes over with us. As for Michelle and Vince ... well ... without meaning to sound too harsh, I hope they had a good time while it lasted.

Money and the monkeys ...

Money is an issue in our household at the moment. Ewan still doesn't have any, due to the fact that the media company is going slowly but surely down the pan. He says some suppliers are now refusing to work with him on the basis that they haven't been getting paid either.

Of course, Ewan had no clue this was happening, but when he brought it to the attention of Heathcliff, he was simply told to keep calling around the picture agencies until he found one that would agree to work with them. When he finally found one, he felt terrible about taking them on. It's happening more and more these days. He knows full well that whoever he hires will never see anything for their efforts, but he needs these people's help to put his magazine together ... what choice does he have?

Heathcliff also recently hired an editor for a new women's magazine without telling the editor already working in the position that she was fired. The first editor, a dowdy, chain-smoking woman from rural Ireland who knew sod-all about women's magazines, had been beyond useless for quite some time and everyone wanted her out. Ewan and his team were called into a conference room one by one to meet the new editor, while the incompetent Irish one was still busying herself with a growing workload in the other room, oblivious to the fact that she'd been usurped. When she was finally given the boot, the poor woman had to slope out quietly under the gaze of a room full of people who'd known for a while what was coming, and there wasn't a damn thing she could do about it.

According to Ewan, the new editor is even worse. She is, in his words, 'an overly confident cockney bitch from London, with no fashion sense', whose daily uniform includes 'the same pair of scuffed suede court shoes'. I don't even know what court shoes are, personally, but judging by the grimace that crosses his face when he mentions them, they are clearly sending shivers down Ewan's spine on a frequent basis. He just won't stand for fashion errors of any sort.

This woman also chucks the 'c' word at him when he gets there in the mornings. Ewan says this was the highlight of her day when she worked at a trashy UK tabloid. 'You're fucking late, you c**t!' she cries, thinking everyone finds her funny. Unfortunately, this deluded way of asserting her past popularity as a fun-loving, easy-going girl in London is driving everybody mental in Dubai. She'd be ruining Ewan's day, every day, even if he was getting paid, but seeing as he's not, he's pretty much suicidal.

I got an early wake-up call from HSBC this morning, demanding I pay the 900 dirhams from a credit card I told them very clearly to cancel a very long time ago. I cleared it before I cancelled it, and I cancelled it because of their total inability to offer a service that didn't feel like it was based on an island full of monkeys. So, why the 900 dirhams, I hear you ask? Well, a TV provider I will leave unnamed, whose managing team are also clearly hanging from a branch somewhere slapping their chests like big baboons, has been charging me a subscription fee every month since I moved out of the old flat, in spite of me calling to cancel that too. So here we have a double case of incompetence, coupled with my tragic, longstanding difficulties with financial situations. Not a good mix.

Money and I have never been the best of friends. I never really used to have any, and now that I do I'm still rubbish with it. Back in London I never used to check my statements for fear of what I might find. Like most of the world I would buy what I wanted on credit, blissfully ignoring my actual poverty-stricken status and skipping joyously through my lavish daily existence like Julie Andrews with armfuls of shopping bags. Like everyone else I thought, 'I'll worry about it later'. And of course, when 'later' came around, I just got another credit card.

Back to the issue at hand. I'm all grown up now — hence the initial cancellation of a credit card I was no longer using. But alas, alack, the banks have turned their evil on the slightly-more-established me. I offered to pay the outstanding balance on the understanding that they would then, finally, cancel my credit card. The bank informed me delightedly that this was excellent news (although they were sad I wouldn't be banking with them anymore) and could I give them my new credit card number. Well, of course, I said: 'No, I have the cash right here. I'll give you my debit card number. How's that?'

'That won't work,' the lady said. 'We only accept credit card payments, and there's a handling fee, too.'

I was outraged. 'Do you mean to say that you don't accept real money?'

'Only MasterCard or Visa, ma'am.'

'But I have real money, in my account, now. Real money that I shouldn't even owe you in the first place but am giving you anyway. And you want me to put it on a credit card, therefore forcing me into more debt?'

'Only MasterCard or Visa, ma'am.'

'What if I don't have a credit card? What if I learned from my past mistakes and cancelled all my credit cards when you should have cancelled this one?'

'Do you have a credit card ma'am?'

'Yes of course I do, but ...'

'Is it MasterCard or Visa, ma'am?'

Demented with the Rage (it was only 8 am), I paid up before she called the cops. Perhaps I'm asking too much, I thought. Am I acting a little spoilt ... expecting customer service people to cancel things when I ask them to, nicely? It's a constant quandary here, that's for sure. But seriously, at a time when the world is now seemingly drowning in debt, why oh why is my bank encouraging me into more?

I called the TV people, who were very nice. They admitted their mistake, filed it somewhere in a tree within their monkey network for a chimp to screw up at a later date, and said a technician would call me back about my 900-dirham refund. Something tells me I could be waiting a very long time.

19/11

Re-biting the Big Apple ...

Baz Luhrmann wrote a song about the dangers of being hardened by New York. I sort of understand it. Spend too much time in Manhattan and its pace would probably drive you crazy. People push, people rush, people chatter in your ears, people shout, people laugh LOUDLY, people mock, joke and poke at you until eventually, you become immune. You take it for granted. You harden and then become oblivious to all the amazing reasons you moved here to begin with.

Being back in New York after two and a half years away is very weird. When Stacey and I arrived at Todd's apartment he welcomed us in, M&M included, cooked for us and set up Rock Band so we could jam into the early hours. The rain was hammering down outside, but it really didn't matter. I heart New York!

I almost married Todd once by the way … for my visa! I was so in love with New York in a way I've never felt for a man. Not that I'd tell this to M&M, of course, who flew from London on a different plane (in business class, obviously), just to be with me on my birthday. He's gone back to Dubai now. I told him he had to stay in a hotel, like he'd offered to do, as we're not together anymore. I'm still not sure that he's entirely clear in his head about our relationship status because something happened one night in his hotel room which shouldn't have. This worries me a bit (*stupid stupid stupid!*). I hope it doesn't make things more complicated. But God … what a wake-up call to be here on my own again, thinking of all the things I've done and the people I've met since I left New York the first time.

I didn't even realise how much I've missed this city till now. In the end, I didn't marry Todd for the visa. It wasn't such a good idea to stay here, once the Libran (the guy I would have married for love) made it clear he didn't really feel the same. I kind of blocked it out like I'm prone to doing with most things that don't pan out the way I want them to. I moved to England, then Dubai — always marching forward, always pushing, always 'too ambitious' (like Stanley said), maybe. It's funny, thinking back over what's played out. I didn't think I'd left New York before it had hardened me, but maybe I was hardened after all.

The streets still smell the same. It's so weird what you remember. Hotdogs, pretzels, coffee and car fumes. There's attitude round every corner. And now that I'm here, in spite of M&M, The Irishman, and every other guy who's entered my life in the time since I left, I can't help but wonder where the Libran is.

I told Stacey all about him as we walked through Central Park, before she left for London. The unfamiliar cold gripped my sun-tanned fingers like a vice but I wouldn't have had it any other way. I've always loved walking in Central Park. It clears your head, helps you make sense of the chaos beyond its borders. This is something Dubai definitely doesn't offer. We have parks, obviously, but the imported grass and palm trees don't thrive naturally in the desert. I don't think anything thrives naturally in Dubai. I don't think I do ... not as well as I used to, anyway. Every time I leave it lately, I wonder whether or not I should actually go back.

Broadway bustles with workers on cell phones, twenty-somethings wrapped up warm in hats, scarves and furry boots. Walking in NYC, you're as invisible as you want to be, and that's without covering up in an abaya. Being crazy is encouraged. Bartenders chat about their lives as you prop up their bars, sipping Jack and Coke where no one needs to know your name: 'I'm an actor from Maine, this is only a part-time job ...' Promoters stop you in Times Square: 'Buy a comedy ticket for 20 bucks — that's half price, lady ... hey, where ya from? Your accent's kinda awesome!'

Men stop you struggling up the subway steps and offer to help carry your suitcase. Waitresses call you 'cutie' as they serve you iced water that you didn't even ask for. Taxis speed and screech, dodging people. People speed and screech, dodging taxis. Crossing the street is a game of patience. When the lights are red cross the other way. Follow the grid till you reach your destination. Stay awake. Stay focused. Take a cab if it's raining. The driver will talk whether you want him to or not, and he'll always know where he's going. Pictures of his family litter the dashboard. His coffee spills precariously from a cup, perched in its holder: 'Tom Hanks was in here last week, I took him to the theatre … hey, where ya from? Your accent's kinda awesome!'

Carrie Bradshaw once described New York as a loveable boy-friend. Perhaps that's why I've thought of it this way myself. New York was strong and tough; it taught me to stand up for myself, to fight my corner. But it was loud and demanding too; it scared me and scarred me. We had some amazing nights, staying up late, cultivating dreams and schemes. It gave me a lot, but it took a lot away, too. Perhaps I was a little too young, a little too na-ive. I should have known New York would move on without me, eventually.

But our fling was beautiful and wild and it changed me. With miles and years between us, and a man on the scene who's quite the opposite of the Libran and doesn't want to let me go, New York is still the ex I can't get over. I wonder now what Dubai brings to our relationship. It's dirty, that's for sure. A little dishevelled and also very loud. It's a dreamer but it fights admirably to put even its wildest plans into action. It's bright with a sunny disposition and buys me an extravagant lifestyle. It takes me further than New York ever did and lavishes me with promises for the future. But I do get a little lost sometimes, wondering what it wants from me really. It's hard to read. It's difficult. But like New York, I guess Dubai is teaching me brand-new things about myself every single day.

Sitting here in Todd's apartment, hours behind Dubai and a whole world away, I'm thinking I couldn't have loved and lived in two more different cities. I wonder, perhaps, if Baz Luhrmann should write a new song: Live in Dubai once, but leave before it makes you ungrateful.

Fireworks ...

Even in New York, people would stop me when I said I was from Dubai and ask, 'Are you going to see the massive fireworks display? They spent more money on them than on the ones in Beijing, you know!' No, I didn't know. Three million dollars! That's a whole lot of money.

Apparently it was all in aid of the official opening of Atlantis — the mega hotel to end all hotels they've been building for ... it feels like about two weeks ... on the crest of the Palm. Atlantis is a pink monstrosity that could well have been created by a hundred Disney fairies in lilac dresses and golden tiaras. From a distance it resembles a giant sandcastle plopped by God in the middle of the ocean. The Irishman can see it from the end of his street, but he wasn't invited to the opening — a star-studded event my new friend Svana got to attend, which was ... well ... another star-studded event in Dubai.

Svana's kind of lucky like that. Being in PR she has a job like the one I used to have, where she either gets invited to, or hosts, the opening of every envelope, bookshop and bar in town. The party at Atlantis was above and beyond as far as VIPs were concerned. Svana reports that aside from a scrambling by the media on the red carpet (Dubai apparently couldn't decipher who deserved to walk the walk and who should be standing on the sidelines, such are the egos in this town), it was really quite impressive.

Kylie Minogue gyrated through five or six songs. Oprah Winfrey bailed, but she sent her two friends instead, which was nice. Lindsay Lohan stumbled about to full expectancy. Richard Branson scoffed at a reporter, causing controversy, and Charlize Theron appeared in a less-than-impressive dress, but was appropriately polite to everyone.

Mary Kate Olsen was small. Michael Jordan 'wasn't really that tall,' the fireworks exploded to rounds of applause — a few 'oooohs', a few 'aaaaaahs' — and at 2.30 am, the lights came on and everyone went to bed. Oh, but thanks to a leaked guest list, including celebrity room numbers, security probably had a hell of a job keeping the normal citizens at bay from those fancy lifts and staircases, hoping for a sight of the stars in sweet slumber.

Back to the fireworks. The Irishman says he had to have written permission to get back to his villa on the Palm after 2 pm on the day of the party. Can you believe that? Some people with jobs who went out all day and didn't go by the rules must have had a problem getting home, and I'm sure there was at least one forgetful soul sitting calmly on the balcony, sipping a cup of tea as a gigantic Catherine wheel started shooting red and yellow sparks across the sand at the end of her 'garden' before launching a stream of rockets into the sky, absolutely terrifying her cat. They lit up the whole Palm, allegedly. Apparently it was quite a display. I wouldn't know. I was in New York. I just had to watch it in small, grainy format on YouTube.

Grucci's of New York (the organiser), has confirmed that the fireworks for the launch party will take pride of place in the next *Guinness Book of World Records*. You'd bloody well hope so, too, if you'd spent that much money and gone to all that effort. According to the *Gulf News*, they planned 'firing positions from 226 floating pontoons across 46 kilometres of water on the

Palm fronds, 40 locations along the 5.5-kilometre monorail on the Palm's trunk and positions on 400 balconies on the south facade and rooftop surfaces of Atlantis.' This is pretty frickin' impressive, seeing as Dubai can't even run a public transport system.

Anyway, if the world was ever in any doubt about Dubai's ability to throw a party, it's definitely not anymore. Just when I was thinking no city could ever impress me as much as the Big Apple, look which city's gone and done just that. Even though I wasn't invited.

29/11

Who wants to be a millionaire?

Today, as we speak, I have one million dirhams in my bank account. As I sit here in my swivel chair, trying to put together a credit card campaign for our lovely local bank, I have one million dirhams at my disposal (oh, the irony) and no one in the office has a clue. I feel wicked and special and almost invincible. I could do anything right now, go practically anywhere. I could shove this project in EGO The Great's face and go shopping. Oh, sweet temptation!

Before you think you've gone insane and missed something huge along the way, you haven't. I didn't win the Dubai lottery — there isn't one. Gambling's a sin, remember? It's actually not my money at all. It's M&M's.

He hasn't given it to me, unfortunately. I am simply keeping it safe for him. He trusts me … which is perhaps slightly unwise in light of many things, least of all my issues with money and spontaneous clothing purchases. But he does. And now I have one million sparkly little Arab dollars in my otherwise empty bank account that I can't touch. It's killing me.

It's not very good for him either, though. One of his many businesses has gone bust. And by bust, I mean the bloke who owns the major share has skipped town having drained the company bank account and M&M is automatically responsible. Apparently, the authorities might come after him for the money his former partner (now AWOL) owes to a number of people. They'll take M&M's own money if they have to, anything to get it back. The lack of legal standing for people in this situation here is bloody scary. If you can't pay back your debts you're guilty of thievery and deceit before you've even muttered the words 'But I thought I had an overdraft!' It's not like it is at home.

In the UK, HSBC would just write a polite letter asking me to please pay something back. If I didn't, they'd write another one. If I still didn't pay, they'd write another one. If I didn't pay for quite a while, they would maybe call me, or my dad. When my dad called me … well, then it was different. Then I'd be scared and definitely have to start paying it back. But no one threatened prison. A court summons, maybe. A severe telling off; a big black mark against my name when it came to requesting that holy TopShop loyalty card, maybe, but no life behind bars, getting yelled at in Arabic for nine hours. Maybe that was the problem.

Anyway, M&M has given me some of his personal money to take care of, until the legalities, if there are any, are sorted out. He's a pretty powerful man who knows a lot of people, so he thinks he'll be OK. Of course, if you have enough of your own money, there are a different set of rules altogether in Dubai. He tried to explain it all in factual business terms but to be honest I was just sitting there in his Porsche, looking at my bank statement, trying to fathom how a million dirhams could be 'some' of his personal fortune. It's more money than I've ever had in my life. It's also a lot of responsibility. M&M and I are not even really together and all of a sudden I'm his financial carer. Me. The girl who less than a year ago couldn't even budget for a Big Mac.

I suppose it's nice to know that he trusts me. I have decided to try and be his friend since the slip-up in his New York hotel room, and friends help other friends out when they need them, don't they — especially if they're millionaires.

After he deposited the cash in my account last night, I took him as my date to a food review at a new steakhouse called Hunters Bar and Grill in the Westin hotel. The dinner was a diabetic's nightmare, featuring five sickly courses of chocolate-themed food, but I thought enjoying a free meal together would be a nice chance for us to talk about all the things I wasn't going to spend his money on.

I also tried not to talk about my upcoming adventure in Nepal … in a matter of days. I know it still annoys him that I'm going and that The Irishman is packing his bags along with me. It doesn't seem to matter that Svana and Sash will be there too, along with another four people. He only sees The Irishman and his non-existent ulterior motives.

What happened in M&M's hotel room in New York has only served to make me feel worse about things. I ended things for good, *forever*, and in a moment of weakness I've buggered it all up again. He's just as keen as ever and now I have 'some' of his money, which kind of makes things difficult. HSBC was one thing; it's a faceless entity I had no problem ignoring. But I can't very well not see M&M when I'm running about with a million dirhams of his hard-earned cash. I hope that's not what he was thinking when he gave it to me. Hmmm …

Stacey says I shouldn't be hanging out with M&M again. She reckons I'm only doing it because The Irishman appears to have lost all romantic interest since our drunken snog and I need to have a man around me who cares. I don't think she's right. She says I'm just trying to convince myself that I don't think she's right. Maybe I'm managing to convince M&M that I'm not still convincing myself that he's wrong for me, but I'm not convincing Stacey that I've convinced myself at all.

My head hurts.

As if to rub it in that we really had nothing to celebrate, the couple on the table next to us cracked open a 5,000-dirham bottle of vintage wine and nuzzled each other all evening. Bastards. Getting a bottle ourselves wouldn't have cracked a dent in the wad sitting comfortably in my bank account, but it would have been nice to feel as though I deserved such a treat. I've only been a millionaire for one day, but already I can see how money really doesn't buy happiness if you're investing in all the wrong things.

05/12

Spinach and the Nepalese concept of time ...

'A brave heart and a courteous tongue. They shall carry thee far through the jungle, manling,' says Rudyard Kipling. (I had to Google that 'cause I didn't know the *Jungle Book* was anything other than a Disney film till I was too old to care.) Anyway, he forgets to mention that a strong stomach helps too. But perhaps Mowgli wasn't raised in Chitwan National Park in Nepal, and perhaps he never ate the suspicious-looking wilted spinach I had to deal with a second time round, when it 'popped up' again before me rather unceremoniously in the toilet.

Oh, the humiliation. Oh, the misery. The bout of food poisoning I experienced last week wasn't too unlike the bowel-based occurrence in Kenya, after I narrowly missed taking a brand-new boyfriend along for the shitty ride. It was only my good friend from school I had to fight for the toilet on that trip. On this one, it was The Irishman. Perhaps there's such a thing as karma after all.

Anyway, a brave heart was definitely necessary in Nepal. Bravery was called upon as we wandered openly through an eerie jungle, reminiscent of the one in the movie *Pan's Labyrinth*, brushing the trees and vines aside like wide-eyed, intrepid explorers with giant sticks. It was very David Attenborough, only with smaller cameras. The guide — a small and tubby man in a sort of off-green policeman-type sweater (weird) — carried no gun and no tranquilliser dart, yet informed us that not one, not two, but thirty-five wild tigers were roaming freely in our general vicinity, and should we come face to face with a charging rhino, we should probably run. He was a very smart man.

A courteous tongue was required in Kathmandu, a city in which the service is so bad, you're never entirely sure that the food you order is going to arrive. That's if you even manage to contact anyone working at the restaurant you've been sitting in for ages in the first place. The Nepalese operate on another time system entirely. I waited more than an hour for a bean burger the night after 'the spinach incident'.

If Ewan had been there, he'd have had his business card out in seconds and hauled the lazy chef into another room for a media interrogation. I wasn't actually sure if I should be eating anything at all, really, but Svana, who was my absolute saviour during the entire bout, told me I should really try and put some lining back in my stomach. The staff at the lodge brought me water and a Panadol tablet when she told them I was in the cabin, emptying my guts of their lunch buffet, but that was the only thing I consumed in a whole two days. I even missed an early-morning elephant trek through the mist, thanks to my sickness. The backs of elephants don't have toilet cubicles in Nepal, in case you were wondering. They'd probably have them installed in Dubai, though.

In regards to the terrible service, Kathmandu isn't unlike Dubai — although it's rare to find yak's milk on a coffee menu in the UAE. For a country that produces coffee by the kilo, it's surprisingly difficult to come by a good cup in Kathmandu.

Anyway, I'd be lying if I said the eight of us who ended up on the trip strapped on those backpacks (or in my case, hot-pink wheelie case from Carrefour, darling) thinking luxury would be following us to Nepal. In the jungle lodge, where we spent two nights surrounded by chirruping grasshoppers and random rhino snorts, I even had a strange urge to see a tarantula. Now, I'm normally terrified of spiders. I'm not sure what I'd do if I saw one except cry and turn blue, but in a funny sort of 'face the fear' way I wanted to see what would really happen if I did. None appeared. Looking back, I'm glad — what was I thinking? I'm all talk in the jungle. And shits.

Back to those. I'm not entirely sure why the plate of soggy spinach affected me and nobody else, but one minute I was walking through the bushes on another of our 'wildlife tours', waving a giant stick with The Irishman and Svana on either side of me, and the next, my entire innards worked in tandem to shift position. I started to sweat. I wanted to puke. I hurried back to the cabin I was sharing with Svana and did exactly that in the toilet. The spinach was the first thing to reappear, but over the course of the next twenty-four hours, my entire stomach lining decided it quite liked the outside world. While I was hugging my porcelain friend, I couldn't help but think that if this was something that happened as often as I suspected it did, the staff at the lodge could at least have put a nice rug on the floor ... maybe even some 'toilet mitts' so I wouldn't have to touch anything nastier than the remnants of my lunch, now hanging in my hair.

The Irishman came to visit me on my sickbed, which made me feel a bit better. He stayed for about ten minutes before the smell of puke drove him back to his beers around the campfire. And as it happened, he left just in time. My grumbling bowels showed no mercy. Lying there, listening to them all having fun without me was the worst part. Why couldn't this have happened in Dubai, when I could have sweated it out in relative comfort in the Jacuzzi, or watched *Peep Show* right through from series one to five with no distractions, sprawled on my giant sofa surrounded by nice squidgy cushions? Being sick on holiday is the most depressing thing in the world, isn't it? The timing is so unbelievably inconvenient that you feel even worse, even more of an outcast, like the universe is laughing in your sweaty, sick-covered face.

I actually thought about texting M&M, just to get a comforting response. But my phone wouldn't work in the jungle. Staring at the damp-covered ceiling I realised I had one million dirhams in my bank account, yet I was all alone. Unreachable — physically, spiritually, metaphorically, mobile-phoneally ...

When I was semi-better, however, Nepal was pretty much a medicine in itself. We passed through a hundred tiny mountainside villages in our rickety bus, listening to tunes on our iPod speakers that didn't match the scenery at all. These places, like many I've seen on my travels in the past two years, are still rooted in the basic and very bare necessities of life. Baloo the bear might not have come out to see us (he'd have been an evil sloth bear in Nepal), Shere Khan the tiger stayed hidden with his thirty-four pals and only a handful of monkeys rustled the treetops for our entertainment, but the real wonders of Nepal, we discovered, sat on the outskirts of the lush green jungle. Lambs frolicked on door-steps, chickens pecked around gravel paths and happy children ran about in fields of bright yellow flowers and golden hay, just as carefree as they seemed to be in India and Yemen.

I've noticed I always look at the children wherever I go now. I can kind of imagine myself as them, you know … growing up the way they do in these places, so far removed from how I was brought up myself. Sometimes I think life would be so much simpler if I'd never had the chance to become 'too ambitious'. Not that I'm ungrateful, but … er … you know what I mean.

Of course, there is poverty in Nepal. Lots of it. But a lot of the time, those who don't appear to have much actually have a lot. It struck me as more peaceful than India, more spiritual perhaps. I want to live in Chitwan, as a self-sufficient citizen of nature. I can actually imagine myself enjoying the lifestyle, living on a diet of everything I'd grow myself (except spinach).

It's funny but in Nepal the fact that I was wandering about in possession of a million dirhams was actually holding me back. I thought to myself as I watched the hills roll past from the bus window, perhaps I'd have stayed, tried it out for a while, if responsibility wasn't tying me down. Obviously, it was just a dream. I'd have been savaged by a rabid monkey in minutes if my bus had driven off without me, but it's nice to let your imagination run wild from time to time. At heart, we're all Nepalese adventurers, on Western remote controls. The Irishman and Svana both said they felt so inspired that they wanted to go back, or go somewhere else for another adventure — maybe even climb a mountain. I told them they could do that by themselves …

Getting out of Dubai tends to bring you back to life, somehow. I couldn't help the odd look at The Irishman, having such a good time. He's infectious when he's messing about like a hyperactive child. We always bounce jokes off each other and the hours we spent on buses between Chitwan and Kathmandu were no exception. He's just such fun to be around, and I think when you spend so much time with happy people, it kind of rubs off on you. The thing I remember most about Nepal is laughter. And spinach, obviously. Though I'll try not to dwell on that.

18/12

The 22 degrees of Christmas …

Someone at the agency just said it was 22 degrees outside, which is quite exciting. That's positively freezing to someone who spends her life in strappy tops and sandals. I'm embracing it. Today I've personally opted for a polo neck dress, leggings and a scarf. Of course, the sun has since decided to come out.

I felt a little bit stupid at lunchtime when a tourist walked past me in shorts, so I made a little *brrrrr* sound and hugged my arms to my chest to emphasise my acclimatisation and consequential clothing needs.

The cold is good for other reasons. We're going ice-skating on Saturday. Ice-skating, in the desert. Well, not technically in the desert, but Dubai is sort of in the desert, so I guess I can make that claim. They've constructed a 300-square-metre rink on the

Marina Promenade, so we can all graze our butt cheeks in the glory of the great outdoors. I'm not sure how much of it is rooted in hope that the sun doesn't come back out and turn it into a pond, but if they hand out lifejackets as well as skates, then I guess we'll know it's another praiseworthy Dubai dream that probably should have stayed on a blueprint.

On Saturday I'm planning to glide, hand in hand, with The Irishman, Torvill-and-Dean-style, laughing gaily as my hair blows beautifully like an auburn flag in the wind. Of course, that's what will happen in my head, before I fall over and cause a heap of angry chaos like I normally do when my fictional abilities clash with reality.

I think Sash, Svana and Ewan are coming too. Sash has recently broken up with another boyfriend, so she's in need of some decent escapism opportunities, and she, The Irishman, Svana and I have become a bit of a gruesome foursome since we got back from Nepal. I didn't actually think Sash, with her perfect model looks and penchant for appearing well groomed twenty-four hours a day, would like Nepal, but as it happens, it's given her a new-found need to work in a poverty-stricken country. She's even looking at teaching English in rural Thailand when she leaves Dubai. Svana and The Irishman are also still talking about climbing a mountain … I think they're actually serious.

It's definitely feeling festive in these parts — surprisingly so. Santa looks a bit disgruntled as he sits in the Madinat's Christmas Market in his itchy beard, listening to kids ask: 'Please get Mummy and Daddy a loan so we don't lose our house and car.' Still, the magic of Christmas can't be completely crushed by a global economic crisis, can it? There's still the 'shopping without your parents to say no' thing. We might not have anyone to buy us a PlayStation, but last night Ewan and I took great joy in treating ourselves to a giant supermarket sweep, a delightfully superfluous calorific affair, so riddled with e-numbers that I half expected that lady from *You Are What You Eat* to pop out from behind a bag of Doritos and start threatening to dissect our poop.

It felt good, carrying our cheap little tree home and then constructing it in our living room, listening to 'Christmas Rock'n'Roll'. Even though Ewan's still a little short on the cash front, he's decided it's the season to be jolly after all. And just like last Christmas in this crazy place, we've no choice but to create these comforts ourselves. It's important. Otherwise we'd be sad and lonely and even more single than we both are already … [*insert violins here*].

Back to that. I had to give the money back to M&M. He's ironed out his problems and has managed to walk away from the whole ordeal without being sent to the slammer, which is a relief. However, I was quite enjoying having that beautiful, imaginary nest egg, while it lasted.

It does take the pressure off our already strained relationship, though. Not having a million dirhams in my bank account is a small price to pay for feeling like I'm free. M&M has been getting very intense again lately. I still don't quite understand why he can't accept how miserable we seem to make each other. His intensity and jealousy suffocate me and my resulting secrecy drives him crazy, but it's almost like he can't admit defeat. At times I wonder if he looks at me like one of his business deals; one that he can't quite close. It annoys him. Anyway, I can only leave him to his own analyses as I feel like the time might be approaching for me to leave Dubai. Things aren't the same anymore, and being single while I sort things out is definitely better than struggling in what's clearly a doomed relationship.

I can't believe that this time next week it'll be Christmas Day! Svana is bringing the turkey from the five-star hotel she works at

— even though she's a vegetarian, bless her. Just like last year we're doing the 'orphan' thing, for which we'll each cook a dish and take it to someone's apartment, where the majority of our lovingly prepared spread will inevitably go cold and in the bin as we get shit-faced on red wine and fall asleep like old age pensioners on the sofa.

Where did the year go again? I remember my nan telling me the years get shorter as you get older. I believed her. I thought she meant it literally, like I'd finally get to 2020 and it would only consist of January. I know what she meant now. Time flies.

04/01

Solidarity, songs and skyscrapers ...

Another year is over. A new world has dawned. The year 2009 is upon us, which means 2012 — the time of robots and spaceships — is another year nearer, too! Can't wait. There have already been some pretty monumental changes around these parts, not least the one that happened at The Irishman's villa over Christmas. I'll come back to that. There was, of course, the quashing of Dubai's eagerly anticipated New Year's celebrations in light of the terrible attacks on Gaza — a decision which angered many mostly because of the credit crunch as well as the general need to 'just have a little bit of fun'.

It seems Dubai was briefly torn over a desire to forget the tragedies of current times and a responsibility to remember them for how such things affect us all, somehow. Parties went on in people's homes, of course. It just meant that a few villas were messier than

usual the next day. I sang 'Auld Lang Syne' with a guitar-playing
stranger and sixty people in masks at The Irishman's pad on the
Palm. And the general consensus was, as we all highfived at midnight against a firework-free sky, that ultimately Dubai made the
right decision to show solidarity in the face of uncertainty.

Then strangely, we were submitted to an orchestra of pan pipes
on the radio. There's nothing like a spot of The Carpenters on
the flute in the key of F-sharp as you're hurtling down the highway in a cab to make you feel a tad uncomfortable. Flags waved at
half-mast all over the city before it was announced that, yes, sadly,
something was indeed wrong. The very important Sheikh Rashid
Bin Ahmad Al Mu'alla passed away on Friday. You may have heard
of him (or not). He was only seventy-seven years old and inevitably enjoyed a carb-laden lifestyle in a palace somewhere, sitting,
scoffing, smoking shisha, stroking lions and passing judgment. He
will be missed.

In other 2009 news, the Dubai Mall Aquarium has opened.
It's the biggest fish tank you've ever seen, right in the middle of
what is essentially another soulless shopping centre. It stretches
51 metres by 20 metres and features the world's largest viewing
panel at 32.8-metres wide and 8.3-metres high. (Dubai loves big
facts and figures.) You can stand there with your face pressed
against the glass, watching sharks, stingrays and occasionally div-
ers swimming about inside, before nipping into H&M next door
for a T-shirt. It's amazing. We're told that 33,000 sea creatures live
inside. It also has the capacity to hold ten million litres of water.
That's a hell of a lot of fluid and a scary amount of beasts with
sharp teeth. I just hope it never breaks.

Anyway, just as 2008 had Atlantis, 2009 will have the Burj
Dubai … another topic that's raising as many eyebrows as it will do

glasses when it's finished, I'm sure. The word on the street is that the 160 or so floors have cost several billion dollars to build. It'll house a hotel designed by Giorgio Armani and some office space, but the question on everyone's lips is how high will it really be?

'If you put the Empire State building on top of the Sears Tower then it's reasonable to say you'll be in the neighbourhood,' says Mr William Baker, the chief structural engineer on this groundbreaking project. But he's not giving much away, really. Come on, won't you give us a clue?

'We're not allowed to say. The client hasn't announced what it is and I don't think they will. It'll turn into urban folklore. You'll have people measuring the shadows on Google Earth and trying to figure it out.'

This all sounds very intriguing … until you apply logic. As my dad pointed out via email: 'Has Mr Baker not heard of triangulation?'

I googled it. It's a very simple formula involving angles. The ancient Greeks, Egyptians, Chinese and the Arabs (maybe) knew about it. Measure a distance to the base of an object, measure the angle from that point to the top and a bit of simple maths will give you the height. It's a bit worrying that the man in charge of building the world's tallest structures isn't familiar with it, but then again, half the fun of Dubai has always been in the 'theory' of it all.

'We could definitely go taller,' says Mr Baker, in a rant that includes predicting the possibility of towers 1,000 metres high. 'The next generation of tall buildings are in a hiatus right now, but there're places with pent-up demand. I see China continuing with that, and India will come into it soon …'

OK, enough. Geek! Our heads are spinning already. It's 2009, almost 2012. Let's just think about shopping malls and robots some more.

P.S. I hate you ...

It could have been because we were high on festive spirits ... and it could have been because we've been keeping something inside since our very close encounter at the party last year, but The Irishman and I shared another surprise snog over Christmas, after a late night out drinking at the Madinat. We cabbed it back to his villa, danced around his room like idiots for a bit and locked lips on the bed till we fell asleep. To be fair, we were hammered again, just like we were when it happened before, but still, this twisted idea of a platonic relationship is all a bit confusing.

I've been talking about it all to Svana, my newest confidante in relationship theory since Stacey only became available via Skype. Svana, like a lot of people, thinks The Irishman and I should be together. She says she noticed something about the way he looked at me in Nepal — and it wasn't swayed by the fact that I couldn't string two sentences together without feeling like my guts were about to explode. And because he hasn't done anything about initiating a date or anything at all since our latest passionate embrace, Svana and I have embarked on Project Snog (or 'P.S.', as we've taken to calling it). She's promised to get some handy information out of him regarding what he really thinks of me, so I can put my mind at rest.

After the first time, when nothing happened as a result of our poolside pash, it was easy to think The Irishman had written me off as a home-wrecking retard, already under the thumb of a man I moan about all the bloody time. I sort of got over it, let my feelings go, decided being single was the way forward ... but now that it's happened again. For God's sake, does he like me or not? A girl needs to know.

I should probably tell you that as all of this has been evolving, M&M has been receiving some very strange text messages from an anonymous stranger, who seems to know his every move. Whoever is sending these messages seems to be able to detail every little motion he makes, and it's creeping him out. They're not threatening, just informative — but it's seriously weird. The other day, after a particularly informative message, M&M called me in tears, demanding to know whether it was true that The Irishman and I had shared a kiss over Christmas. It appears whoever his secret texter is, they have inside information on me as well. Freaky or what?! I hung up and called The Irishman in his workplace, asking who he'd told about our festive frolics. He said no one. I've only told a few people myself, and they're all people I trust implicitly.

M&M called back in even more of an emotional state. I was forced to admit right there, as I slouched on a comfy red beanbag that yes, I had made out with The Irishman over Christmas. I was very sorry, and yes, of course, I knew that The Irishman was the one person with the power to upset him the most etc., etc. And then I realised that I'd been single at the time of our kiss.

Now, I might be a little silly, a little secretive, a little psycho in other areas, but I never raise my voice to people usually, unless it's in Harry Ghatto's and I'm holding a mic singing 'Cheesebread', which is our own special, drunken version of 'Total Eclipse of the Heart' (don't ask). But on this occasion, as he ranted tearfully down the phone I stepped out of the room, calmly took the lift to the ground floor, strolled casually out into the scorching desert sun and screamed at him in the car park.

We yelled even more insults at each other from the front seats of his air-conditioned Porsche that night. He managed to convince me beforehand that he was calm and just wanted to talk things over, and I was dying to find out more about the mysterious text messenger. It's still making me nervous, knowing that someone out there hates me, or M&M, so much that they're trying to sabotage what's already a pretty fucked-up relationship. But our talks ended very, very badly. With nothing whatsoever resolved, he sped off down the street, still hysterical. And I was so angry that I needed to go out for more booze, naturally. I called Svana, who was already out in a bar with The Irishman. They were planning their mountain trekking expedition no less. In that moment, I could think of nothing better than being with my two favourite friends, so I called a cab and was on my way.

My phone rang off the hook, flashing M&M's face at me from the screen the entire journey. He always does this — rants and raves about me breaking his heart and then begs for another conversation. I'll never understand it at all!

I rocked up to the bar, visibly pissed off, and ordered a huge cocktail. The Irishman and Svana, who were already eating chips and mayo in a corner, could obviously tell something major had gone down, so I proceeded to tell them the whole story as I chugged on my drink, feeling like a boring, broken record.

I don't even know how many times The Irishman has heard about my dull-as-shit relationship issues with M&M now. But looking at their frowning faces, hearing my phone ring yet again with his desperate plea for attention, it suddenly occurred to me that I was ruining their night with my drama. There in that bar, I felt like more of a moron than ever before and seriously ... I cringe about it now. How is it that I'm constantly putting myself in such a lame position, letting M&M and his controlling actions affect me in front of a guy I actually quite want to like me? When did my life get so complicated?

Svana finally ordered me to turn my phone off, so I obliged, prior to which the gadget, now low on battery, kindly informed me I had no less than sixty-two missed calls from M&M. 'Is he insane?' she asked, her eyes wide as dinner plates. To this day, I consider it a very good question. Maybe I drove him that way.

The Irishman says he has no idea who the texter could be, but reckons it's someone from the company that just went bust wanting a slice of that million, no doubt, and trying to find an angle that intimidates. Svana suggested that there's no mysterious texter at all — perhaps M&M just got wind of our snog somehow and is trying to trick me into admitting it. God knows how many times he's checked my phone when my back's been turned.

When I got back to the apartment a few hours and a few more cocktails later, M&M was there, snoring very loudly on the sofa. I was so angry I almost marched over to him, but I suddenly realised he was clearly waiting to yell at me in another burst of jealousy. He must have asked Ewan to let him in … or forced his way past him in a fit of fury.

I crept past him, but he heard my bedroom door shut. Just as I locked it behind me, he was wide awake, banging on it violently. He'd worked himself into such a state that he was sobbing, ramming his fists against the door and begging me to let him in. Of course, I refused. I actually screamed at him to go away, told him in a drunken slur at a very high volume that he was ruining my life, and oh yeah, I hated him. I would have said anything to make him leave me alone and stop harassing me; to stop him begging for me back when clearly we do nothing but piss each other off. But he wouldn't leave.

Ewan stayed in his room throughout the whole sorry saga, though he tells me now that he woke up when the screaming started. He was just as freaked out as me. I've never experienced such an intense display of emotions from any man before. It was actually terrifying. I dialled Svana in the midst of it all, who at that point was on her way home from the bar. She called M&M herself on his mobile to tell him to leave me alone.

It was only after we both threatened to call the police that he actually straightened himself out and announced that he was going. I was mortified, sitting there on my bed in my going-out frock, mascara running down my face, looking like the victim of a very bad episode of *The O.C.*, I'm sure. I can't believe it's come to this. I have seriously messed with M&M's head, perhaps even more than his possessive streak has messed with mine. And now we have a friendly stalker, stirring things up for good measure. Honestly, could things go any more tits-up round here?

22/01

When two worlds collide ...

I got to work this morning, only to be accosted by Nina in the brainstorm room. Apparently, a very cool campaign she concocted against drink-driving in her spare time was picked up by some advertising big-wigs a few weeks back, who wanted to feature it in an industry magazine. Awesome! Only … EGO The Great's been up to his old tricks again. Apparently, he got the call about her creative genius and decided to conduct the interview with the magazine on her behalf. Nina only got to hear about it when he popped his bespectacled head out of his office and asked for a close-up photo of her face. They wanted to picture her next to the campaign shots.

She was outraged not to have been invited to speak to them herself about her idea. She was even more infuriated when the magazine was delivered this morning, and she discovered that they didn't even use her photo. They used EGO's instead. Her name might be in there, somewhere, in the fine print. But at first glance … well, it's all him and his amazing work. If it wasn't so utterly exasperating for poor Nina, it would be laughable, right? His soul must be bullet proof.

It's been a weird day in general. I saw Stanley today. It was most unsettling. I was simply doing my thing in the food court of the building next door, tucking into a sneaky cinnamon bun with my coffee (*sssshhhh*), when I looked up and spotted those familiar flappy sleeves, that somewhat lopsided smile and the same thinning, mousy brown hair.

'Hello, Rebecca,' he said, looking down at me. He always did call me by my full name, even when I signed off my emails with 'Becky'. I'm never really sure why people do this, when you give them full permission to call you by the name you prefer. It's almost as irritating as when the people who hardly know you decide to shorten your name to something you've never, ever been called before in your life, because they feel some sort of unrequited familiarity.

Anyway, I was thrown for a second. A number of things went through my head: What is he doing here? Why is someone who fired me for absolutely no valid reason approaching me with a smile and assuming I wish to acknowledge him? Why the hell is he still wearing that suit?

Fuck, I have a face full of cake.

At first I kept my face expressionless. Obviously I didn't want him to assume I was actually pleased to see him … the last time I saw him I was marching past him with my nose in the air, having just been given the boot. I nodded to confirm I had registered his presence and waited for him to leave, but he hovered, looking at me struggling with my sinful snack.

'What are you doing here, Rebecca?'

'I was going to ask you the same thing, Stanley.'

'I work here.'

'So do I.'

We were like two soldiers from opposing sides, standing on the frontline, ready to battle each other to the death. His weapon — the fact that he'd fired me; mine — well, a cinnamon bun.

He smiled slightly and nodded his head, raising his eyebrows as if he was impressed that I'd actually got another job. It struck me that maybe he'd been fired from the publishing company himself. He was on the wrong side of town. I felt a minor pang of sympathy for him in that moment. Perhaps they hired another monkey and shoved Stanley out on the street. I imagined for a split second that he might apologise, sit down next to me and have a rant about how shittily they treated him too … maybe buy me another bun.

Instead, he made small talk from his standing position. I told him where I was working, at which point he actually folded his arms and said: 'Oh, well I suppose you're glad you left, then.'

I looked up at his pasty face. 'I didn't leave. You fired me, Stanley.'

He shuffled, nervously. 'Hmmm, well it looks as though I did you a favour,' he said.

The effing cheek of it. Clearly he was trying to say that my job at the agency was so impressive in his eyes that had I still been working for him, I wouldn't have climbed as many rungs of the career ladder as I've done to date. But as usual, Stanley fucked it up. He actually implied that he had personally contributed to my success, even though he'd done nothing but make my life hell in that morgue. I felt like shoving my bun in his hair and wiping icing down the front of his shirt so the flies would stick to him as soon as he went outside. Instead, I just sipped my coffee and pretended he didn't exist.

He could probably tell he'd screwed up. The silence was excruciating for both of us. Eventually, he told me he'd see me around and sloped off in his normal, sloth-like style towards his new, unfortunate place of employment. As he left, I found myself wondering what the future holds for people like Stanley in Dubai. Maybe he simply got another job, but what if he really was fired? There must be hundreds of people who came here years ago for a taste of the good life, who've now been tossed to the curb as their companies experience the backlash of spending far too much money way too quickly on some seriously ridiculous things.

At the end of the day, EGO The Great might be tough to endure, but at least he still needs me to help with his spelling.

12/02

Geese and guilt-free cookery ...

To keep from engaging in a sorrowful textual exchange with M&M the other night (who's still sending quite a few, I can assure you), I went to the launch of a vodka bar that's been open since before Christmas. I couldn't really see the logic in it either but who am I to turn down free cocktails these days? So off I trudged with Svana to Souk Al Bahar, where we found a host of girls in white dresses awaiting us at the entrance of a place called Left Bank.

To be honest, I wasn't really in the mood. Lately, I often think that I've turned into a bit of a snob; that maybe I just don't appreciate the glitz, glamour, fawning and faux niceties, business-card bashing and air-kissing quite as much as I once did. Maybe I really would just like a night on the sofa with Ewan, watching Nigella slicing and dicing something delicious. I always did enjoy the televised treat of what's essentially the joyfully slow expansion of a woman's bottom half before an entire nation. It makes me feel better about myself somehow, watching her spoon that ice-cream into her mouth at midnight in the secrecy of her dimly lit pantry. I know I should be out, getting over a bad relationship in the company of other people, but as long as she's bigger than me and not afraid of growing, another night in with my feet up is acceptable.

But before we knew what was happening, it was too late to back out. Svana and I were surrounded by the aforementioned media luvvies all brandishing glorious free cocktails. It turned out I knew the Vodka Man too — the guy who sells it to bars. He's a walking, talking cocktail of suave sophistication and limitless free booze. Sash and I had once had dinner in his luxurious apartment, which was full of art and trinkets, remember? He recognised me, we exchanged a few words, did the obligatory air-kissing as he glided over to hand us both a nice watermelon concoction and promised to meet again soon, before he sidled off into the ether, oozing charm and smiles.

I remember when I used to do that. I never used to stand in one place for long in a bar. Before things with M&M got serious, I thought absolutely nothing of gliding round a room in that hot red TopShop dress and high heels, talking to absolutely everyone. It wasn't even that long ago that this room would have been mine — a goldmine of opportunity. I wonder how many other people have grown tired of it all, too, for one reason or another.

As we huddled by the bar, I tried probing Svana for some news on the 'P.S.' front. Since the whole drama with M&M, I've not really seen The Irishman much. My freelance work and the agency have been keeping me busy, and to be honest my own embarrassment has been keeping me away a bit. For this reason, I didn't think it would be good news at all … though of course being an idiot I harboured a little hope in my heart.

When I brought it up, Svana glanced sideways, after throwing me a little apologetic look, which told me all I needed to know. I've fucked it up royally. The fact that the whole M&M affair ended with him still being married, refusing to believe we were over, banging down my door in the dark of the night and crying over texts from a stalker has put The Irishman off me once and for all. He probably thinks I attract drama. He's probably right.

We still don't even know who's sending the text messages. M&M is still getting them. Each one comes from a different number that proves not to exist when he calls it back. The latest theory is that someone who used to work for M&M has contacts in the government. They're tracking him with ultra-modern super radar devices that have yet to be released to the public. Anything's possible in Dubai. Well, it used to be …

In spite of the show of glitz and glamour, things are really crumbling now. The agency is pitching ideas like crazy to anyone who'll listen at the moment. The property and development companies and the banks that all used to bring in the big bucks have started to zip up their wallets. People are starting to leave the city. Everyone's noticing a difference. The publishing company, which may or may not have fired Stanley, is rumoured to be discussing even more layoffs. This means the girls I went with to Jaipur all those months ago might soon be packing their bags. And of course, Ewan's company is seriously in the shitter.

Standing there with Svana, watching the ladies sipping cocktails and the men swanning round, laying on the charm to anyone who'd listen, I had a sudden jolt of not belonging — not in the bar, nor here in Dubai. Leaving has been playing on my mind a lot more lately, but in that moment I really felt it.

One good thing about Dubai getting quieter by the day is that even if we do waste three hours schmoozing, boozing and air-kissing people with no intention of ever seeing them again, we can still cab it home in time to catch Nigella disappearing into the pantry.

20/02

Holes, moles and guillotines ...

I had drinks with my friend Sam last night. He's making an extortionate amount of money in Dubai; not that he'd ever admit it but you can tell.

Most people don't discuss their salary here. You can usually guess what they're earning by how much they flash it about in bars, restaurants and (occasionally) seedy hotel joints frequented by Russian women in leopard print. Sam's not like that. He's earning a mint, yes, but unlike lots of other people, he's stashing it all away in order to buy a house back in his home country, and go on some very nice holidays to exotic places. Very sensible, I say.

Sam's company in Dubai provided him with everything when they moved him here, on top of his ludicrous salary. They shipped over all his furniture, too! I'm told lots of companies used to do this, though the travel publishers never offered to ship mine over when I first got the job, way back when. It's a shame. Lucy and I had a great, white leather sofa that we found on the street outside our flat and got the neighbor to drag upstairs for us. It would have looked great in my place.

Anyway on top of paying him more per month than I'll probably earn in my life, Sam's company pays the rent for his fancy apartment in the Marina, too. You know, I reckon, if I'd moved to Dubai a few years before I did, it would have been a different story. I could have demanded all sorts of things, like Sam. I could have asked for a home cinema, or a pony, or a private jet to work every morning. Maybe. I'm not as important as Sam but still, I could have had a go. These days newbies don't get anything special for the effort it takes to move and live here. Times have definitely changed.

I digress. Last night, over a couple or more of the most ridiculously expensive Gin Slings, Sam told me the most amazing stories about some of the stuff going on behind closed doors. I don't know where he gets his information, but he's a gossip queen's goldmine..

He said, the other day, a friend of his arrived at work to find a little Indian man sitting in the stationery cupboard, slicing up sheets of paper with a guillotine. He asked him what he was doing. The man stared at him blankly. He asked his manager what the man was doing, only to be told it was a cost-cutting exercise. The poor guy was basically hired to hack an entire stack of A3 paper down into A4 sheets. In Dubai, you see, it's cheaper to hire an Indian man for the week than it is to buy a new stack of A4 paper and a recycling bin for the rest.

This has to be the most ridiculous thing ever … right? Wrong. What's even more ridiculous, Sam continued, is that allegedly, a gigantic hole was being dug at the command of the sheikh, who was so eager to get the project for a new plaza or something started that he evacuated hundreds of people from their homes on the site first, demolished their villas and ordered his men to get to work, without obtaining proper planning permission. When the water started seeping in it became pretty obvious the exercise was pointless. The hole was too deep and too close to the sea, so all those people, now without homes were just left looking at a giant, useless hole. Imagine! Sam says you can see it for yourself if you look down from a building high enough. I made up my mind to check it out!

Apparently, so says Sam, this isn't the first time that work has been started on a project without the approval of a qualified engineer, architect or property developer. These people are all on the team from the get-go, of course, carefully hired and plied with oodles of cash. But at the end of the day, what the sheikh wants done is done, no arguments. He's got a city to build, dammit! Why let a simple thing like structural engineering get in the way? Surely physical laws were made to be broken in the name of such a beautiful dream?

The laws of the land are broken also, at times, when it comes to new projects. Sam thinks it might just be a rumor but apparently the Burj Al Arab, which markets itself as a seven-star hotel out on its own little island, was originally intended to house a casino on the top. Being 'offshore', officials thought the no-gambling rule might not apply once inside. Someone overruled the decision, obviously, but it might explain why what is now the very expensive Sky Bar has some truly, head-fuckingly awful patterned carpets.

Sam also told me how the sheikh has apparently invested in a glorious new 130-metre yacht, which he'd quite like to dock in the bay of a brand-new private island, being built for him out at sea. Sam's good friend Rocko is involved in this project — a guy I'm set to meet in a couple of weeks when we all go on a snorkelling trip to the Musandam peninsula.

The beautiful Burj Al Arab at night.

Unfortunately though, the bay to this piece of land, specially dredged up to please his Highness, is only 80 metres wide and 6 metres deep. The sheikh doesn't like this. According to Rocko, he's having to dock his fancy yacht about a mile out at sea and then take a speedboat across. This is highly inconvenient, especially as he usually rides a Segway (a two-wheeled, electric vehicle in case you've never seen one) everywhere and it's difficult to transport a

Segway on a little boat. It won't be long before he deserts his very own desert island.

This said, Rocko deems the sheikh as a pretty awesome bloke, albeit a bit of a dangerous dreamer. He's spent a lot of time with him, thanks to his line of work. He's hobnobbed with his people in various palaces all over the UAE and even helped to build a swimming pool for him in the grounds of one of them.

Apparently, when it came to testing the paths around it, they had to be exactly wide enough for his Segway to pass. Even a little bridge, which took him to a beautiful grotto, had to be a certain width. Rocko was there when he tested it out.

He stood there with bated breath and watched the mighty sheikh whiz about in his dishdasha, careful not to get the robes caught up in the wheels of his toy. As you can imagine, Rocko experienced the ultimate career high, and the absolute career low all in the same breath, as the man stepped off his Segway and told them all he was very pleased with his new paths.

Perhaps more interesting is the fact that the sheikh hangs out with cage fighters. He is also a black belt in Brazilian jiu jitsu— a form of martial arts for which there are no rules. Anything goes in a fight, except eye-gouging and biting. The sheikh loves this sport so much that in an act of kindness, he adopted twenty underprivileged kids, gave them schooling, encouraged them to keep fit and helped each one of them take up the martial art of their choosing. According to one of Rocko's palace sources, they're now pretty much a miniature army squad, taking part in international competitions and generally kicking arse. How cool is that? The man's a walking, Arabic-talking legend. Building an entire city out of dust is just a side-project, clearly.

I love hearing inside secrets about this place! I could have sat for hours with Sam, but our coffee was getting cold and we'd eaten all the complimentary chocolates, and even people on ridiculously massive salaries can only stomach so many expensive Gin Slings. Makes me wonder what else is going on behind our backs around here.

Coffin for two, please ...

I think 'Project Snog' is well and truly over. I'm feeling like such an idiot. I spoke to The Irishman today during my lunch break and he sounded a little more quiet than usual, a bit subdued. I thought perhaps his job was getting him down again but he said he had something to tell me ... about Svana. I panicked. I thought something horrid had happened to her; I've not heard from her for a few days. But then he said: 'Oi really, really loike her,' which in my head of course translated as 'We've fallen head over heels in love and have already done the deed behind your back, so there'.

I didn't really know what to say, so I said nothing. I just sort of stood there gaping into the phone like a retard. His words, plus the things they'd already done together, were getting bigger and badder in my imagination — so much so that perhaps the truth got a little lost, but still. Basically, my current best mate and the object of my somewhat skewed affections have seen the light and hooked up with each other. Great.

As my brain was going crazy, swinging from denial into furious acceptance, The Irishman asked, 'Are you OK?'

This was what upset me most. He might as well have kneed me in the stomach. When a guy tells you gut-crunching news himself and then asks if you're OK, you know he's only asking in order to make himself feel better. If he really cares how you're feeling, he wouldn't be telling you things to make you upset, would he? (Or shagging your friend.)

I felt so alone right there in the car park, where I always seem to be lately when I scream at people, or cry. I tried not to cry, however. I sucked it up and put on my happiest voice, making it sound like I really didn't care at all. Me, bothered? Of course not! I'm so happy for you. She's great, you're great, what great news, thanks for sharing! Was there anything else?

I'm not sure he was convinced. He knows me too well. And Svana surely must have questioned him about me, prior to falling for his cocky Irish charms herself. This whole thing has been screwed up from the start, thanks to my own pathetic weaknesses round M&M. It's no wonder he's pushed our dalliances into the past and moved on with someone better. But still ... ugh ugh ugh.

'We loike each other,' he said, before asking again if I was OK. I felt my chin wobble. His confirmation that these feelings were mutual, plus his second caring question as to the state of my well-being was like a double smack in the face; proof, I suppose, that he gave up liking me in return ages ago but didn't know how to tell me. He obviously found himself liking Svana far more than me, but was having to witness me acting like a total tool. Being a nice, caring guy, he pitied me for it. Ugh ... The Irishman actually felt sorry for me.

His words were the final nail being slammed into the coffin, into which he'd just lain what was left, if anything, of our twisted romance. I can picture it clearly ... me, banging from the inside with my fists, screaming to be heard as he and Svana cast an evil glare over my pent-up soul, skipping off together, free of me, into the mountains. The mountains! That's what made it all happen, isn't it! They're still planning their trip, inspired by Nepal. They found a common interest, a binding thread right in front of my face, which grew and grew and grew into something else. They really are skipping off into the bloody mountains. They always were, and I didn't even realise. They didn't realise, The Irishman went on to say. It just sort of … happened.

I did less work at the agency today than I've ever done in my life — and that's saying something. I just couldn't concentrate, couldn't even finish an email to Stacey explaining what had gone on. Couldn't even update my Facebook status to: *Becky: loathes the world and everyone in it.*

I suppose I should have seen it coming … but then again, maybe not. How can you ever see what's coming, when you're stuck in a rut of denial in the first place? They were already out together in the bar that night … the night it all came to a head with M&M. I hadn't even known they were going out that night until I called Svana … and we usually all go out together. At the media-luvvie launch party, she didn't elaborate on the topic of 'Project Snog', as we'd done a million times before. She just stared into her cocktail, probably wanting to tell me she had feelings for him herself, but not really knowing how to say it. I should have seen it then. Am I really so selfish and stupid these days, so caught up in my own pathetic life and ambitions that I can't even see what's right under my nose? Is this what Dubai's done to me, or what I've done to myself as a result of getting so caught up in Dubai?

One thing I do know. The way I feel right now — the absolute emptiness as I picture him with her and me with no one — it's far more painful than when M&M dumped me way back on New Year's Day. It's worse than being dumped, I can tell you that much.

I haven't been dumped on this occasion because I never gave us a proper chance to be together. It's the not knowing that's the killer with things like this, isn't it. It's all the what-ifs.

I was too much of a coward to finish things with M&M for good when I first had the chance to pick up where The Irishman and I left off in Spain. I was too scared. Too controlled. Too guilty for liking someone else when M&M had taken it upon himself to fall totally in love with me. I didn't know how to face his utter misery and outbursts whenever I let it show that he wasn't my number one priority. So I endured it while letting my heart wander anyway. I tried to break up with him, sure, but I always went back. Even if I didn't go all the way back, I still let him think I was available. I shouldn't have let him think I was available, not for one second. For the most part, now that I think about it, my heart was never properly available. If it was, then why is it breaking now?

Svana tried to call me tonight but I couldn't pick up the phone. I watched her name flash on the screen, feeling like a total bitch, knowing she probably feels bad. I'm her closest friend in Dubai these days. But I still just can't imagine what I'd say to her. I know she didn't do anything on purpose. She would never do that. These things happen. She's a gorgeous, clever, fun-loving girl and he's an amazing guy. And at the end of the day, I introduced them. I brought this on myself. My own boring, insufferable shit contributed to bringing them together. I know all this, but I feel so stupid and I really, really don't want to have this whole conversation with her.

Nope. This is all my fault, so I suppose I must face the consequences. I want to shut myself away for three weeks, eat chocolate, watch my thighs expand and do a Bridget Jones; I want to be eaten by Alsatians. Dubai has to have the biggest of everything. And I think I'm officially its biggest ever loser.

The boat that rocked ...

I almost pulled out of Kathy's snorkeling trip to the Musandam Peninsula, but Ewan told me I should really make the effort to get myself out and mix with some new people. I think he's just a bit sick of seeing me slouching round the flat. As you can imagine, our household hasn't exactly been full of delight lately. Just as Ewan's probably sick of hearing about my stupid boy dramas, I'm sick of hearing about his miserable company not paying anyone. In a show of friendship and solidarity, however, we carry on confiding in each other, pissing each other off and generally making things worse. It's just what friends are for really, isn't it?

The Musandam Peninsula is the northernmost part of Oman. It's a pretty nice drive from Dubai, takes a few hours if you stop along the way and gives you the perfect opportunity to appreciate just how modern Dubai really is ... or will be, if they ever finish it. Everything else on the outside of our booming city exists just as it did thirty years ago. Camels, cows and goats are everywhere. Women cover up fully. Dusty carts selling fruit and veg still sit on the roadsides, as do carpet-sellers and bearded men making ceramic pots. It's a bit like stepping back in time to the UAE before oil came along.

Kathy organised a dhow for about fifteen people. It was a large, wooden barge affair, moored in a beautiful spot surrounded by mountains. We spent the night aboard and didn't have to get off once, except to swim. Our Indian crew took full control of the sailing and all our food was included; they cooked up some fabulous fish and incredible salads too — very impressive! Oh, and between us we took enough booze to last a week.

Rocko was one of the first people I met. He bounded up to me as I was examining my legs for nasty, itchy mosquito bites, which I must have got a couple of nights before in the Yacht Club. The Yacht Club in the Marina is right on the water and lately the mozzies have been out in force. Anyway, I looked up from my scratching and there he was, all smiles and sparkly eyes and saying he's heard a lot about me from Kathy. Obviously I'd been hearing a lot about him too. I was dying for more details on the Sheikh's shenanigans! He doesn't actually look at all like the kind of person who mixes in royal circles for a living, but then … who does?

One thing I'll say about the Musandam is that I've never seen water that colour in my life. The Maldives were pretty awesome, but the bird's-egg blue of the seemingly bottomless waters just a few hours' drive from Dubai are in another league entirely. The water in Dubai probably used to be the same; so clear that you could see 10 meters to the floor. All the dredging that's killing the fish is also churning up the sand, so you can hardly see your kneecaps when you're waist-deep off Jumeirah Beach anymore. It's such a shame. Makes me wonder what else is still in the water … hmmm … maybe that's what's causing the mosquito population to explode.

When I jumped from the dhow with my snorkel, I jumped straight into swarms of tiny, darting fish. That was a bit freaky — they'll nibble your fingers and toes if you stay still enough. We could see them waiting for us below as we leaned over the edge of the dhow. They swam in a colourful swirl of yellow and silver, like an underwater storm cloud. Rocko knew the name of them but I can't remember now.

I even saw a stingray on the bottom! I've never seen a stingray directly below me before. It was massive. I'll admit, pathetically, thoughts of Steve Irwin's early demise flashed through my head as I was looking at it and I suddenly felt an urge to get away. Being a Kiwi, Rocko had a blow-up sheep on hand to save me, naturally. It served as a floating device and later on became a prop for photos as we all got slowly shit-faced in the moonlight — my absolute favourite part of the trip! You can't beat a game of drunken truth or dare with a bunch of strangers in the middle of nowhere.

As I drank my vodka and Cokes, I listened to Rocko and Kathy as they regaled us with tales of Australia and New Zealand. It's obvious he misses home. We might have been in the most beautiful corner of the Middle East, but the difference between the harsh desert landscapes and the lush green canvas painted by nature in New Zealand is pretty huge. I spent a month there once.

We also witnessed a magical, neon sea at night. I watched it shimmer and shine as we chatted. Apparently, tiny bioluminescent creatures in the water make this light by combining oxygen with other body chemicals. Clever, eh? It's a really weird effect. In the black of night, the water round our dhow looked like it was glistening with fallen stars.

Rocko's hilarious, by the way! I haven't laughed as much in ages as I did around that random group of people on the dhow. He lives in Abu Dhabi and as well as all his stories about ridiculously wealthy people and projects doomed for failure, he's got this infectious chuckle that makes you want to squeeze his cheeks. He's pretty hot too … although obviously I was determined to stay in a bad mood and look to the mountains for reflection on my

traumatic situation. Self-pity is the new black in my current wardrobe of woe.

I still haven't really spoken to The Irishman and Svana. I just
can't seem to do it. Stacey's telling me to suck it up, get over it, accept that I've been a knob and wish them well. I know she's right.
But it's been more than two weeks now and the longer I go without answering their calls, or calling them myself, the less I feel like
I can deal with them.

I'm probably just being a coward because I actually do wish
them well. I want them to make each other smile. I want them to
climb lots of mountains and dance off into the hills for a Disney-
style happy ever after, I really do. They're two of my favourite people and I miss them both like mad … but I just don't want to know
about their relationship. I don't want to hear about it. I don't want
to see them, even individually, because it really fucking hurts.
And it makes me hate myself for being such an idiot over M&M. I
know I'm being selfish, but I don't want to hate myself every time
I look at them together. I just want to take my mind off the whole
thing.

Obviously, Dubai hasn't been floating my boat for a while, but
now … now I'm just killing time, I suppose, floating on boats. It's
good to meet new people, though, do different things. I think I
need to work more on rediscovering this happier side of myself
and make it stick — which is exactly why I've just accepted Rocko's
offer of a date. Well, why not?

I didn't even know he'd taken a shine to me until Kathy told
me when we got back. I thought my relatively morbid frame of
mind and the state of my unshaven, mosquito-bitten legs would
have put anyone off, and romance was the last thing on my mind.
To be honest, it still is. But Rocko's a fun guy to be around, so
confident and positive and full of the optimism I had myself

when I first got here. I definitely need some of that around me right now.

Cat Woman going solo …

Poor Ewan. His constant moaning is justified. He's now roughly four months behind in his salary and no one can ignore the fact that his company is well and truly buggered. Heathcliff came over with a measly pay-off when he demanded his monthly check the other day, almost three weeks after it was due. Three hundred dirhams in cash was all anyone in the company got, and apparently they only got that if they literally had no money to buy food with.

Because Ewan can't afford rent for too much longer, he's having to move out of the flat, which is why in the space of just a week I have signed the lease for my own studio apartment in the Marina. It's all happened so quickly, but our lease is up soon anyway. I'm actually really excited, but of course I can't say so to Ewan because he's my friend and he's being treated really badly. I'm trying to be sympathetic, but the prospect of having my own place in a matter of days is filling me with complete and utter joy. I'm carrying more joy around in my heart this week than I have in ages — and it's got nothing to do with a couple of totally excellent dates I've had with Rocko … honest.

Ewan's planning to stay in a friend's spare room until he finally gets some money and then he's leaving Dubai.

'I'm going travelling,' he announced in my doorway the other day, before asking if I'd borrowed his eye-mask with the aloe vera eye pads and could he please have it back. I can't for one second imagine Ewan attempting to live out of a suitcase. He has more stuff than me and scored the en-suite with the biggest bathroom when we first moved in because he's got an entire pharmacy's worth of designer products to store. I, on the other hand, have a Dove deodorant stick and some two-year-old make-up from Priceline. But travelling he must go, apparently: 'Anything to be away from this place!'

I always wanted a studio flat. Back when I lived in New York I went to my friend Martin's studio on the Lower East Side and he had one of those beds that you pull down from the wall at night to save space in the day. I thought that was the greatest thing I'd ever seen and spent about ten minutes lifting it up and down, determined that one day I'd have one too. I probably won't, though. I have to transport the furniture I've already got and sell whatever won't fit, but it's all an adventure, isn't it? My own space! I can hardly believe I've graduated from living on an Iranian's landing with Stacey, to getting my own studio flat in a swish new building that isn't even on a construction site!

Rent's come down so much in Dubai now that I managed to get my studio for just 55,000 dirhams a year. That's almost 8,000 dirhams less per year than I'm paying to live in TECOM with Ewan, and it's in the Marina, right opposite the Yacht Club. I will actually have the Yacht Club as my local, which definitely beats the dodgy English pub that can't make a pie properly in the Media Rotana. As long as I remember the mosquito repellent I'll be able to take advantage of their happy hour after work, when it's two glasses of wine for the price of one. Imagine! I'll be looking out at all the yachts I can't afford and it won't bother me, because I'll have a flat that I can more than afford just over the road, and two glasses of wine in my hands. Yay!

In retrospect, I've paid a price higher than the cost of my new rent for a year. I've had to watch a lot of my friends leave, or listen to them talk about leaving. Ewan's not the only one. Nearly two years after moving to Dubai as an impoverished, debt-ridden nobody, I can live the unimaginable dream in the Marina — but I can't have all my friends round to enjoy it with me. I can now catch a cab in five minutes and know that I'll be somewhere within the hour, but who will meet me at the other end? This kind of sucks if I think about it too much. But still, I'm looking on the bright side. It'll be such a luxury to be able to walk everywhere — the Marina has pavements. And the Marina Mall round the corner has a Waitrose in it. This makes Mum happy because now she knows I might be buying food and cooking, instead of ordering it in. (I said 'might'.)

The pool is great and there's even a bubbling little Jacuzzi next to it, a bit like the one we had in Garhoud overlooking the Irish Village. This one's not on the roof, though, but in a space at the front of the building that just screams 'party'. Sash has already eyed it up for this purpose, and Rocko's planning an entire weekend of drinking beers on inflatable Li-Los and getting KFC delivered to his deckchair. (He's a true Kiwi, I'm discovering little by little.)

Even though it's stupidly exciting, the idea of living alone always scared me a little bit. Of course, there are the good parts that everyone raves about, like being able to walk around butt naked. Like, playing my *Wicked* soundtrack on full volume, prancing about, pretending to be the witch in Oz while letting the teacups pile up in the corner like my own ceramic version of the Emerald City. (I used to do this with Ewan anyway, but never in the nude.)

I'll do everything from my bed because I can, and because there isn't anywhere else to do it from. I'll have the full 42 inches at my disposal, whenever I please, in whichever direction I choose …

every flat needs a big-screen TV. But I am slightly worried that once the luxury wears off I'll be lonely. I might buy another cat to keep me company, one that's not possessed. And then I might like it and buy another one. And then it will have kittens and I won't have the heart to get rid of them. And the place will smell of litter trays and Whiskas and no one will come over anymore, and before I know it I'll be Becky the Cat Woman, who used to be quite cool, but now is just a little bit weird and doesn't have any friends.

There are also a lot of annoyances about moving in alone — like having to pay the full deposit, having to stump up the full whack for TV and Internet, having to clean the floors ... or search for someone else to do it on the cheap (maids are cashing in on clean-ups lately). Rent's come down but it might actually wind up costing more than sharing with Ewan. I'm trying not to think about it. I'm also trying not to think about how I'm going to fit everything I own into a studio flat. I might not have too many beauty products, but I haven't got any better at ignoring the calls of new clothes. I'll be storing shoes in the oven and T-shirts on hooks on every wall ... well hey, it might look 'arty'? Hmmm ... maybe I need to sell some stuff. That would be good for a bit of spending money, too. I wonder if anyone would like my red rug from IKEA. It's only got a couple of wine and pie stains on it and with a power vacuum it could easily be rid of all my hair.

Leaving TECOM and living without Ewan in the next room will be the end of an era, but I feel as though I've made a very sensible decision. I'm all about making sensible decisions lately and getting my life back on track, in case you hadn't noticed. I messed it all up for a while, that's for sure. But I always say when life hands you lemons, you're far better off making some lemonade ... unless you just buy some from Whole Foods, obviously.

Flights of fancy ...

I had to leave my lovely new apartment early today. I felt really bad because the maid was there again and there was absolutely no place to escape as she cleaned. Ewan says I'm a spoilt little brat, hiring a maid to clean my studio apartment. It's only 10-feet square. But I'm really very busy, you know, getting a suntan now that it's not a zillion degrees outside, and shopping, and ... stuff. Oh, all right, I know it's a bit silly, but really, her services are very reasonably priced.

This maid even does my ironing. It's amazing. Rocko was here the other day and left a shirt behind by mistake. After I washed it, my maid ironed it. I watched her do it as I got ready for work. She even hung it on a hanger for me, ready to present to him when he comes back. I can't help feel a bit bad, though, being there when she's there. It makes me feel mean. She's probably only a few years older than me and doesn't speak any English. Although I try to make conversation with her, we only end up miming to each other like members of a Parisian circus troupe. She did manage to tell me she cleans several other apartments in the building, though. She's probably got quite a lucrative little business going on in the grand scheme of things; one of the few people able to cash in on the current economic downfall. There's a lot of mess to clean up around here.

Which actually leads to me to a friend's little problem. I just heard about it. Well, it's quite a big problem really. Remember Rochelle, the Australian girl who was hired by a random banking employee to do absolutely nothing but make him feel important? Well, just yesterday she tried to leave Dubai for a month-long holiday back home. But she was detained at the airport and hauled into an interrogation room for an entire day! Basically, she was told that her bank was suing her, so she couldn't leave the country. Rochelle didn't know what to think. She hadn't been told by the bank that they were suing her at all — no phone call, nothing. Having dealt with the banks here in Dubai myself, well … HSBC still gives me the Rage. Also, keep in mind this girl is only twenty-two years old and the sweetest little thing you've ever seen.

Apparently, Rochelle's car loan repayment check bounced. She's got money in her account, but she recently lost her job and in order for her to leave the country the loan company has to have a new guarantor for the repayments. The poor girl was never told any of this, however. Rochelle missed her flight, was kept at the airport for five hours with no food, then put in a police car and taken to the police station for another two.

The police at the station spoke to her in Arabic, refused to get her a translator and tried to make her sign a form in Arabic that she obviously couldn't read. She refused and eventually her boyfriend (who for legal reasons couldn't actually admit he was her boyfriend, nor that they were living together), had to bail her out. It was all so humiliating for her. She even got followed to the bathroom! Luckily, Rochelle has an open one-way ticket, so she can eventually go back to Australia, where she's now thinking about staying.

It seems the issues facing the entire world at the moment are increasingly more concerning in Dubai than in most other places, due no doubt to the outlandish regulations imposed on the recession's unfortunate victims. I still have a job and a maid, and a brand-new lease on a studio flat, and I seem to have a new man in my life, too … but have I really done the right thing, choosing to stay here? I thought I had, but now I'm having doubts again. Christ!

The thing is, the employment situation back in the UK is terrible. I know more people who've been laid off than have actually got work back at home. Those people, some of them friends of mine who've recently lost their jobs in Dubai, have gone back and not been able to find any work. I also have debts. No one can escape Dubai with debts and I still have a few grand left to pay on my last loan. The more I think about it, I'm actually trapped here — albeit in a very nice studio apartment with a swimming pool and a Jacuzzi and a security guard and a Waitrose round the corner and a maid — but I'm trapped here nonetheless. If I wanted to go anywhere more permanent than a weekend jaunt on a cheap airline, I'd be hauled into a cell and chanted at in Arabic … and who would bail me out?

I'm literally living my life in a glitzy prison at the moment; a glorious 10-by-10 foot gilded cage. I'm waking up, watching the maid iron my sundress collection and my half-boyfriend's shirts, thinking how lucky I am, how happy, finally … when in actual fact, I'm no more free than a hamster running on a treadmill, slowly going nowhere behind bars.

16/04

The Twilight hour...

M&M found me lounging in the shallow end of my swimming pool, reading *Eclipse*. My heart jumped into the back of my throat as he walked slowly around the edge towards me and I considered ducking my head under the water in the hope that he wouldn't see me … only he already had. Somehow I knew what was coming.

He bent down way too close to my face and asked if I was seeing someone. Bit of a silly question really, as he wouldn't have been there, standing by my pool, perspiring profusely and interrupting my session with Edward and Bella if he thought I wasn't. Someone must have told him about Rocko.

I blocked M&M on Facebook ages ago, but he has a habit of texting Stacey in the UK, fishing for information about me. He probably thinks she doesn't tell me when he does this, but obviously she gives me word-by-word breakdowns on an almost daily basis, in spite of the fact that she's in London. Although, admittedly, Stacey has been getting a little sick of his constant probing and has started to ignore his questions. He must have taken her silence on the matter to mean we're hiding something and assumed the worst.

I told him it was none of his business and swam to the other side of the pool, away from him. God, I've come to dread his outbursts. Fear of his somewhat manic reactions was what led me to hide things from him in the first place. It's exactly what put the initial vicious circle in motion! I said nothing but he walked around towards me again and told me he couldn't believe I'd started seeing someone else so soon, and did I know how much this was hurting him, and blah blah blah …

I still said nothing. I buried myself in my book, hoping it looked like I was actually still reading. I pictured myself as Bella, springing onto Edward's back and being carried up into a tall tree, away from the scary monster.

It's not like I intended to start 'seeing' Rocko. In fact, I'm not sure I would even class myself as being 'in a relationship'. He's just a fun guy to hang around with. In fact, the first time he called me, when we got back from the Musandam, we spent two whole hours on the phone discussing, among other things, the merits of sweet corn. When he came all the way from Abu Dhabi to get me, he drove me all the way back again on a whim and took me to a dark, grimy club full of prostitutes. He thought watching them grind with little Indian men on the dance floor would be fun … more fun than sitting down to another fancy five-star dinner. And he was absolutely right!

Rocko even let me buy some drinks when I offered. Now, obviously I came to expect men to buy the drinks in these parts ages ago, but there's actually something really refreshing about getting them myself. I feel like an equal, instead of someone's well-kept possession or trophy. It's funny how something so small can make such a massive difference to your mindset. Sweet corn, prostitutes and buying my own drinks in a bar is all it really takes to make me happy these days. I don't know why men aren't lining up, quite frankly.

Of course, Rocko initially took my mind off The Irishman and Svana, who themselves took my mind off M&M, who I suppose was and still is the root of my emotional difficulties in Dubai. But there's no denying that Rocko and I exist on the same level. We talk utter shit and make ridiculous plans to take over the planet. I think Rocko gets the real me, instead of a version of me I have to pre-prepare to impress someone, similar to the way it was with The Irishman when we first met. In some ways, actually, they're pretty similar.

As M&M stood there waiting for me to speak, I read the same paragraph of my book about fifteen times. He asked me to try and think about things from his point of view, so I gave it some consideration. I guess there's always one person who moves on before the other after a break up, isn't there? And it must suck to know you've been replaced so quickly. But M&M didn't have to find out about Rocko. Like I said, he probably went fishing for information and didn't much like what he discovered.

Looking up at him, still sweating through his rugby shirt and pleading with his eyes for answers, I felt a sudden pang of pity. It surprised me. I was all set on being defensive and snooty, and then … it struck me. I was doing to M&M exactly what The Irishman had done to me. I absolutely hated it when The Irishman had pitied me.

When I was on the phone to The Irishman in the car park, it felt like a midget with a knife was stabbing my knees, willing me to fall down and crumble. But I'd stayed strong, like M&M was trying to do now. A new-found respect for the man washed over me; this man who was standing there, so blindly in love with me for reasons I still can't even fathom. I offered him what I'm sure was a pretty lame smile and shrugged my shoulders, in the hope that it would be enough. Well, what else could I do? I didn't want to hurt him with a final confirmation that he'd lost me, but I didn't want to experience another emotional tirade right there on the edge of my swimming pool either.

In that moment, M&M straightened himself up and said I'd made him think about a few things. He told me he was flying to meet his wife, in order to get a divorce. I felt my mouth fall open. A divorce? Now?

I watched him walk away. Once I'd given him sufficient time to think I was still reading, unaffected by his presence or statement and deep in the world of vampires and werewolves, I raced back upstairs and called Stacey. I fired the questions down the phone: Does he really think getting a divorce will make me love him, after all this time, after everything we've been through? Does he think I'll go back to him when I've shouted the words 'I hate you' in his direction more than once? Would he have thought about a divorce if it wasn't for the fact that I'm now with someone else? Would he have ever even told his wife he didn't love her anymore

all those months ago, if he hadn't been caught in an affair …
with ME?

That night Rocko called me and I let it go to voicemail. I just
felt so guilty for being angry and upset at M&M … it didn't feel
right to talk to him. Stacey probably had something to do with my
decision. Basically, she thinks that if M&M is still getting to me,
I'm really not ready to be with anyone else. She thinks I should
take a step back and re-think rushing into a relationship, just for
the sake of having someone around.

Of course, I protested that I didn't mean for it to happen, and
that it's not even serious, but she was pretty adamant that my
head and my heart are still fighting a battle over three different
men. While that's the case, I shouldn't be with anyone. Not even
Rocko — who aside from the fact that he'll never sparkle in the
sun or fly me through the treetops like Edward Cullen, seems
pretty bloody perfect, really.

I hate it when she's right.

09/05

Another one bites the dust …

Uh oh. It's happened again. Another company's gone bust,
another businessman's dream has turned to ruin — and this
time I'm a part of it! The lifestyle and experiences company
I've been working for on the side, pretty much ever since I got
to Dubai, has just gone down the toilet. And they owe me
3,000 dirhams!

Obviously, the cracks have been showing for a while. Payments
have been late, demands have been unreasonable and timelines

have been ridiculous for a good few months now. I've been working for them harder than ever lately to meet what's been looking like impossible expectations. But they paid me decent money when they actually got around to writing me the checks. And besides, I tend to do all my freelance work from my desk in the ad agency during my 'spare time', so it's kind of like getting paid twice to be in the same place.

Unfortunately, though, it's looking a lot like this business is one of many that have fallen victim to the current economic situation that most definitely has not escaped Dubai, in spite of what the media are choosing to tell us. Dubai's twisted laws and regulations have now driven the poor MD — a British man, no less — to despair. Plagued by debt he's packed up his wife and kids and legged it. The MD's house on the Palm, once full of furniture, is now totally barren — his mate went round to check.

He's sent an emotional letter 'To the people of Dubai' in an effort to explain these tragic circumstances. It's just so very sad. He flocked to the UAE in its boom with his family and lived in extravagant luxury. He had the nice car, the big house on the Palm, but pushed himself to the max in order to turn his money-making dreams to reality. He was passionate to the point of fighting for more than he could ever have, on borrowed funds and time.

His departure is not good news for his full-time employees. Jobs are scarce round here lately and I read in the paper this morning that Dubai police have over 450 people locked away from the public right now because of outstanding debts! You might be lucky enough to land a job elsewhere, with the full intention of paying off your dues in Dubai from afar, but you might not even make it out of the UAE in order to do so.

As we learned from the people suffering at Ewan's place, if a company cancels a work visa and informs the bank, the bank can enforce a travel ban until all outstanding payments are made. Under Sharia law, the punishment for defaulting on a debt is serious; even bouncing a check can land you with a prison sentence. Look at how strict customs were with our Rochelle when she failed, through no fault of her own, to make a car loan repayment.

Prison is obviously what the MD of the lifestyle and experiences dot com was terrified of. His official letter says:

> I am not running away from debt, I am purely protecting those dearest to me and getting out of a country which, due to the lack of structured bankruptcy laws and a banking system which has zero flexibility on loan repayments, drives people to make horrible decisions.

As much as I hate to lose the 3,000 dirhams he owes me, I can't very well say I've been that hard done by in this whole situation — not when his wife and children are living in hiding somewhere, probably going through hell, knowing they've left innocent, hardworking people in a lot of trouble. Having that on your shoulders would be truly, soul-crushingly awful.

The MD adds that although a hunt for investors was ultimately unsuccessful, he's now taking personal responsibility for paying back everything that's owed to his employees, suppliers, customers who can no longer redeem their gift vouchers, and investors, no matter how long it might take. This is a noble offer indeed. But then, like many others round here who are failing miserably in ambitious endeavors, he always did dream a little too big.

Waving Dubai-bye ...

M&M's divorce hasn't really changed anything between us, but the fact that he's deposited a large sum of money into my bank account to help me pay off my outstanding debts is something that renders me somewhat dumbstruck! He says he's doing it because he still loves me, and even though I've made it very clear that we're over for good, he doesn't want me to feel like I'm stuck in a place I just don't want to be in anymore.

Obviously, I'm more grateful for this act of generosity than I know how to put into words. In spite of everything we've been through, in spite of how I've hurt him, he's chosen to help me out, even though he knows damn well that if he pays off my debts, I'll leave him behind once and for all. I'm thinking that this might mean M&M's learned what I wanted him to figure out all along: that if you love someone, clinging to them too tightly, trying to control a future they're quite happy not to plan, dictating who they can and can't see isn't going to make them love you back. The old cliché is totally true. If you love someone, you really do have to let them go.

I still can't believe he's doing it. He knows his money hasn't necessarily made me happy in the past, but on this occasion, he's really not trying to buy me or my time, or my heart. He's paying for my freedom.

I've promised M&M I'll pay him back some day ... God knows how ... but he still insists he doesn't want me to. He says he wants me to go make something more of myself, somewhere else ... which is kind of what I want, too. If I'm honest with myself, I've been enduring Dubai rather than enjoying it for a long time now.

I've had the experience of a lifetime. I know this; I can really feel it. The things I've done in Dubai will stay with me forever, and even though I've started to appear ungrateful, a little miserable at the way certain events have unfolded, I'm pretty sure that when I look back on all of this, I'll never fail to appreciate what this place has done for me.

Right now, however, the novelty has well and truly worn off. Just as I suspected might happen when the buzz died down, things like having a Yacht Club for a local and a steady job that pays the bills aren't really making me happy — especially when all my friends are being made redundant, or leaving me to move elsewhere.

Ewan's gone. We had a final farewell for him in Harry Ghatto's, which isn't at all like it used to be when Stacey and I started going there, back when the staff all knew our names. It's full of losers in suits now, and the exclusive vibe has been replaced by one of a cheap, booze-soaked pub … not unlike Waxy O'Connors, where Stacey and I had our first filthy brunch with The Trader. Harry's even has a happy hour now, to encourage more people to squish through its doors. I guess they weren't making enough money.

Sash was fired a few days ago. She's been sitting at her desk, twiddling her thumbs for weeks, hoping for another project to land on her desk, but in the end her company just didn't have enough work for everyone. She called me up in tears, said she was going to have to do a runner back to Canada with her credit card debts outstanding. Credit card debts, apparently, won't get you stopped at the airport. It's the massive personal loans for things like rent, cars and property that are causing people all these problems. A friend of mine said she knows a woman who's sleeping in her car at the moment. She has nowhere else to go. And apparently, down at JBR, the car park attendants are being paid to wash the dust off all the abandoned sports cars, so the people who still live there won't realize exactly how many have been left behind.

The agency laid off a few people the other week, too. Nina was convinced she was going to get the boot, but in the end they fired some Filipino employees and kept the Westerners, which doesn't really make too much sense. We weren't supposed to discuss our salaries at the agency, but obviously we all did. Some of the Filipinos doing exactly the same jobs as Westerners were getting much less money, so technically, they should have kept them on and booted out the more expensive people. I'm sure there's a lot we weren't told about the situation, but I'll never get Arabic logic.

Telling EGO The Great I was leaving was a bit weird. I just walked into his office, sat down in front of him and told him straight out I'd decided to move on ... that my love life was in turmoil, that my friends were all getting fired, that it was just time to do something else — somewhere that wasn't Dubai. I felt the need to connect with him emotionally for the first time ever, as I knew he'd probably be quite upset that I wasn't going to be around to help him spell stuff anymore.

He nodded his head as I spoke and looked at me over the top of his designer glasses. I waited for some sort of sentence expressing his disappointment; I waited for him to tell me I'd be missed. But after a few seconds of silent contemplation he offered the following: 'Well, to be honest, I always thought you were a better editor than a "creative". It bothered me for a while, but then I just endured it and let you get on with it.'

I bit my lip and frowned, trying to process his words in a way that made them seem less insulting. I thought perhaps he'd made a mistake, as he so often did in English, but no ... no mistake. He'd obviously decided to be an arrogant asshole to the very end.

I fought the urge to tell him I'd had trouble 'enduring' him too, but decided I didn't really care enough to bother. Let's face it, advertising never was and never will be the career for me.

I've decided to sub-let my beautiful studio flat and meet up with Ewan in America, where he's been 'travelling' for the past few weeks. The media company still hasn't paid him the majority of what they owe him and he's now threatening legal action ... not that it'll get him anywhere, by the looks of it. Heathcliff is ignoring all of his emails on the topic, while desperately trying to cling to his own job, swanning about the city, sleeping with every girl who hasn't cottoned on to his antics yet.

I will miss a lot of things about Dubai — but mostly shallow things, I guess. Like the ability to take a taxi door to door, the convenience of having a maid to tidy up after me, the independence of having my very own studio flat (albeit one I don't actually own), the financial security of a well-paid job. Even before M&M wiped them out entirely, I only would have had to make repayments for another six months in order to clear the debts that have plagued me since I left university with a degree in drunken shenanigans and way too many clothes. This is something I'm pretty proud of, all things considered.

In spite of all this, Dubai to me was never a place I saw myself living forever. Let's face it. It's not like the rest of the world. I don't have any emotional attachment to the place itself. There's nothing real to miss. My heart broke over leaving New York City. I mourned for the place itself, as well as the friends I made. I sat on my bed in London and cried for Manhattan — the streets, the sights, the smells, the energy. But Dubai isn't finished yet, and to me it has no soul.

The billboards that used to offer promises of things to come, like large residential development projects and exciting family-based theme parks, now show mostly chicken ads and options for phone contracts. There isn't as much to brag about these days. The Sheikh still looms above it all, still as ominous and powerful as when Stacey and I discovered him during our sweaty walks home, back when we first arrived. Only, he doesn't seem as credible

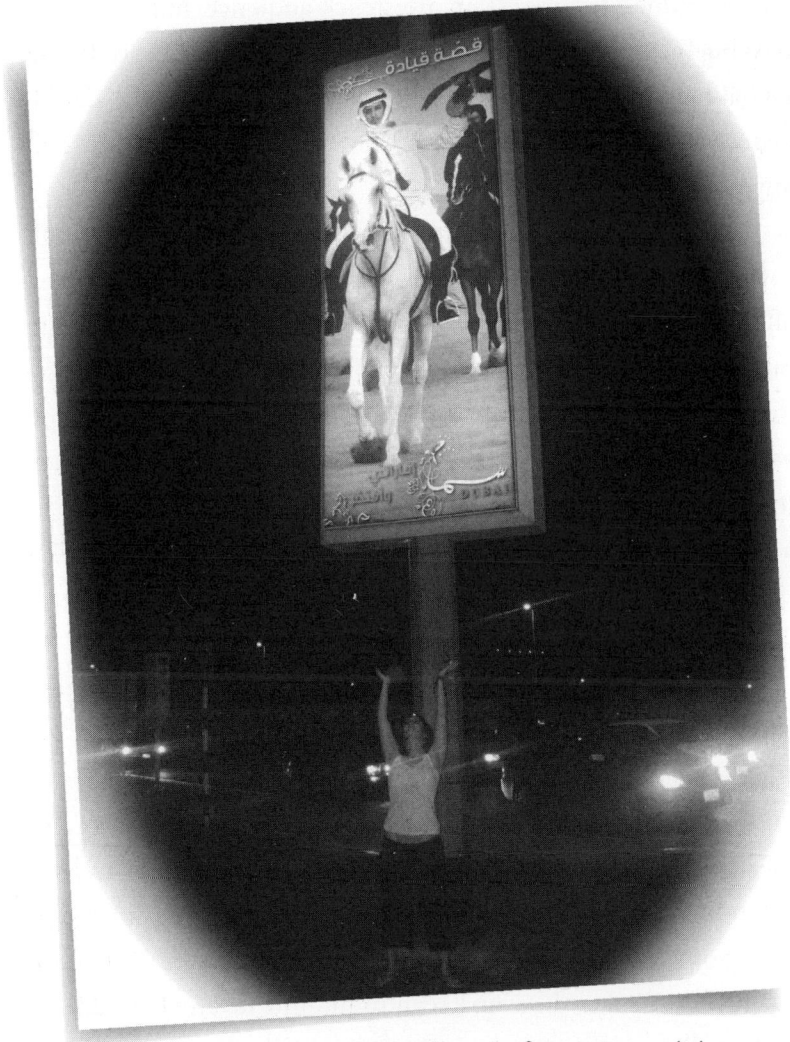

The billboard of promise! It didn't seem quite so exciting after a while.

anymore. All he stands for has faded in my mind, just as his image on the billboard weakens day by day in the scorching sun.

The World, The Universe, Fashion Island — a thousand projects that blew my mind, made my head spin, made me feel like I was living in the greatest, most up-and-coming city in the world — where are they now? They're still just dreams on press releases, timed to impress an awestruck audience, hungry for the next big thing. Ultimately, most of the things I once believed about Dubai have crumbled into dust; they've blown away like sand to be reclaimed by the desert. They're not even building Jurassic Park anymore.

It makes me wonder, was it all really as great as I once thought it was? Pamela Anderson, Brad Pitt, David Beckham — they were all sold a slice of this dream in the hope that the rest of us would buy into it, but the cynicism's long since set in. I wonder now, looking at my boxes waiting to be shipped back home to London, were these people ever really as excited about Dubai as we were told? I mean, I've been a part of the media, plugging this city for a living. I took the piss … repeated these stories to my friends at home, just to make them laugh … but still, there's no escaping the fact that in the end, Dubai and its lifestyle have affected me. I believed the hype. I fell for a dream. I craved the money, power and attention, just like everyone else.

I've helped create Dubai's advertisements. I was actually, up until a few days ago, one of those people hired to make the greatest sales pitch of all: *Dubai — a city where anything's possible!*

So many people have passed in and out of my life since I got here. Some I'll always keep close, but others, like The Trader and the Private Banker, I haven't seen in months. Even Heidi doesn't really call anymore. Somewhere along the line, in the mess of it all, she went from rooting for me and The Irishman, to thinking what an awesome bloke M&M was. They go for dinners now. He's a good bloke, as a friend. I should have known where to draw the line, all those months ago. I've seen a side of him they haven't seen, I suppose. But then, he's seen a side of me I'd rather not reveal to anyone ever again.

Telling Rocko I was leaving was kind of hard. He drove from Abu Dhabi once again and we went for a drink. He hugged me goodbye, sighed, and told me, 'Someday, you'll see how awesome I am.' The night after I let my voicemail pick up his call, I rang him back and explained I wasn't really ready for wherever it was we were going. At times I think I am, but when I told him later that getting out of Dubai was the healthiest option for me to explore, he took it so well. His own company isn't looking very stable at the moment anyway, and he may have plans afoot to move himself, at some point in the near future.

So what's next after travelling with Ewan? I've decided to head back to London, see the family, spend some time with Lucy and my other friends, eat chips and curry sauce and revel in the luxuries of non-censored trash mags and daytime TV. And then, I don't really know, if I'm honest! I didn't really know what Dubai would have in store for me when I packed my bags in my little east London flat two years ago, and I'm equally unsure about what's next, once I leave here. Ewan wants to go to Sydney, and so does Stacey, who's getting pretty fed up with the cold and the misery in London. Apparently, we can still have a house with a swimming pool over there. We can still spend weekends on the beach and walk about in flip-flops. It does sound appealing ... and Rocko's got family in Sydney. Not that I can entertain that thought right now.

Whatever's next, I'm waving Dubai bye. It's over and out. It's time for a new beginning, away from dusty buildings, hollow dreams and shallow people. I'm happy. Of course, I'm not looking forward to unpacking my boxes at the other end, or getting the tube from Heathrow to my brother's house, or cooking my own dinner, or cleaning my room, or … dammit!

You can take the girl out of Dubai, I guess. But I reckon it's probably going to take an entire lifetime to get Dubai out of me.